Fiction Catalog Author

D1054233

Twenty-One
Stories

APR 1 9 2005

Twenty-One Stories

Stories

S. Y. AGNON

Edited by Nahum N. Glatzer

SCHOCKEN BOOKS · NEW YORK

Copyright © 1970 by Schocken Books Inc.

All rights reserved under International and
Pan-American Copyright Conventions. Published
in the United States by Schocken Books Inc.,
New York, Distributed by Pantheon Books,
a division of Random House, Inc., New York.

Library of Congress Catalog Card Number 71-108902
ISBN 0-8052-0313-3

Manufactured in the United States of America
9

Contents

The Tale of
the Scribe

(Dedicated to my wife, Esther)

1

THIS IS THE STORY of Raphael the scribe. Raphael was a righteous and blameless man who copied Torah scrolls, phylacteries, and *mezuzot* in holiness and purity. And any man in the household of Israel who was childless, Mercy deliver us, or whose wife had died, Mercy deliver us, would come to Raphael the scribe and say: "You know, Reb Raphael my brother, what are we and what are our lives? I had indeed hoped that my sons and my sons' sons would come to you to have you write phylacteries for them; but now, alas, I am alone, and my wife, for whom I had thought I would wait long days and years in the upper world, has died and has left me to my sorrows. Perhaps, Reb Raphael my brother, you can undertake to write a Torah scroll under the good guidance of God's hand, and I will compensate you for it. Let us not be lost both in this world and the next, my dear Reb Raphael. Perhaps God will be gracious unto me and the work of your hands will be found acceptable." And Raphael then would sit and write a Torah scroll to give the man and his wife a name and remembrance in the household of Israel.

What may this be likened to? To a man who travels far from his own city, to a place where he is not known, and the watchmen who guard that city find him and ask: "Who are you and where do you live?" If the man is wealthy and a property owner, then as soon as he says I am So-and-so, the son of Thus-and-so, from such-and-such a place, they check the record books and documents, and find out how much he had given to the king's treasury, how much in property taxes he had paid, and they welcome him immediately, saying: "Come in, you blessed of God, the entire land is before you, dwell wherever you wish." But if the traveler is an ordinary man, and has neither property nor wealth, then he shows them a document written and signed by officials of his own city, which states that So-and-so is a resident of our city. Then he is permitted to remain and they do not hurry him out.

Likewise, when a man comes to the next world, and the evil angels meet him and ask, "Who are you and where are you from?"; if in his earthly life he had been an upright and blameless man, and left behind him good deeds, or sons busy with Torah and commandments, then these certainly serve as his good advocates. But if he had had none of these then he is lost. However, when Jews come to the synagogue to pray and take a Torah scroll out of the Ark and read from it, if the scroll was written as a memorial for the ascent of this man's soul, then it is immediately known on high that he had been So-and-so, a resident of such-and-such a place, and that is his identification. They then say to him, enter and rest in peace.

Raphael the scribe sat and wrote, and his wife, most blessed among women, the pious Miriam, stayed home and made life pleasant for him in a fine house with fine utensils which she scrubbed and cleaned and purified, so that her husband would do his work in a clean and pure atmosphere. She delighted him with delicate foods and savory beverages, and for Sabbaths and holidays, and sometimes even for the New Moon, she would buy a goose, cook the meat in a pot, or roast it; and Raphael would prepare the quills for writing

Torah scrolls, phylacteries, and *mezuzot*. He sat at the Torah and at God's service in holiness and purity, wielding the scribe's pen and fashioning crowns for his Creator.

2

Before we begin telling part of the story itself, let us tell about his way in his holy work. This was his way in holiness:

At midnight he would rise, seat himself on the floor, place ashes on his head, and weep for the destruction of Jerusalem, for the death of the righteous, the burning of the Temple, the length of the exile, the exile of the Divine Presence, the suffering under enslavement, and all sorts of hard and cruel decrees that are inflicted on the people of Israel day in and day out, and for our just Messiah, who is held in iron chains because of the sins of our generation. After that he would study the *Path of Life* and the *Book of Splendor* until the morning light, thus tying together what is proper for the night with what is proper for the day.

In the morning he would go down to the ritual bath and immerse his thin body in the water, then recite the morning prayers, return home and eat a piece of honey cake dipped in brandy, and fortify his weak body with a very light repast. After that he would go back and immerse himself again in the ritual bath, and then turn his heart away from all worldly matters. All day he sat in his house communing with his soul in solitude, completely within the frame of Torah. He did not mingle with other human beings and was thus saved from any of the transgressions between man and man, and remained holy in his speech, thought, and deed, and was spared all temptation and distraction. He sat secluded and isolated and no one was with him except His Name, may He be blessed, and he studied a portion of the Talmud in order to tie together the oral teachings with the written ones, and concentrated on all the sacred meanings hinted at in Scripture. He was careful never to write the Holy Name without first having purified his body. For this reason he often wrote an entire sheet of parchment but left blank the spaces for the Holy Name, and later he wrote the Name in the blank spaces only after having immersed himself again in the purifying ritual bath.

He may thus be likened to a craftsman making a crown for a king: does he not first make the crown and then set into it the diamonds and other precious stones? Thus Raphael sat and wrote, until the beadle came, knocked on the window, and announced that the time had come for the afternoon prayers.

3

How good is a word in its proper time. Having told of his way in his sacred work, let us now note the place of this work.

He lived in a small house close to the big synagogue and to the old House of Study and to other houses of prayer, a few steps from—not to be mentioned in the same breath —the bathhouse which contained the ritual bath. His house was small and low. It had only one room which was divided in the middle by a partition made of boards. On the other side of the partition there was an oven and a range for pots, and between oven and range the pious and modest mistress of his house sat, and she cooked and baked and preserved and wove and knitted and looked to the needs of her home. Children they had none. Because the Holy One, blessed be He, desires the prayers of the righteous, He closed her womb.

When she completes the tasks that a wife is required to perform for her husband, she takes out a used garment and remakes it into clothing for an orphan. She is especially fond of this task because it enables her to sit quietly, to pull thread after thread, and in her thoughts take stock of the world. And in order to avoid doubts, Heaven forfend, about God's ways, and not to complain, Heaven forfend, against Him, she recalls several pious tales of salvation. For example, the story of a childless woman like herself who saved money in a stocking to buy a ruby, which is a proven remedy against child-lessness. Then she saw the officials of the Society for Clothing the Naked, and gave them all the money, and in addition sewed clothes for the orphan children. Not many days later her womb was blessed, and out of her came affluent men who served God in comfort.

Or another story about a woman who was making a small prayer shawl for an orphan, and suddenly she felt that the ritual fringes were being pulled and drawn upward, and a fragrance like that of the Garden of Eden was all around her. When she looked up she saw Reb Gadiel, the infant who had been born by virtue of his father's having taught Torah to Jewish children; Reb Gadiel was kissing the ritual fringes she had made, and she heard him say to her: "Know that your deeds are acceptable on high, and that you will yet merit making ritual fringes for your own sons and sons' sons." Not many days later she was rewarded and her womb was blessed, and out of her came righteous, God-fearing, good men, taken up with Torah and God's commandments. And this birth was out of the ordinary, because that woman had been barren by nature.

Thus the pious Miriam sits, drawing thread after thread, and a thread of mercy is drawn and extended on high, and good angels bring up before her various fantasies: for example, that she is preparing a garment for her son who is sitting in his schoolroom and studying Torah.

From time to time she raises her pure eyes toward Raphael, the husband of her youth, who sits on the other side of the partition, near the window, at the clean table covered with a prayer shawl. Also on the other side of the partition there are a wardrobe and a bed. The bed is covered with a colored, clean spread, and the wardrobe contains rolls of parchment and sacred implements. In it her white wedding dress hangs, and in it also earth from the Land of Israel lies hidden away.

Across the top of the room a dark beam stretches from one end of the house to the other. On top of the beam there are a number of sacred books: some new, some old; some thick, some thin; some bound in cured sheepskins and some in a plain binding.

Near the beam, to the right, on the eastern wall, is the embroidered wall-hanging which Miriam had made in her youth at her father's house. It depicts a garden full of fruit trees, with a palace in the garden, and two lions watching over the garden. The lions' faces are turned toward each other, lion facing lion, one tongue reaching out toward the other; and stretching from tongue to tongue there is an inscription in large letters of gold, which says, "The earth is the Lord's and the fullness thereof," as if it were one mighty roar. In each of the four corners of the embroidery there is a square which contains the words: "I have set the Lord always before me."

Facing the east-wall embroidery, on the opposite wall, there is a mirror, and on top of its frame lies a bundle of willow twigs. Every year, on Hoshana Rabbah, Miriam brings home a bundle of the twigs that had been beaten against the prayer lecterns in the synagogue as part of the liturgy. A number of women had already been helped at childbirth by water in which such willow twigs were boiled. Only she herself has never yet made use of that water. The willow twigs continue to wither, and leaf after leaf is shed into the web that the spider has spun over the amulet that is near the bed. Her mother had given her the amulet on her wedding day to help keep away from the house the evil spirits that prevent births.

The amulet is written in the letters of the sacred alphabet but in the tongue of the gentiles, *Yak krova mloda*, etc., meaning, "When the cow is young and healthy why should she not give birth to a calf?" It was written for her mother, peace be upon her, who had been childless for a number of years, by Rabbi Simon of Yaroslav during his stay at the inn operated by her mother. He wrote it at the insistence of several righteous rabbis, while she cooked red borsht and potatoes for them after they had gone without food for three days on their journey to their saintly rabbi, the "seer" of Lublin. And since at that time Rabbi Simon had not yet been ordained, he did not write the amulet in the sacred tongue; but the Hebrew letters in which the amulet was written spelled out the name of the angel in charge of pregnancy, with the Holy Name interwoven among them. Miriam tied the amulet with seven threads from seven veils of seven women from whom had come sons and sons of sons, none of whom had died during the lives of their parents.

From time to time Miriam comes softly to her side of the partition, and stands there letting her pure eyes rest on her husband as he sits at his work in holiness and purity. And if Raphael should interrupt his work and notice her standing there, immediately the pallor leaves her face and a blush takes its place, and she offers him the excuse that she had only come to fetch the Sabbath candlesticks to polish them in honor of the Sabbath. This is the rule of the house. Outside of the house nothing unclean ever appears, because the schoolchildren drive away any dog or pig that may wander into the street. The only animal present is the cat, which was created for the purpose of keeping the house free of mice. Geese and other clean fowl wander around the house. And the birds of heaven, at the time of their migration to the Land of Israel when the Torah portion *ki tavo* is read in the synagogue, and again at the time when they return on Passover to hear the recitation of the Song of Songs in the classroom, sing their own song at his window every morning.

4

Inside the house there is quiet and peace. A feeling like Sabbath rest prevails. And the beauty of the place is reflected in its dwellers. The beloved Miriam's head is always covered by a clean white kerchief knotted below her throat, with its ends resting upon her heart like a dove's wings. Unlike most women she uses no pin in her kerchief so that not even the smallest part of the covered area may become exposed, Heaven forbid. And if her hands were not busy with her work, one might mistakenly think that every day is Sabbath unto the Lord.

At times a poor man comes to the house to ask for alms, or a traveler comes in to have his phylacteries repaired, and they tell Raphael what they had seen and heard in the dispersion of Israel. "What shall we say and what shall we relate, Reb Raphael? If told it would not be believed. In the house of Thus-and-so the scribe, I saw with my own eyes a number of young men sitting day and night writing Torah scrolls, phylacteries, and *mezuzot*, thus making factory work of the sacred Torah. Not only this, but I have heard that another scribe even employs girls to sit and write."

Raphael listens respectfully and replies humbly: "Do not say this, my dear fellow Jew. Why should we slander the people of God? Indeed, we have reason to rejoice that we have reached a time such as this when the Torah is spread so widely that a single scribe for a city is no longer enough."

At times a woman neighbor comes in to consult Miriam on something related to cooking, or to ask when the new month will begin. And if there is a difficult birth in town, someone comes running to her to borrow her willow twigs. The woman says to her: "My dear Miriam, surely you wish to save two human souls, therefore please lend me your willow twigs. Tomorrow, God willing, I shall go from one end of the town to the other end and find other willow twigs to replace these." And Miriam answers with a sigh: "Take the willow twigs, my dear soul, and may they bring good fortune and long life. As for me, I am not worthy of your going to any trouble about me; for myself, what will these willow twigs give or add, even if they were boiled in tears?" And her neighbor replies: "Don't, Miriam, don't, my precious life, let us not give Satan a foothold by complaining. We have a mighty Father in Heaven and His mercies are over all His works. Many barren women have given birth, and children have clung to their breasts. There is a women's prayerbook that has been brought from the Holy Land; nothing I can say matters, but in that book you will discover God's acts and miracles, and in it also you will learn how to entreat God."

When Miriam visits the bathhouse Raphael remains in the House of Study. When she returns home she dresses in fine clothes like a bride on her wedding day, and stands before the mirror. At that moment it seems as if the days of her youth were returning to her. She recalls an inn on a main road, frequented by gentile lords and ladies, and cattle dealers sojourning there, and herself sitting with her father and mother, and with Raphael the husband of her youth. She recalls the crown her mother placed on her head on her wedding day, and at that moment the thought enters her mind to make herself beautiful for her husband. But then she sees reflected in the mirror the east-wall embroidery with its scenes and those two lions with their mouths open; immediately she is startled and shrinks back: "The earth is the Lord's and the fullness thereof."

And when Raphael returns home after the prayers and sees his wife in her true beauty reflected in the mirror, he is immediately attracted to her. He goes toward her to make some pleasing remark. But when he is near her, His Name, may He be blessed, flashes before him out of the mirror. Immediately he stops and recites devoutly and in holiness: "I have set the

Lord always before me," and shuts his eyes before the glory and awe of the Name. Both turn away silently. He sits in one corner and studies the *Book of Splendor*, and she sits in another corner reading the women's prayerbook, until sleep invades their eyes. They take the large bucket of water with the large copper fish embossed on its bottom, and wash their hands in preparation for reciting "Hear, O Israel" before retiring.

5

When hope and patience came to an end and she no longer had the strength to weep and pray for children, she stood before her husband heartbroken and with great humility. Said Raphael to Miriam, "What is your wish, Miriam, and what is your request?" And Miriam replied: "My wish and my request, if I have found favor in my husband's eyes, and if it please my husband to do my wish and fulfill my petition, then let him write a Torah scroll for us also."

At that moment Reb Raphael took Miriam's head and placed it on his knees, then he placed his eyes upon her eyes, his face upon her face, his mouth upon her mouth, and said to her: "Please don't, my daughter, God has not yet withdrawn His mercy from us. We shall surely still behold seed upon the earth." Miriam lowered her eyelids and replied: "May the words of your mouth enter the ears of the Holy One, blessed be He." From then on her hands were busy making a mantle for a Torah scroll, and other sacred implements, as does a woman whose hands are busy making decorative ribbons, sheets, and coverings for the expected newborn baby.

6

"Good fortune is not forever." God chastises those He loves. One Sabbath morning Miriam returned from the synagogue, put down her prayerbook, and, before she was able to remove her outer garment and prepare her heart and soul to greet her husband properly, a sigh escaped from deep within her, she began to feel alternately chilled and hot, her face turned green, her bones began rattling in their joints, and her whole skin sought to escape from her body. She lay down on her bed and remained there and never again rose or left her bed. She had not been inscribed on high for a long life, and was plucked while still in her youth.

Miriam died in the prime of her days and left her husband to his sorrows. She died in the prime of her days and left behind her neither son nor daughter.

7

At the end of the seven days of mourning Raphael the scribe arose, put on his shoes, went to the marketplace, and obtained sheets of parchment, bundles of quills, a string of gallnuts for ink, soft gut-thread for sewing together the sheets of parchment, and set his heart to the writing of a Torah scroll in memory of the soul of his wife whom God had taken away.

What may this be likened to? To a great gardener who raised beautiful plants in his garden, and all the officials who were to see the king would first come to his garden and buy beautiful flowers to take with them. Once the gardener's wife was to see the king, and the gardener said: "All others who visit the king take flowers from my garden. Now that my own wife is to visit the king it is only proper that I go down to my garden and pick flowers for her."

The comparison is clear. Raphael was a great gardener. He planted beautiful Torah scrolls in the world. And whoever was invited to appear before the King—the King over kings of kings, the Holy One, blessed be He—took a Torah scroll with him. And now that Miriam's time had come to appear before the King—the Holy One, blessed be He—Raphael immediately went down to his garden—that is, to his pure and holy table—and picked roses—that is, the letters of the Torah scroll which he wrote—and made a beautiful bouquet—that is, the Torah scroll he had prepared. Thus the work began.

8

Raphael sat and wrote. He wrote his Torah scroll day and night, interrupting the work only for prayers with the congregation and for the recitation of the kaddish. A prayer shawl was spread over the clean table, its fringes drooping below the table and getting intertwined with the fringes of the little prayer shawl he wore. On the prayer shawl lay a lined sheet of parchment dazzling in its whiteness as the sky itself in its purity.

From morning to evening the quill wrote on the parchment and beautiful black letters glistened and alighted on the parchment as birds upon the snow on the Sabbath when the Song of Moses is read. When he came to the writing of the great and awesome Name he would go down to the ritual bath and immerse himself.

Thus he sat and wrote until he completed the entire Torah scroll.

9

But the doing does not flow as fast as the words. Raphael sat at his toil a long time before he completed the writing of the scroll. His face shrank, his cheeks became hollow, his temples sunken, his eyes larger and larger, as he sat bewildered in the emptiness of his desolate house. Near its hole a mouse plays with a discarded quill, and the cat lies dejectedly on the abandoned oven. A month comes and a month goes, and time sprinkles his earlocks with gray. Raphael prods himself with the sage's saying: "Raphael, Raphael, do not forget death because death will not forget you." Month comes and month goes and there is no action and no work done. The sheet of parchment lies on the table and the quill lies in the sunshine, and the sun's reflection out of the quill shines as the hidden light from among the wings of the celestial creatures. Sunbeams come down to bathe in the scribe's inkwell, and when they depart in order to bid welcome to the shadows of the night, the sheet of parchment lies unchanged.

At times Raphael summoned strength, dipped the pen in ink, and wrote a word, but this did not lead to any more work because his eyes filled with tears. When he sat down to write a single letter in the Torah, immediately his eyes brimmed with tears which rolled down to the parchment.

> In vain do builders build palaces
> If a flooding river sweeps away their foundations;
> In vain do people kindle a memorial candle
> If the orphans extinguish it with their tears.

And when he swallowed his tears and said to himself, Now I will work, now I will write, he would reach such a peak of devout ecstasy that his quill spattered droplets of ink, and he was unable to write even a single letter properly.

It is told of the Rabbi of Zhitomir that he once asked the
Rabbi of Berditchev about the biblical verse "And Aaron
did so," on which the commentator Rashi, of blessed memory, commented that Aaron did not deviate from God's instructions. This is puzzling; how could it have been otherwise? The Holy One, blessed he He, told Aaron to kindle the
lights; would it have been possible for Aaron to deviate? Had
God instructed an ordinary man to do this, would that man
have deviated? Therefore, what is so praiseworthy about
Aaron's not having deviated? However, if the Holy One,
blessed be He, had told the Rabbi of Berditchev to kindle
the lights, he would surely have felt ecstasy and awe and
fervor, and if he tried to kindle them he would spill the
oil on the ground, and, because of his awe, would not succeed
in kindling them. But Aaron, even though he surely possessed
ecstasy and awe and fervor more than any other person, when
he came to kindle the lights, he did as God commanded,
without any deviation.

That winter it once happened that the bathhouse in Raphael's town was closed down by the authorities because it was
near collapse, and when Raphael reached a place in the Torah
scroll where the Name had to be written, he could find no bath
of purification. He took an ax, went down to the river on the
outskirts of the town, broke the ice, immersed himself in the
water three times, and returned and wrote the Name with the
joy of wondrous fervor. At that moment Raphael attained the
merit of discovering the divine secret that before a man is able
to rise to the height of joyous fervor he has to be like a man
who stands in icy water on a snowy day.

From then on Raphael sat, physically weakened, in the joy
of silence, and with emaciated hand he wielded the quill on the
parchment until he completed his scroll. The wooden rollers
on which the parchment sheets are rolled, and other sacred implements, he made by himself. In this he may be compared
to a host who always had guests in his house and had several

servants waiting on them. Once he made a feast for the king. Who should properly wait on the king? Surely the host himself.

10

And now let us recall the custom—a custom in Israel is like a law—observed at the completion of the writing of a Torah scroll.

When a scribe is about to complete a scroll, he leaves several verses at the end unfinished, in outlined lettering, in order that any Jew who had not himself had the privilege to fulfill the biblical admonition "And now ye shall write down this song for yourselves" may be afforded the opportunity to come and fill in one of the letters of the Torah. And whoever is so favored takes a pen, dips its tip in ink, and fills in the hollow, outlined letter. Raphael put down his quill, having left several verses in outlined letters, and said to himself: "I shall go and invite a quorum of ten Jews, so that the Torah will not be lonely, and saintly Jews may see and rejoice in the completion of a Torah." He walked over to the mirror to look into it and straighten out his earlocks and his beard in honor of the Torah and in honor of those who would come to rejoice with him.

The mirror was covered with a sheet. From the day of Miriam's death, peace be with her, no one had removed this sign of mourning. Raphael pulled aside the end of the sheet, looked into the mirror, and saw his own face, and the east-wall embroidery across the room, and the scroll he had written, with the hollow, outlined letters at its end. At that moment his soul stirred and he returned to the table, took the quill, and filled in the letters in the scroll he had written in memory of his wife's soul. When he completed the task he rolled up the scroll, raised it high, dancing with great joy, and he leaped and danced and sang in honor of the Torah. Suddenly Raphael stopped, puzzled about the melody he was singing in honor of the completion of the scroll. He felt sure that he had heard this melody before but could not remember where he had heard it. And now, even when he closed his lips the singing of the melody continued by itself. Where had he heard this melody?

11

Having mentioned the melody, I shall not refrain from relating where he had heard it.

It was the evening of the Festival of Rejoicing in the Torah. That evening the rabbi's House of Study was full of bright lights, every light fixture glowing with a radiance from on high. Righteous and saintly Hasidim clothed in white robes of pure silk, with Torah scrolls in their arms, circled the pulpit, dancing with holy fervor, and enjoying the pleasures of the Torah. A number of Hasidim as well as ordinary householders get the privilege of dancing with them, and they cling to the sacred Torah and to those who selflessly obey the Torah, and they forget all anger and all disputes and all kinds of troublesome trivialities. And their young children form an outer circle around them, each child carrying a colored flag, red or green or white or blue, each flag inscribed with letters of gold. On top of each flag is an apple, and on top of each apple a burning candle, and all the candles glow like planets in the mystical "field of sacred apples." And when young boys or girls see their father receive this honor, carrying a Torah scroll in his arms, they immediately jump toward him, grasping the scroll, caressing, embracing, kissing it with their pure lips that have not tasted sin; they clap their hands and sing sweetly, "Happy art thou, O Israel," and their fathers nod their heads toward the children, singing "Ye holy lambs." And the women in the outer lobby feast their eyes on this exalted holiness.

When the seventh round of the procession around the pulpit is reached, the cantor takes a Torah scroll to his bosom and calls out to the youths: "Whoever studies the Torah let him come and take a Torah scroll," and a number of fine youths come and take scrolls in their arms.

Then the cantor calls out again: "The distinguished young man, Raphael, is honored with the honor of the Torah, and with the singing of a beautiful melody."

Raphael came forward, went to the Ark, accepted the scroll from the cantor, and walked at the head of the procession. The elders stood and clapped their hands, adding to the rejoicing. The children stood on the benches chanting aloud "Ye holy lambs" and waving their flags over the heads of the youths. But when Raphael began to sing his melody all hands became still and everyone stood motionless without saying a word. Even the older Hasidim whose saintly way in prayer and in dancing with great fervor is like that of the ancient sage Rabbi Akiba—of whom it is told that when he prayed by himself, his bowing and genuflecting were so fervent that "if when you left him he was in one corner, you found him in another corner at the next moment"— even they restrained themselves with all their might from doing this. They did not lift a hand to clap because of the ecstatic sweetness, even though their hearts were consumed with fire. The women leaned from the windows of the women's gallery, and their heads hung out like a flock of doves lined up on the frieze of a wall.

Raphael held the scroll in his arm, walking in the lead with all the other youths following him in the procession around the pulpit. At that moment a young girl pushed her way through the legs of the dancers, leaped toward Raphael, sank her red lips into the white mantle of the Torah scroll in Raphael's arm, and kept on kissing the scroll and caressing it with her hands. Just then the flag fell out of her hand, and the burning candle dropped on Raphael's clothing.

After the holiday Raphael's father brought an action before the rabbi against the girl's father in the matter of Raphael's robe that had been burned because of the girl. The rabbi, indulging himself in the pleasure of a wise remark, said to the girl's father: "God willing, for their wedding day you will have a new garment made for him." Immediately they brought a decanter of brandy and wrote the betrothal contract. And for Raphael's and Miriam's wedding a new garment was made for him. This is the story of the melody.

And Raphael continues to circle the pulpit, singing sweet melodies. His voice is lovely and sad, numbing the senses but wakening the soul to rise and dance the dance of the Divine Presence. That dance without sound or movement, in which even the earlocks and beard remain motionless, and only the fringes of the prayer shawl drip down to the knees. The house is still, the feet are stilled, and the hands unmoved. The girls come down from the women's gallery to the House of Study to watch the youths dance. The youths continue to circle the pulpit, and the girls reach out with the tips of their fingers toward the Torah scrolls in the hands of the youths.

The sun has set, her last rays shine through the cracks in the shutters, and their light adorns Miriam's white dress. Raphael came toward Miriam and bowed before her with the Torah scroll held in his arm. He could not see her face because she was wrapped in her wedding dress. Silently Raphael stood and wondered where her wedding dress had come from, because he had taken it out of her wardrobe to have a curtain for the Ark made out of it. He walked over to see whether her dress hung there, but when he got there he no longer remembered what he had come for. He stood facing the wardrobe and looked into its black void. Suddenly he noticed the little bag of earth from the Land of Israel. He had placed some of this earth on Miriam's eyes in her grave. Raphael took the little bag of earth in his hand and his heart trembled violently. His hand faltered and the earth spilled to the floor of the house. His heart became agitated as that of a man who stands on sacred soil.

The lamp flickers. Raphael is wrapped in his prayer shawl, a Torah scroll in his arm, and the scroll has a mantle of fine silk on which the name of Miriam the wife of Raphael the scribe is embroidered. The house becomes filled with many Torah scrolls, and many elders dancing. As they dance they neither lift their feet nor bend their knees, but move as if they had no joints. They dance without motion, revolving their bodies, and Miriam stands in the center, her face covered, dancing with her shoulders, her arms raised into the emptiness of the room. She approaches Raphael's scroll. She takes off her veil and covers her face with her hands. Suddenly her hands slide down, her face is uncovered, and her lips cling to the mantle of the Torah scroll in Raphael's arms.

The Holy One, blessed be He, removed His robe of light, and the world stood in silent evening prayer. The lamp flickered and the wick sank into the oil. Suddenly a tongue of flame leaped up and illumined the room. Its light framed the face of Raphael the scribe who sank down with his scroll. His wife's wedding dress was spread out over him and over his scroll.

Translated by ISAAC FRANCK

Fable of the Goat

THE TALE IS told of an old man who groaned from his heart. The doctors were sent for, and they advised him to drink goat's milk. He went out and bought a she-goat and brought her into his home. Not many days passed before the goat disappeared. They went out to search for her but did not find her. She was not in the yard and not in the garden, not on the roof of the House of Study and not by the spring, not in the hills and not in the fields. She tarried several days and then returned by herself; and when she returned, her udder was full of a great deal of milk, the taste of which was as the taste of Eden. Not just once, but many times she disappeared from the house. They would go out in search for her and would not find her until she returned by herself with her udder full of milk that was sweeter than honey and whose taste was the taste of Eden.

One time the old man said to his son, "My son, I desire to know where she goes and whence she brings this milk which is sweet to my palate and a balm to all my bones."

His son said to him, "Father, I have a plan."

He said to him, "What is it?"

The son got up and brought a length of cord. He tied it to the goat's tail.

His father said to him, "What are you doing, my son?"

He said to him, "I am tying a cord to the goat's tail, so that when I feel a pull on it I will know that she has decided to leave, and I can catch the end of the cord and follow her on her way."

The old man nodded his head and said to him, "My son, if your heart is wise, my heart too will rejoice."

The youth tied the cord to the goat's tail and minded it carefully. When the goat set off, he held the cord in his hand and did not let it slacken until the goat was well on her way and he was following her. He was dragged along behind her until he came to a cave. The goat went into the cave, and the youth followed her, holding the cord. They walked thus for an hour or two, or maybe even a day or two. The goat wagged her tail and bleated, and the cave came to an end.

When they emerged from the cave, the youth saw lofty mountains, and hills full of the choicest fruit, and a fountain of living waters that flowed down from the mountains; and the wind wafted all manner of perfumes. The goat climbed up a tree by clutching at the ribbed leaves. Carob fruits full of honey dropped from the tree, and she ate of the carobs and drank of the garden's fountain.

The youth stood and called to the wayfarers: "I adjure you, good people, tell me where I am, and what is the name of this place?"

They answered him, "You are in the Land of Israel, and you are close by Safed."

The youth lifted up his eyes to the heavens and said, "Blessed be the Omnipresent, blessed be He who has brought me to the Land of Israel." He kissed the soil and sat down under the tree.

He said, "Until the day breathe and the shadows flee away, I shall sit on the hill under this tree. Then I shall go home and bring my father and mother to the Land of Israel." As he was sitting thus and feasting his eyes on the holiness of the Land of Israel, he heard a voice proclaiming:

"Come, let us go out to greet the Sabbath Queen."

And he saw men like angels, wrapped in white shawls, with boughs of myrtle in their hands, and all the houses were lit with a great many candles. He perceived that the eve of Sabbath would arrive with the darkening, and that he would not be able to return. He uprooted a reed and dipped it in gallnuts, from which the ink for the writing of Torah scrolls is made. He took a piece of paper and wrote a letter to his father:

"From the ends of the earth I lift up my voice in song to tell you that I have come in peace to the Land of Israel. Here I sit, close by Safed, the holy city, and I imbibe its sanctity. Do not inquire how I arrived here but hold onto this cord which is tied to the goat's tail and follow the footsteps of the goat; then your journey will be secure, and you will enter the Land of Israel."

The youth rolled up the note and placed it in the goat's ear. He said to himself: When she arrives at Father's house, Father will pat her on the head, and she will flick her ears. The note will fall out, Father will pick it up and read what is written on it. Then he will take up the cord and follow the goat to the Land of Israel.

The goat returned to the old man, but she did not flick her ears, and the note did not fall. When the old man saw that the goat had returned without his son, he clapped his hands to his head and began to cry and weep and wail, "My son, my son, where are you? My son, would that I might die in your stead, my son, my son!"

So he went, weeping and mourning over his son, for he said, "An evil beast has devoured him, my son is assuredly rent in pieces!"

And he refused to be comforted, saying, "I will go down to my grave in mourning for my son."

And whenever he saw the goat, he would say, "Woe to the father who banished his son, and woe to her who drove him from the world!"

The old man's mind would not be at peace until he sent for the butcher to slaughter the goat. The butcher came and slaughtered the goat. As they were skinning her, the note fell out of her ear. The old man picked up the note and said, "My son's handwriting!"

When he had read all that his son had written, he clapped his hands to his head and cried, "*Vay! Vay!* Woe to the man who robs himself of his own good fortune, and woe to the man who requites good with evil!"

He mourned over the goat many days and refused to be comforted, saying, "Woe to me, for I could have gone up to the Land of Israel in one bound, and now I must suffer out my days in this exile!"

Since that time the mouth of the cave has been hidden from the eye, and there is no longer a short way. And that youth, if he has not died, shall bear fruit in his old age, full of sap and richness, calm and peaceful in the Land of the Living.

Translated by BARNEY RUBIN

Agunot

1

IT IS SAID: A thread of grace is spun and drawn out of the deeds of Israel, and the Holy One, blessed be He, Himself, in His glory, sits and weaves—strand on strand—a prayer shawl all grace and all mercy, for the Congregation of Israel to deck herself in. Radiant in the light of her beauty she glows, even in these, the lands of her exile, as she did in her youth in her Father's house, in the Temple of her Sovereign and the city of sovereignty, Jerusalem. And when He, of ineffable Name, sees her, that she has neither been sullied nor stained even here, in the realm of her oppressors, He—as it were—leans toward her and says, "Behold thou art fair, my beloved, behold thou art fair." And this is the secret of the power and the glory and the exaltation and the tenderness in love which fills the heart of every man in Israel. But there are times—alas!—when some hindrance creeps up, and snaps a thread in the loom. Then the prayer shawl is damaged: evil spirits hover about it, enter into it, and tear it to shreds. At once a sense of shame assails all Israel, and they know they are naked. Their days of rest are wrested from them, their feasts are fasts, their lot is dust instead of luster. At that hour the Congregation of Israel strays abroad in her anguish, crying, "Strike me, wound me, take away my veils from me!"

Her beloved has slipped away, and she, seeking him, cries, "If ye find my beloved, what shall ye tell him? That I am afflicted with love." And this affliction of love leads to darkest melancholy, which persists—Mercy shield us!—until, from the heavens above, He breathes down upon us strength of spirit, to repent, and to muster deeds that are pride to their doers and again draw forth that thread of grace and love before the Lord.

And this is the theme of the tale recounted here, a great tale and terrible, from the Holy Land, of one renowned for his riches—Sire Ahiezer by name—who set his heart on going up from the diaspora to the holy city Jerusalem—may she be rebuilt and established—to work great wonders of restoration in the midst of her ruins, and in this way to restore at least a corner of the anteroom which will be transformed into our mansion of glory on the day when the Holy One, blessed be He, restores His presence to Zion—may it be soon, in our day!

And credit him kindly, Lord—credit him well for his wishes, and for his ministrations to his brethren, sons of his people, who dwell before Thee in the Land of the Living, and this though he ultimately failed.

Sire Ahiezer fathered no sons, but he praised the Ineffable sevenfold daily for the daughter who fell to his lot. He cherished her like the apple of his eye, and set maidservants and tirewomen to wait on her, that her very least wish might be honored. And, surely, she was worthy of all this respect, for she was the pattern of virtue, and all the graces were joined together in her person: princely the radiance of her countenance; like the matriarchs', her straitness of virtue; her voice pleasing as the harp of David; and all her ways modest and gentle. But all this pride was inward, and dwelt apart, in the innermost chambers, so that only the intimates of her father's house might behold her, at twilight, when— at times—she went down to walk in the garden, among the spice trees and the roses, where the doves fluttered about her

in the twilight, murmuring their fondness in her ears and
shielding her with their wings, like the golden cherubs on the
Ark of the sanctuary.

And when her season came, the season of love, her father
sent couriers to all the dispersions of Israel, to spy out a
youth that would be her match, such a paragon, a cluster of
virtue, as had no peer in all the world. Here it was that the
evil one intervened, and not in vain were the words bruited
about, by the men of Jerusalem, to the effect that Sire
Ahiezer had slighted all the seminaries and academies, all the
seats of learning in the Land of Israel when he sent to find
a match for his daughter among the sons of the exile abroad.
But who might admonish so mighty a man—who might
tender him counsel? They all began eagerly to await the
match that the Holy One, blessed be He, would provide for
this cloistered grace, glorious child, vaunted daughter of
Jerusalem.

And then, months having passed, a scroll was received
from the emissaries, declaring: "We hereby proclaim with
joy: with the aid of the Lord we have found in Poland a
boy, a wondrous lad, in virtue clad, with wisdom blest, head
and shoulders above all the rest; pious, modest, pedigreed;
model of virtue and good deed; paragon and worthy son,
wreathed in blessings from the sages, who bless this match
with all their hearts and wages." And so forth.

The grandee, Sire Ahiezer, seeing his designs were pros-
pering, thought it only fitting that the above-mentioned bridegroom hold forth at a great academy in Jerusalem, that
scholars might stream from the ends of the earth to hear
the law from his lips. What did he do? He convened all
manner of craftsmen, built a great mansion, adorned it
inside and out—painted it and gilded it, and furnished
it with several cartloads of precious texts, no jot of godly
wisdom lacking among them. And he designated a hall for
prayer, adorned it with all manner of adornment, and called
on the scribes to prepare the scrolls of the law, and on the

gold- and silversmiths to design the ornaments of the scrolls
—and all of this in order that the prayers of the sage might
be neighbor to his studies, so that he might truthfully say,
"Here is my God, and I will praise Him." The grandee, wish-
ing to consummate his work of glorifying the sanctuary, set
his heart on an Ark for the scrolls—an Ark such as the eye
of man had never seen.

He began to ask after a proper craftsman. Among the
journeymen he came on one said to be versed in the subtlest
of crafts, one Ben Uri by name—a man both modest and
diffident, a mere craftsman as met the eye were it not for the
spark that flashed from his glance, and was reflected in the
work of his hand. Ahiezer took note, and placed the work of
the Ark in his hand.

2

Sire Ahiezer took Ben Uri and lodged him by the garden,
at the bottom of his house. Ben Uri brought his tools and
readied himself for the task. Immediately, another spirit possessed him. His hands wrought the Ark; his lips uttered song
all the day.

Dinah, lovely child of Ahiezer, stood by her window, gazing into the trees, and heard. Dreaming, she was drawn to
the singer as though—God save us!—a spell had been cast.
So she went down, she and her handmaidens with her went
down, to examine the work of the man. She peered into the
Ark, she stirred his paints, examined his carvings, and picked
up his tools. All the time Ben Uri worked, singing as he
worked, working even as he sang. Dinah heard his song and
did not know her heart. And he, even as he wrought, all the
time aimed his song at her heart, to wrap it in his rapture,
so that she might stand there forever, never depart.

But as Ben Uri pursued his work, he cleaved more and

more to it, until both eyes and heart passed into the Ark; no part of him was free of it. Memory of Dinah fled him; it was as though she did not exist. Not many days passed before he stopped singing altogether; his voice rang out no more. Ben Uri stood by the Ark all day, carving figures on the Ark and breathing the soul of life into them. Lions mounted upon it, a mane of gold on each of the pair, their mouths brimming with song, uttering the glories of the Lord. On the hangings that draped the doors of the Ark, eagles poised above, their wings spread, to leap toward the sacred beasts above. At the sound of the golden bells when the Ark was opened, they would soar in their places, flap their wings, and wrap the universe in song. Already the worthies of Jerusalem awaited the day the Ark would be borne up to the House of the Lord the hand of the grandee had builded, when the scrolls of the law, crowned with silver and lapped in gold and decked out in all the jewels of sanctity, would find their place within this Ark.

Rapt, Ben Uri wrought, possessed by a joy he had never known before. In no kingdom, in no province, in the course of no labor had he exulted as he exulted here, in the place where the Divine Presence was revealed and then reviled, in the multitude of our transgressions. Not many days passed before his labors were ended. Ben Uri looked at the work of his hands and was astonished how the Ark stood firm while he himself was like an empty vessel. His soul was sad and he broke out in tears.

Ben Uri went out to seek the air among the trees in the garden, to restore his spirits a little. The sun set in the west; the face of the heavens crimsoned. Ben Uri went down to the far corners of the garden, he laid himself down, and he slept. At just that moment Dinah left her chamber. Her robe clung to her flesh; fear was on her countenance. It was many days since she had heard Ben Uri's voice, since she had looked on the man. She went to his chamber to look at the Ark. She came, but did not find him there. Dinah stood in Ben Uri's chamber, and the Ark of God stood at the open window, where Ben Uri had worked. She stood near the Ark, and examined it. The evil one came, and poured a potion of vengeance into her heart. He pointed at the Ark and said, "It is not for nought that Ben Uri takes no thought of you; it is the Ark that separates you twain." At that moment Dinah lifted her arms, and smote the Ark. The Ark teetered, and fell through the open window.

The Ark fell, but no part of it was broken, no corner of it was blemished. It lay there among the trees in the garden below. Roses and lilies nodded over it, like mourners at the ark of the dead. Night drew a mantle of black silk over the Ark. The moon came out of the clouds, and, weaving its silvery web, traced a Star of David on the shroud.

3

On her couch in the night Dinah lies and her heart wakes. Her sin weighs heavily upon her: who could bear her burden of guilt? Dinah buries her head in her pallet, oppressed by sorrow, by shame. How can she look to Heaven, how call to it for grace? Dinah springs from her couch and lights the taper in her room. In the mirror opposite, light flares out in her eyes. It had been her mother's glass, but held no trace of her mother's glance. Were Dinah to look into it now, it is only her own countenance she would see—the countenance of a sinner. "Mother, Mother!" her heart cries out. But there is no answer. Dinah rose and crossed to the window, she rested her chin on her hands, and looked out. Jerusalem is cradled in mountains. The wind swept down and entered her chamber, extinguishing the light, as in a sickroom, where some invalid sleeps. It played around her hair and through her ears, whispering sweet melodies, like the songs Ben Uri had sung. Where, oh where, is he now?

Among the trees in the garden he sleeps, like a lyre whose strings are rent, whose melodies have forsaken it. And the Ark lies prone, in the garden. The Guardian of Night unfurls his pinions of darkness, and the lions and eagles in the Ark nestle under his wings. An unspotted moon slips out of the clouds; another moon rises to meet her in the waters of the pond. They stand, face to face, like a pair of Sabbath candles. To what might the Ark have been compared at that moment? To a woman who extends her palms in prayer, while her breasts—the Tables of the Covenant—are lifted with her heart, beseeching her Father in Heaven: "Master of the Universe, this soul which Thou hast breathed into him Thou hast taken from him, so that now he is cast before Thee, like a body without its soul, and Dinah, this unspotted soul, has gone forth naked into exile. God! Till when shall the souls that dwell in Thy kingdom suffer the death of this life, in bereavement, and the service of Thy habitation sound out in suffering and dread?"

All Israel which was in Jerusalem had foregathered to consecrate the Ark, to bear it up from Ben Uri's chamber to the synagogue. They thronged into Ben Uri's chamber, but the Ark was not there. Bewildered, they cried, "Where is the Ark?—the Ark of the Lord?" "Where is the Ark?" "The Ark, where is it?" They were still crying out when they spied it, under the window, prone in the yard. Directly they began to heap abuse on its creator, saying that the ne'er-do-well, the scoundrel was surely an infamous sinner, quite unqualified for the hallowed work of the Ark: having presumed to undertake it, he had surely called down the wrath of the Heavens, which had overturned it. And, having revered the Ark, they loathed it. The rabbi immediately condemned it to banishment. Two Ishmaelites came, and heaved it into the lumber room. The congregation dispersed in torment, their heads covered with shame.

The morning star glimmered and dawned, lighting the skies in the east. The folk of Jerusalem awoke as from an evil dream. The Ark had been banished, their joy had set, Ben Uri had vanished, none knew whither. Misery reigned in the house of the Sire.

Night and day Dinah keeps to her window. She raises her eyes to the heavens, and casts them down again, like a sinner. Sire Ahiezer is dogged by worries. The synagogue his hands had builded stands desolate, without Ark, without prayer, without learning. Sire Ahiezer bestirred himself and commissioned an Ark to replace Ben Uri's. They installed it in the synagogue, but it stood there like an emblem of loss. Whoever comes to pray in the synagogue is at once struck by dire melancholy; he slips away from that place, and seeks some place of worship, humble and poor, where he can pour out his heart before God.

4

The time of rejoicing is come; the wedding day is near, and in the house of Sire Ahiezer they knead and they bake and they dress all the viands, and prepare fine draperies to hang in the gateway, for the day his daughter will enter under the bridal canopy with her partner in joy, the esteemed and the learned Ezekiel, God preserve him.

And—see!—upon the hillsides the feet of a courier—a special emissary with scroll in hand: " 'Twill be the third day hence!" They were preparing themselves to delight in the bride and the bridegroom on the day of their joy, saying, "A precious pearl it is the couriers have drawn from the sea of learning which is Poland, and the festivities will be such as Jerusalem shall not have seen the likes of, since the day her sons were driven into exile." All the men of Jerusalem went forth to welcome the bridegroom, and they brought him into the city in great honor, with tabor and cymbal and dancing. They escorted him to the house of Sire Ahiezer,

and the great ones of the city, assessing his virtues, were
dazzled by a tongue dropping pearls, and by his regal presence. Then the wedding day arrived. They accompanied the
bride to the house of the rabbi, to receive her blessing from
his lips. Suddenly, she raised her voice in weeping, and cried,
"Leave us alone!" They left her with the rabbi. She told him
all that had happened, how it was she who had overturned
the Ark. The rabbi stood mute with terror, his very vision
was confounded. But, deferring to the eminence of the bride
on this, her day of grace and atonement, began to ply her
with comfort. "My child," he said, "our sages of blessed
memory tell us that when a person takes a wife to himself,
all his sins fall away. Notice that it was person they said,
not man, and thence we gather that it was not man, the male,
that was meant, but mankind in general, so that man and
wife are one in this, that on the day of their marriage the
Holy One, blessed be He, pardons their sins. And should
you ask, How is a woman to earn her absolution, on whom
the yoke of works weighs so lightly?—know that the good
Lord has called you to the greatest of all works. And should
you ask, What could that be?, I will tell you: it is the rear-
ing of children in the ways of the Lord." And he proceeded
to speak the praises of her bridegroom, to endear him to her,
and draw her heart to his virtues. And when the rabbi came
to the matter of the Ark, he intimated that silence would
be seemly, and held that the Ark would be restored to its
rightful place, to the synagogue, and that merciful God would
grant Dinah forgiveness. After the bride had left the house
of the rabbi, the latter sent Sire Ahiezer word regarding
the restoration of Ben Uri's Ark to the synagogue. They
sought it, but did not find it. Stolen? Hidden? Ascended to
Heaven?—who could presume to say?

Day ebbed and the sun set. All the great ones of Jerusalem foregathered with Sire Ahiezer, in his house, to celebrate
his daughter's marriage. Jerusalem glowed in precious light,
and the trees in the garden were fragrant as spices. The musi-

cians plied their instruments, and the servants clapped for
good cheer. Yet, none the less, a sort of sadness has found
a place among them. This sadness attacks the bridal canopy,
and rips it into shreds. They assemble at the grandee's table,
to partake of the wedding feast. The throats of the scholars
are filled with delicate viands and wines, with song and
hymns of praise. The jester calls for a dance for the righteous,
and they move out in a ritual ring to cheer the bride and
the groom. But this dear pair are afflicted by some sadness;
it drives a wedge between them, and forces their elbows
apart. And neither drew near to the other all that night,
even in the seclusion of their chamber. The groom broods
in one corner, his thoughts straying elsewhere. He dwells on
his father's house, on Freidele, whose mother had tended his
father and him since his sainted mother had died. And Dinah
broods in the other, her thoughts going back to the Ark and
its builder who has vanished from the city, no one knowing
where he has turned.

At morning prayers the young man stood wrapped in a
prayer shawl and crowned with phylacteries. He reigns as
bridegroom all the seven days of the feast, and is not left
alone, lest envious spirits assail him. But how to ward off
the spirits that hold sway in his heart, and afflict him greatly?
Just when he is preparing to give himself over, heart and
soul, to the *shema*, and shields his eyes with his palms in
order to shut out anything that might intrude on his devotions—just then his Freidele slips into the palm of his hand,
and stands there before his eyes. And once she has accom-
modated herself there, she stays there till the end of the
service, when he unwinds his phylacteries and lays them in
their reticule. This reticule—Freidele has made for him with
characters embroidered upon it! He folds the reticule, and
wraps it in his prayer shawl, and furtively puts it away. His
father, come from Poland for the nuptials, watches him, angry and troubled. What might he be wanting in the house
of Sire Ahiezer? If wealth he craved, here was wealth, so

prodigal; if love of woman, his wife was comely and gracious; if a home, this one was fit for a king. Why, then, was he restless? They went in to breakfast, and chanted the seven blessings of nuptial felicity, and seated the couple side by side. Their bodies are close, but their hearts have been given to others.

5

And they never drew near. Month comes and month goes. In numbers the scholars assembled, to attend the law from Ezekiel's lips, and the academy was filled with holy lore. Gracious learning was on his tongue, and whatever his mode of expounding—simple or subtle or mystic—bright angels gathered around him, shedding the light of the law on his brow. But even as he teaches, anguish gnaws at his heart, as though—God forbid!—he lacks gratitude for having been deemed worthy to go up to the Holy Land.

And Dinah—Dinah sits, despondent. At times she goes out for a while, and stands by the spot where Ben Uri had wrought, and stares at his implements, which are gathering dust. She clasps her hands, and murmurs some few of the songs Ben Uri had sung, sings until her eyes are dimmed by tears. Her soul weeps in secret for her pride. Once, as Rabbi Ezekiel was passing by, he heard a pleasing melody rising within that chamber. When he paused to listen, they told him that it was no mortal voice he heard singing, but rather the evil spirits that had been created out of Ben Uri's breath as he sat and sang at his work. Rabbi Ezekiel hastened away. Thenceforth, when forced to walk in that part of the house, he averted his head, in order to avoid lending his ears to the chants of such as these.

Toward evening, Rabbi Ezekiel goes to walk in the hills. The mighty ones of Israel walk out at that hour, and their retainers go before them, striking the earth with their staffs, and all the people hasten to rise in awe and deference before them, and the sun casts purple canopies over each of the righteous as it goes down to greet its Creator. The elect, who are deemed worthy of this, are granted the privilege of finding their place in the Holy Land in their lifetime, and not only this, but those deemed worthy of dwelling there in their lifetime are privileged to enjoy the Holy Spirit for ever and ever. But Rabbi Ezekiel? His feet are planted in the gates of Jerusalem, and stand on her soil, but his eyes and his heart are pledged to houses of study and worship abroad, and even now, as he walks in the hills of Jerusalem, he fancies himself among the scholars of his own town, strolling in the fields to take the evening air.

It is told that once they found there Freidele sitting with her friends, singing:

> They have borne him far away
> To wed a dowered maiden.
> His father did not care to know
> Our hearts were heavy laden.

One day an emissary of the rabbis returned to Jerusalem from the diaspora, and brought a letter for Rabbi Ezekiel. His father was pleased to inform him that he had negotiated the home journey in safety, and now, as ever before, was bearing up under the burdens of justice and learning in their town. In passing, he thought his son might care to know that Freidele had found her mate and had moved—together with her mother—to another city, so that the sexton's wife was therefore looking after his needs. Rabbi Ezekiel read the letter and began to weep. Here was Freidele, decently wedded, and here was he, fancying her still. And his own wife? When they pass each other she stares off in one direction, he in another.

Month comes, month goes, and the academy grows ever

more desolate. The scholars, one by one, steal away. They cut a staff from some tree in the garden, take it in hand, and set off on their separate ways. It is obvious for all to see —Heaven help us!—that Rabbi Ezekiel's soul is tainted. Sire Ahiezer perceived that his works had not prospered, that the couple was ill-matched, that the marriage, in fact, was no marriage at all.

The couple stand silent before the rabbi, their eyes downcast. Rabbi Ezekiel is about to divorce his wife. And just as he did not look at her at the hour of their marriage, so he does not look at her in the hour of their parting. And just as Dinah did not hear his voice as he said to her, "Lo, thou art sanctified unto me," so she does not hear it as he says, "Lo, I cast thee forth." Our sages of blessed memory said that when a man puts his first wife away from him, the very altars weep, but here the altars had dropped tears even as he took her to wife. It was not long that Sire Ahiezer left Jerusalem with his daughter. He had failed in his settlement there; his wishes had not prospered. He went forth in shame, his spirit heavy within him. His house was deserted, the House of Study stood desolate. And the quorum that had gathered in the synagogue to honor Sire Ahiezer so long as he was there, now did not assemble there for even the first round of afternoon prayers on the day of his departure.

6

That very night, after the departure, the rabbi, seated at study, nodded over his Talmud. In a dream he saw that he would suffer exile. Next morning, following the council of our sages, he put the best possible interpretation on his dream, and fasted all day. After he had tasted a morsel and returned to his study, he heard a voice. He raised his eyes, and saw the Divine Presence in the guise of a lovely woman, garbed in black, and without adornment, nodding mournfully at him. The rabbi started out of his sleep, rent his garments, again made good his dream, and sat fasting for a day and a night, and in the dark of the following evening inquired as to the signification of his dream. Providence disclosed to him a number of things concealed from mortal sight, and he beheld with eyes of spirit the souls of those bereaved of their beloved in their lifetimes groping dismally in the world for their mates. He peered hard and saw Ben Uri. Ben Uri said to him, "Wherefore hast thou driven me out, that I should not cleave to my portion in the Kingdom?" "Is it thy voice I hear, Ben Uri, my son?" the rabbi cried, and he lifted his voice and he wept. Weeping, the rabbi woke out of his sleep, and knew that his doom had been sealed. He washed his hands, drew on his mantle, took up his staff and his wallet, and, calling to his wife, said, "My daughter, seek not after me in my going forth, for the doom of exile has been levied upon me, to redeem the forsaken in love." He kissed the *mezuzah*, and slipped away. They sought him, and did not find him.

They say he wanders still. Once an aged emissary from the Holy Land stopped at a House of Study in the diaspora. One night he nodded at his devotions, and in his sleep he heard a voice. He awoke, and saw that selfsame rabbi, holding a youth by the hem of his robe and trying to draw him away. Frightened, the emissary cried out, "Rabbi, are you here?" The rabbi vanished. The youth then confided to the emissary that when the House of Study was emptied of its worshippers, he had begun to fashion an ornament for the easterly wall of the synagogue, and the emissary had borne witness to the loveliness of that ornament, and to the craft with which it was fashioned. But as soon as he had begun, that old man had stood at his side, drawn him by the hem of his robe, and whispered, "Come, let us rise and go up to Jerusalem."

Since that time innumerable tales have been told of that rabbi, and of his sojourning in the "world of confusion,"

Mercy shield us! Rabbi Nissim, of blessed memory, who traveled about in the world for many years, used to say, "May I forfeit my portion in the redemption of Israel, if I did not behold him once floating off into the Great Sea on a red kerchief, with an infant child in his arms. And even though the hour was twilight, and the sun was setting, I swear by all that we yearn for in prayer that it was he, but as for that child—I do not know who that was."

At the present time it is said that he has been seen wandering about in the Holy Land. The world-wise cavil and quibble, and even—some of them—mock. But little children insist that at times, in the twilight, an old man hails them, and peering into their eyes drifts into the gathering dusk. And whoever has heard the tale here recounted surely knows that the man is that rabbi, he, and no other. But God alone knows for a fact.

Translated by BARUCH HOCHMAN

The Kerchief

1

EVERY YEAR my father, of blessed memory, used to visit the Lashkowitz fair to do business with the merchants. Lashkowitz is a small town of no more consequence than any of the other small towns in the district, except that once a year merchants gather together there from everywhere and offer their wares for sale in the town's marketplace; and whoever needs goods comes and buys them. In earlier times, two or three generations ago, more than a hundred thousand people used to gather together there; and even now, when Lashkowitz is in its decline, they come to it from all over the country. You will not find a single merchant in the whole of Galicia who does not keep a stall in Lashkowitz during the fair.

2

For us the week in which my father went to the market was just like the week of the Ninth of Ab. During those days there was not a smile to be seen on Mother's lips, and the children also refrained from laughing. Mother, peace be with

45

her, used to cook light meals with milk and vegetables, and all sorts of things which children do not dislike. If we caused her trouble she would quiet us, and did not rebuke us even for things which deserved a beating. I often used to find her sitting at the window with moist eyelids. And why should my mother sit at the window; did she wish to watch the passersby? Why, she, peace be with her, never concerned herself with other people's affairs, and would only half hear the stories her neighbors might tell her; but it was her custom, ever since the first year in which my father went to Lashkowitz, to stand at the window and look out.

When my father, of blessed memory, went to the fair at Lashkowitz for the first time, my mother was once standing at the window when she suddenly cried out, "Oh, they're strangling him!" Folk asked her, "What are you saying?" She answered, "I see a robber taking him by the throat"; and before she had finished her words she had fainted. They sent to the fair and found my father injured, for at the very time that my mother had fainted, somebody had attacked my father for his money and had taken him by the throat; and he had been saved by a miracle. In later years, when I found in the Book of Lamentations the words "She is become as a widow," and I read Rashi's explanation, "As a woman whose husband has gone to a distant land and who intends to return to her," it brought to mind my mother, peace be with her, as she used to sit at the window with her tears upon her cheeks.

3

All the time that Father was in Lashkowitz I used to sleep in his bed. As soon as I had said the night prayer I used to undress and stretch my limbs in his long bed, cover myself up to my ears and keep them pricked up and ready so that in case I heard the trumpet of the Messiah I might rise at once. It was a particular pleasure for me to meditate on Messiah the King. Sometimes I used to laugh to myself when I thought of the consternation that would come about in the whole world when our just Messiah would reveal himself. Only yesterday he was binding his wounds and his bruises, and today he's a king! Yesterday he sat among the beggars and they did not recognize him, but sometimes even abused him and treated him with disrespect; and now suddenly the Holy One, blessed be He, has remembered the oath He swore to redeem Israel, and given him permission to reveal himself to the world. Another in my place might have been angered at the beggars who treated Messiah the King with disrepect; but I honored and revered them, since Messiah the King had desired to dwell in their quarters. In my place another might have treated the beggars without respect, as they eat black bread even on the Sabbaths, and wear dirty clothes. But I honored and revered them, since among them were those who had dwelt together with the Messiah.

4

Those were fine nights in which I used to lie on my bed and think of Messiah the King, who would reveal himself suddenly in the world. He would lead us to the Land of Israel where we would dwell, every man under his own vine and his own fig tree. Father would not go to fairs, and I would not go to school but would walk about all day long in the courts of the House of our God. And while lying and meditating thus, my eyes would close of their own accord; and before they closed entirely I would take my fringed garment and count the knots I had made in the fringes, indicating the number of days my father stayed in Lashkowitz. Then all sorts of lights, green, white, black, red, and blue, used to come toward me, like the lights seen by wayfarers in fields and woods and valleys and streams, and all kinds of precious things would be gleaming and glittering in them; and my heart danced for joy at all the good stored away for us in the days to come, when our just Messiah would reveal himself, may it be speedily and in our days, Amen.

While I rejoiced so, a great bird would come and peck at the light. Once I took my fringed garment and tied myself to his wings and said, "Bird, bird, take me to Father." The bird spread its wings and flew with me to a city called Rome. I looked down and saw a group of poor men sitting at the gates of the city, and one beggar among them binding his wounds. I turned my eyes away from him in order not to see his sufferings. When I turned my eyes away there grew a great mountain with all kinds of thorns and thistles upon it and evil beasts grazing there, and impure birds and ugly creeping things crawling about it, and a great wind blew all of a sudden and flung me onto the mountain, and the mountain began quaking under me and my limbs felt as though they would fall asunder; but I feared to cry out lest the creeping things should enter my mouth and the impure birds should peck at my tongue. Then Father came and wrapped me in his prayer shawl and brought me back to my bed. I opened my eyes to gaze at his face and found that it was day. At once I knew that the Holy One, blessed be He, had rolled away another night of the nights of the fair. I took my fringes and made a fresh knot.

5

Whenever Father returned from the fair he brought us many gifts. He was very clever, knowing what each of us would want most and bringing it to us. Or maybe the Master of Dreams used to tell Father what he showed us in dream, and he would bring it for us.

There were not many gifts that survived long. As is the way of the valuables of this world, they were not lasting. Yesterday we were playing with them, and today they were already thrown away. Even my fine prayerbook was torn, for whatever I might have had to do, I used to open it and ask its counsel; and finally nothing was left of it but a few dog-eared scraps.

But one present which Father brought Mother remained whole for many years. And even after it was lost it was not lost from my heart, and I still think of it as though it were yet there.

6

That day, when Father returned from the fair, it was Friday, after the noon hour, when the children are freed from school. This fact should not be mentioned to children. Those Friday afternoon hours were the best time of the week, because all the week around a child is bent over his book and his eyes and heart are not his own; as soon as he raises his head he is beaten. On Friday afternoon he is freed from study, and even if he does whatever he wants to, nobody objects. Were it not for the noon meal the world would be like Paradise. But Mother had already summoned me to eat, and I had no heart to refuse.

Almost before we had begun eating my little sister put her right hand to her ear and set her ear to the table. "What are you doing?" Mother asked her. "I'm trying to listen," she answered. Mother asked, "Daughter, what are you trying to listen to?" Then she began clapping her hands with joy and crying, "Father's coming, Father's coming." And in a little while we heard the wheels of a wagon. Very faint at first, then louder and louder. At once we threw our spoons down while they were still half full, left our plates on the table, and ran out to meet Father coming back from the fair. Mother, peace be with her, also let her apron fall and stood erect, her arms folded on her bosom, until Father entered the house.

How big Father was then! I knew my father was bigger than all the other fathers. All the same I used to think there must be someone taller than he—but now even the chandelier hanging from the ceiling in our house seemed to be lower.

Suddenly Father bent down, caught me to him, kissed me, and asked me what I had learned. Is it likely that Father did not know which portion of the week was being read? But he only asked to try me out. Before I could answer he had caught my brother and sisters, raised them on high, and kissed them.

I look about me now to try and find something to which to compare my father when he stood together with his tender children on his return from afar, and I can think of many comparisons, each one finer than the next; yet I can find nothing pleasant enough. But I hope that the love haloing my father, of blessed memory, may wrap us around whenever we come to embrace our little children, and that joy which possessed us then will be possessed by our children all their lives.

7

The wagoner entered, carrying two trunks, one large, and the other neither large nor small but medium. Father looked with one eye at us and with the other at the medium trunk;

and that second trunk too seemed to have eyes and smile with them.

Father took his bunch of keys from his pocket and said, "We'll open the trunk and take out my prayer shawl and phylacteries." Father was just speaking for fun, since who needs phylacteries on Friday afternoon, and even if you think of the prayer shawl, my father had a special one for Sabbath, but he only said it in order that we should not be too expectant and not be too anxious for presents.

But we went and undid the straps of the trunk and watched his every movement while he took one of the keys and examined it, smiling affectionately. The key also smiled at us; that is, gleams of light sparkled on the key and it seemed to be smiling.

Finally he pressed the key into the lock, opened the trunk, put his hand inside, and felt among his possessions. Suddenly he looked at us and became silent. Had Father forgotten to place the presents there? Or had he been lodging at an inn where the inn people rose and took out the presents? As happened with the sage by whose hands they sent a gift to the Emperor, a chest full of jewels and pearls, and when he lodged one night at the inn, the inn folk opened the chest and took out everything that was in it and filled it with dust. Then I prayed that just as a miracle was done to that sage so that that dust should be the dust of Abraham our father, which turned into swords when it was thrown into the air, so should the Holy One, blessed be He, perform a miracle with us in order that the things with which the innkeepers had filled Father's trunk should be better than all presents. Before my prayer was at an end Father brought out all kinds of fine things. There was not a single one among his gifts which we had not longed for all the year around. And that is why I said that the Master of Dreams must have revealed to Father what he had shown us in dream.

The gifts of my father deserve to be praised at length, but

who is going to praise things that will vanish, and be lost? All the same, one fine gift which my father brought my mother on the day that he returned from the fair deserves to be mentioned in particular.

8

It was a silk brocaded kerchief adorned with flowers and blossoms. On the one side it was brown and they were white, while on the other they were brown and it was white. That was the gift which Father, of blessed memory, brought to Mother, peace be with her.

Mother opened up the kerchief, stroked it with her fingers, and gazed at Father; he gazed back at her and they were silent. Finally she folded it again, rose, put it in the cupboard, and said to Father, "Wash your hands and have a meal." As soon as Father sat down to his meal I went out to my friends in the street and showed them the presents I had received, and was busy outside with them until the Sabbath began and I went to pray with Father.

How pleasant that Sabbath eve was when we returned from the House of Prayer! The skies were full of stars, the houses full of lamps and candles, people were wearing their Sabbath clothes and walking quietly beside Father in order not to disturb the Sabbath angels who accompany one home from the House of Prayer on Sabbath eves: candles were alight in the house and the table prepared and the fine smell of white bread, and a white tablecloth spread and two Sabbath loaves on it, covered by a small cloth out of respect so that they should not feel ashamed when the blessing is said first over the wine.

Father bowed and entered and said, "A peaceful and blessed Sabbath," and Mother answered, "Peaceful and blessed." Father looked at the table and began singing,

"Peace be unto you, angels of peace," while Mother sat at the table, her prayerbook in hand, and the big chandelier with the ten candles—one for each of the Ten Commandments—hanging from the ceiling, gave light. They were answered back by the rest of the candles, one for Father, one for Mother, one for each of the little ones; and although we were smaller than Father and Mother, all the same our candles were as big as theirs.

Then I looked at Mother and saw that her face had changed and her forehead had grown smaller because of the kerchief wound around her head and covering her hair, while her eyes seemed much larger and were shining toward Father, who went on singing, "A woman of valor who shall find?"; and the ends of her kerchief which hung down below her chin were quivering very gently, because the Sabbath angels were moving their wings and making a wind. It must have been so, for the windows were closed and where could the wind have come from if not from the wings of the angels? As it says in the Psalms, "He maketh the winds His messengers." I held back my breath in order not to confuse the angels and looked at my mother, peace be with her, who stood at such a lofty rung, and wondered at the Sabbath day, which is given us for an honor and a glory. Suddenly I felt how my cheeks were being patted. I do not know whether the wings of the angels or the corners of the kerchief were caressing me. Happy is he who merits to have good angels hovering over his head, and happy is he whose mother has stroked his head on the Sabbath eve.

9

When I awakened from sleep it was already day. The whole world was full of the Sabbath morning. Father and Mother were about to go out, he to his little prayer room and she to the House of Study of my grandfather, peace be with him. Father was wearing a black satin robe and a round shtreimel of sable on his head, and Mother wore a black dress and a hat with feathers. In the House of Study of my grandfather, where Mother used to pray, they did not spend too much time singing, and so she could return early. When I came back with Father from the small prayer room she was already seated at the table wearing her kerchief, and the table was prepared with wine and cakes, large and small, round and doubled over. Father entered, said, "A Sabbath of peace and blessing," put his prayer shawl on the bed, sat down at the head of the table, said, "The Lord is my shepherd, I shall not want," blessed the wine, tasted the cake, and began, "A Psalm of David: The earth is the Lord's and the fullness thereof." When the Ark is opened on the eve of the New Year and this psalm is said, the soul's awakening can be felt in the air. There was a similar stirring in my heart then. Had my mother not taught me that you do not stand on chairs and do not clamber onto the table and do not shout, I would have climbed onto the table and shouted out, "The earth is the Lord's and the fullness thereof"; like that child in the Talmud who used to be seated in the middle of a gold table which was a load for sixteen men, with sixteen silver chains attached, and dishes and glasses and bowls and platters fitted, and with all kinds of food and sweetmeats and spices of all that was created in the six days of creation; and he used to proclaim, "The earth is the Lord's and the fullness therof."

Mother cut the cake, giving each his or her portion; and the ends of her kerchief accompanied her hands. While doing so a cherry fell out of the cake and stained her apron; but it did not touch her kerchief, which remained as clean as it had been when Father took it out of his trunk.

10

A woman does not put on a silken kerchief every day or every Sabbath. When a woman stands at the oven, what room is there for ornament? Every day is not Sabbath, but on the other hand there are festivals. The Holy One, blessed be He, took pity on His creatures and gave them times of gladness, holidays and appointed seasons. On festivals Mother used to put on a feather hat and go to the House of Prayer, and at home she would don her kerchief. But on the New Year and the Day of Atonement she kept the kerchief on all day long; similarly on the morning of Hoshana Rabbah, the seventh day of Tabernacles. I used to look at Mother on the Day of Atonement, when she wore her kerchief and her eyes were bright with prayer and fasting. She seemed to me like a prayerbook bound in silk and presented to a bride.

The rest of the time the kerchief lay folded in the cupboard, and on the eves of the Sabbaths and festivals Mother would take it out. I never saw her washing it, although she was very particular about cleanliness. When Sabbaths and festivals are properly kept, they themselves preserve the clothes. But for me she would have kept the kerchief all her life long and would have left it as an heirloom.

What happened was as follows. On the day I became thirteen years old and a member of the congregation, my mother, peace be with her, bound her kerchief around my neck. Blessed be God, who has given His world to guardians. There was not a spot of dirt to be found on the kerchief. But sentence had already been passed on the kerchief, that it was to be lost through me. This kerchief, which I had observed so much and so long, would vanish because of me.

11

Now I shall pass from one theme to another until I return to my original theme. At that time there came a beggar to our town who was sick with running sores; his hands were swollen, his clothes were rent and tattered, his shoes were cracked, and when he showed himself in the street the children threw earth and stones at him. And not only the children but even the grownups and householders turned angry faces on him. Once when he went to the market to buy bread or onions the shopwomen drove him away in anger. Not that the shopwomen in our town were cruel; indeed, they were tender-hearted. Some would give the food from their mouths to orphans, others went to the forest, gathered twigs, made charcoal of them, and shared them free among the beggars and poor folk. But every beggar has his own luck. When he fled from them and entered the House of Study, the beadle shouted at him and pushed him out. And when on the Sabbath eve he crept into the House of Study, nobody invited him to come home with them and share the Sabbath meal. God forbid that the sons of our father Abraham do not perform works of charity; but the ministers of Satan used to accompany that beggar and pull a veil over Jewish eyes so that they should not perceive his dire needs. As to where he heard the blessing over wine, and where he ate his three Sabbath meals—if he was not sustained by humankind he must have been sustained by the grace of God.

Hospitality is a great thing, since buildings are erected and administrators appointed for the sake of it and to support the poor. But I say it in praise of our townsfolk, that although they did not establish any poorhouse or elect any administrators, every man who could do so used to find a place for a poor man in his own house, thus seeing the troubles of his brother and aiding him and supporting him at the hour of his need; and his sons and daughters who saw this would learn from his deeds. When trouble befell a man he would groan; the walls of his house would groan with him because of the mighty groaning of the poor; and he would know that there are blows even greater than that which had befallen him. And as he comforted the poor, so would the Holy One, blessed be He, in the future comfort him.

12

Now I leave the beggar and shall tell only of my mother's kerchief, which she tied around my neck when I entered the age of Commandments and was to be counted a member of the congregation. On that day, when I returned from the House of Study to eat the midday meal, I was dressed like a bridegroom and was very happy and pleased with myself because I was now putting on phylacteries. On the way I found that beggar sitting on a heap of stones, changing the bandages of his sores, his clothes rent and tattered, nothing but a bundle of rags which did not even hide his sores. He looked at me as well. The sores on his face seemed like eyes of fire. My heart stopped, my knees began shaking, my eyes grew dim, and everything seemed to be in a whirl. But I took my heart in my hand, nodded to the beggar, and greeted him, and he returned the greeting.

Suddenly my heart began thumping, my ears grew hot, and a sweetness such as I had never experienced in all my days took possession of all my limbs; my lips and my tongue where sweet with it, my mouth fell agape, my two eyes were opened, and I stared before me as a man who sees in waking what has been shown him in dream. And so I stood staring

in front of me. The sun stopped still in the sky, not a creature was to be seen in the street; but He in His mercy sat in
Heaven and looked down upon the earth and let His light
shine bright on the sores of the beggar. I began loosening my
kerchief to breathe more freely, for tears stood in my throat.
Before I could loosen it, my heart began racing in strong
emotion, and the sweetness, which I had already felt, doubled
and redoubled. I took off the kerchief and gave it to the beggar. He took it and wound it around his sores. The sun came
and stroked my neck.

I looked around. There was not a creature in the market,
but a pile of stones lay there and reflected the sun's light.
For a little while I stood there without thinking. Then I
moved my feet and returned home.

13

When I reached the house I walked around it on all four
sides. Suddenly I stopped at Mother's window, the one from
which she used to look out. The place was strange; the sun's
light upon it did not dazzle but warmed, and there was perfect rest there. Two or three people passing slowed their
paces and lowered their voices; one of them wiped his brow
and sighed deeply. It seems to me that that sigh must still be
hanging there.

I stood there awhile, a minute or two minutes or more.
Finally I moved from thence and entered the house. When I
entered I found Mother sitting in the window as was her
way. I greeted her and she returned my greeting. Suddenly
I felt that I had not treated her properly; she had had a fine
kerchief which she used to bind around her head on Sabbaths
and festivals, and I had taken it and given it to a beggar to
bind up his feet with. Ere I had ended asking her to forgive
me she was gazing at me with love and affection. I gazed back

at her, and my heart was filled with the same gladness as I
had felt on that Sabbath when my mother had set the kerchief about her head for the first time.

The end of the story of the kerchief of my mother, peace be
with her.

Translated by I. M. LASK

To Father's House

1

CLOSE TO THE Passover holiday it happened. I was far away
from my father's house and my home town, and I was going
about my work, which has neither beginning nor end, work
which you start to no advantage and which never sets you
free. Two men smeared with plaster and paint arrived, one
of them holding a ladder. Actually I should say that the
ladder stood by itself and he, that is, this man with the
ladder, weaved his arms through the rungs. I asked them,
"What do you want?" They told me, "We were sent here
to whitewash the room."

I was involved in my work, and it was difficult for me to
stop. Yet I was bothered not so much by the interruption
as by the dirt, for these painters certainly would not go out
of their way to spread a sheet over the books, and protect
them from being soiled.

To avoid their reading my thoughts, I pretended not to
see them and stared at a hole in the wall, near the ceiling.
Straw and palm-branches hanging down from the ceiling
covered the hole, and flies and mosquitoes clustered there.
I said to myself, What do you gain with your windows
screened if flies and mosquitoes come in through that hole?

I left the workers and went up to the attic, to clear away

the straw and palm-branches so that the hole would be readily visible until I could find a board to cover it.

My little niece came to help me. For some reason which is beyond me, I scolded her: "I don't need you and the likes of you!" She shrugged her shoulders and disappeared.

Meanwhile, the workers began acting in my room as if it belonged to them. I thought to myself, I'm superfluous here, and I can't do my work, so I'll go to my home town, to my father's house. I haven't seen my father for many years now, and I haven't fulfilled the commandment of respect for Father. At the railroad station I boarded a train going to my town. Through no fault of my own, the train was delayed on the way, and when I reached town the festival had already begun; it was Passover night.

2

Passover night had come, and I had come to my home town. Since it was time for prayer, I went to pray, but I did not go where my father usually prays, for if he should see me so suddenly it would confuse his praying.

When I reached the courtyard of the House of Prayer I hesitated slightly, because I saw a lighted candle suspended in the air in a bottle swinging in the wind but not extinguished, and because at that moment one of the men whose avocation is interpreting the Bible—Isaac Euchel by name— came over to show me an explanation of a difficult verse at the end of the book of Joshua, or perhaps it was the beginning of the book of Hosea. Isaac Euchel's explanation was a bit forced, and medieval commentators had already interpreted the verse in a simple style and in clear, lucid language. Nevertheless, I nodded my head, as if the world needed his interpretation.

While talking, he took out a cigarette and asked for a light. A child came over to light a match, but it went out. He took another match and gave it to me, saying "Give it to that gentleman there." I told Isaac Euchel, "Your generation, with all its expertise in grammar, didn't know how to adorn this splinter with a word as suitable as 'match.'" And when I had said this it occurred to me he would answer that since there had been no matches in his day there had been no need for this word. Euchel took the match and said, "Now, then, we can make a flame with this metch" (he said "metch," with an "e" not an "a"). "But what good is a metch which goes out before serving its purpose?"

Alas, I tried to outsmart him and I was outsmarted.

3

I do not remember how we took leave of each other. When I left him, I found myself standing in a large room which had a set table, with bottles, jars, and glasses on it. And two women were standing there, one old and one young. And a candle was suspended in the air in a bottle, like the one I had seen in the courtyard of the House of Prayer. Or perhaps there were two candles which seemed to be one. The room opened directly onto the street, with two doorways facing each other. I turned to the doorway facing my father's house and started to leave.

The old woman said, "Is that the way it's done, coming in and going out?" I realized that I had come upon an inn and that they had made no profit from me. Placing my hand over my heart as an oath and a promise, I said, "Believe me, I'll come again."

The old woman's face lit up. "I know, sir, that you will keep your promise." I nodded my head, saying to myself,

"I only hope I don't forget, I only hope I don't forget," even though it is difficult to keep such a promise. First of all, I had come to my father's town and my father certainly would insist that I stay at home, and not allow me to go to inns or hotels. And second—I've forgotten the second reason.

When I took leave of the old woman I started to run, for it was Father's custom to sit down to the Passover meal immediately following services. While I was running, it occurred to me that I might have passed his house. I raised my eyes to see. My eyes shut themselves firmly, and I did not see a thing. With great effort I opened them just a narrow crack, and saw three or four men running in haste and confusion. I meant to ask them where my father's house was, but they were strangers, even though they were dressed like the men of my town. I let them pass, without asking them.

Time does not stand still, but I was standing still, seeking my father's house, not knowing where it was. For I had not been in the town in many years and I had forgotten many of its roads, and the town itself had changed somewhat. Then I remembered that Father lived next to a man who was known by everyone.

I looked for someone who would tell me where the house was. My eyes shut themselves again. With all my might I struggled to open them. They opened just a narrow crack again. The moon came out, to shine upon them dust and ashes. I saw a little girl. Pointing with her finger, she said, "That's it." I wanted to ask her, "How do you know what I am looking for?" My eyes opened and I saw Father, holding his cup of wine, about to chant the blessing over the wine, hesitating, waiting.

Afraid that I might disturb the quiet of the house, I wanted to explain to Father, letting my eyes speak for me, telling him why I had delayed coming for so long. My eyes closed again. Struggling, I opened them. Suddenly I heard a noise like that of a sheet being torn. Actually, no sheet was being torn, but one small cloud high above was being torn, and once it was torn the moon came out, splitting the clouds, and a sweet light shone upon the house and upon Father.

Translated by Jules Harlow

To the Doctor

FATHER LAY ILL, and a moist cloth was bound about his head. His face was weary from illness, and a heavy worry dulled his blue eyes—like a man who knows his death is near but doesn't know what will happen to his young sons and daughters. Opposite him, in another room, lay my little sister. Each was ill with a different illness for which the doctor had not yet given a name.

My wife stood in the kitchen and shelled peas from their pods. After she placed them in the pot she put on her wrap and went with me to the doctor.

As I was leaving the house, I stumbled upon some peas, for when my wife was busy preparing them for eating they had rolled out of her hands and scattered on the stairs. I wanted to sweep them away before the mice would smell them and come, but I was rushed; it was already past eight-thirty, and at nine o'clock the doctor used to visit his friends and drink with them all night, while at home there lay two sick persons who needed special attention—particularly my little sister, who used to caper and sing, exciting our anxiety lest she fall from her bed or disturb Father from his sleep.

Those peas began to bother me because they turned into lentils, and lentils are a food of trouble and mourning. It is easy to understand the sorrow of a man who has two sick persons at home, and things put this kind of thought into his heart.

It is not proper to tell that I was a bit resentful toward my wife and I thought to myself: What good are women? She had toiled to prepare a meal for us and at the end all the peas had scattered. When I saw she was running and knew why she was running my resentment disappeared, and love entered my heart.

On the way, right next to the black bridge, Mr. Andermann met me and greeted me. I returned his greeting and wanted to leave him. He held my hand and told me that he had just arrived from the city of Bordeaux in England and today or tomorrow he and his father would come to see our new house. "Ay, Ay, Ay," said Mr. Andermann, "they tell all sorts of wonders about your house." I contorted my face to give it a pleasing expression and reflected, Why does he say he will come with his father? Does Mr. Andermann have a father? And I reflected further: Couldn't this excessive attempt to give my face a pleasing appearance leave an impression after it? I remembered the peas which had turned into lentils and I began to worry about retribution.

So that Mr. Andermann might not realize what was in my heart, I put my hand into my pocket and took out my watch; I saw that nine o'clock was near, and at nine the doctor used to go to his club and get drunk, while there at home lay two sick persons whose illness had no name. When Mr. Andermann saw I was in haste, he understood in his usual way that I was hurrying to the post office. He said, "The postal arrangements have changed and you don't have to hurry."

I left Mr. Andermann in his error and I didn't tell him about the sick persons lest he bother me with advice and detain me.

There came a stately old man in whose House of Study I used to pray on the High Holy Days. I have heard many cantors, but I have not heard a precentor like him whose prayer is beautiful and clear even during his crying. I had wanted to speak to him many times, but I never could. Now he set upon me his eyes which were bleary from crying and looked at me affectionately, as if he were saying, "Here I am; let us talk, if you wish." Mr. Andermann grasped my hand and didn't let me go. Actually, I could have removed my hand from his and gone off, but on that very same day a dog had bitten me and torn my clothes, and had I turned my face from Mr. Andermann and gone he would have seen the tear.

I remembered the time when the old man stood before the reader's desk during the prayer "And because of our sins . . ." and beat his head on the floor until the walls of the House of Study quaked. My heart quaked and I was drawn toward him, but Mr. Andermann grasped my hand. I stood and twisted my face and tried to give it a pleasing expression.

My wife crossed the bridge and reached the doctor's house which was next to the post office and stood before the entrance of the house, her shoulders twitching from sorrow and waiting. I removed my hand from Mr. Andermann's hand and went toward my wife. The black bridge quaked under my feet and the waves of the river swelled and rose, rose and swelled.

Translated by Arnold J. Band

The Document

THREE DAYS I spent in the office of the gray bureau. A certain relative, whose name I didn't even recognize, had written to me from a certain city I'd never heard of, asking me to go to a certain office and obtain for him such-and-such a document on which his whole life depended.

My throat was sore—and my whole body. Just the same, I got up very early and went to get my relative's document—thinking all the time that I would find it immediately and then go back to bed. I was fighting a cold which had troubled me all winter and which had returned that day with renewed force. I entered the office humbly and timidly. As I had gotten up early and not a soul was there before me, I was sure there would be no long delay before they gave me the document.

At that hour the cleaning woman was sweeping the building and raising clouds of dust. My lungs became blocked and my voice choked off. I said to myself, I'd better wait a minute until my throat clears; otherwise the official won't know what I want, and all my efforts will be wasted.

As I was standing, the office suddenly filled with hordes of people pushing one another, standing in angry, sullen compliance, and looking avidly toward the men and women clerks who sat at their battered desks scratching away with gray pens on pads and ledgers. I too was pushed first to this clerk and then to another, and I kept my head lowered timidly in the hope they would turn to me and ask what I want. But they paid no attention to me and of course asked me nothing. This was all to the good, for had they asked I doubt whether I could have said a word with all that dust clogging my throat.

So one day passed and so a second. From dawn to dusk I stood in that office. My feet became leaden and my spirit exhausted. Occasionally I was moved from one spot to another, from one room to another; I stood before this clerk or that clerk; I was pushed again and returned to the room from which I started. The clerks sat on—their faces bent over their papers and their pens writing automatically, incessantly. The clock ticked gloomily away. Its hand moved slowly, and a dead fly was stuck to it and moved along with it.

On the third day things got a little better for me. A new clerk came in to replace one of the clerks who had died. This new clerk, by the name of Nahman Horodenker, was a blond, well-built youth with clear spectacles over his good eyes. From his name and facial expression, as from his bear-like movements, I could tell that he was a countryman of mine. All I had to do was announce publicly that he was a Galician Jew, and immediately I would have had the upper hand. But some indefinable misgiving, something like conscience, stopped me. I swallowed my words and was silent.

Meanwhile I was getting sicker and sicker, and I could think of nothing else. I had been ill twice that winter, and each time the first symptoms had been the same—a swelling of the tongue, a tickle in the throat, dry and cracked lips. Now the symptoms were appearing again. My eyes blurred, my forehead began to sweat, and my throat became hoarse. I took a cigarette from my pocket and lit it. Without waiting to finish, I lit another. I had already forgotten why I had come to this office, and why I was standing here, and why I was being pushed and was running from room to room and from clerk to clerk.

Suddenly I heard a noise and felt my left foot expanding

in its shoe. I looked down and saw that the shoe lace had snapped, but before I had a chance to tie it, they called my name. Looking up, I saw a man sitting alone at a small table covered with a soiled black oilcloth, and with files of papers to his right and left; his eyes smiled in his bent head.

I relaxed and rejoiced as one does in recognizing a man one knew before the war. It was the druggist of the municipal hospital in my home town, who always had a glass of soda to offer me whenever I came to visit a sick friend. The druggist looked up and motioned me to be seated. This gesture of compassion touched me, yet I didn't feel right about sitting down because of the papers that were on the chair. He took out a bar of chocolate and offered it to me.

I said to myself, It's now three days and three nights that I haven't seen my wife and children, and they're undoubtedly complaining about me; now I'll be able to placate them with some chocolate.

As I stretched out my hand to take it, though, I saw that the druggist had not intended to give me the whole piece. I became ashamed of my greediness, I blushed and lowered my eyes.

Slowly looking up I saw some professor sitting to the right of my acquaintance. He had a short, blond beard, a cane rested between his knees, and a hidden sneer played on his lips. I nodded and greeted him.

At this he grasped my hands and informed me that he had ingeniously solved a great problem. That letter "L" in a certain word, which everyone mistakenly believes to be part of its root, is not etymologically related to the word and should be substituted with another letter.

The professor's pronouncement was clear to me and the word he was talking about was completely explained. Yet, I was puzzled by a different problem of phonology. . . .

In the meantime the day had cleared up, and I knew that in a certain spot near the edge of the table my acquaintance

had left me a piece of bread—except that I couldn't tell where
it was. But in any case, the mass of people had begun once
again its squeezing and shoving. I was pushed outside and
found myself standing on a large balcony floating on an end-
less ocean.

Translated by JOSEPH MOSES

Friendship

MY WIFE HAD RETURNED from a journey, and I was very happy. But a tinge of sadness mingled with my joy, for the neighbors might come and bother us. "Let us go and visit Mr. So-and-so, or Mrs. Such-and-such," I said to my wife, "for if they come to us we shall not get rid of them in a hurry, but if we go to them we can get up and be rid of them whenever we like."

So we lost no time and went to visit Mrs. Klingel. Because Mrs. Klingel was in the habit of coming to us, we went to her first.

Mrs. Klingel was a famous woman and had been principal of a school before the war. When the world went topsy-turvy, she fell from her high estate and became an ordinary teacher. But she was still very conscious of her own importance and talked to people in her characteristic patronizing tone. If anyone acquired a reputation, she would seek his acquaintance and become a frequent visitor in his house. My wife had known her when she was a principal, and she clung to my wife as she clung to anyone who had seen her in her prime. She was extremely friendly to my wife and used to call her by her first name. I too had known Mrs. Klingel in her prime, but I doubt whether I had talked to her. Before the war, when people were not yet hostile to each other, a man could meet his neighbor and regard him as his friend even if he did not talk to him.

Mrs. Klingel was lying in bed. Not far away, on a velvet-covered couch, sat three of her woman friends whom I did not know.

When I came in I greeted each of them, but I did not tell them my name or trouble myself to listen to theirs.

Mrs. Klingel smiled at us affectionately and went on chattering as usual. I held my tongue and said to myself: I have really nothing against her, but she is a nuisance. I shall be walking in the street one day, not wanting anyone to notice me, when suddenly this woman will come up to me and I will ask her how she is and be distracted from my thoughts. Because I knew her several years ago, does that mean that I belong to her all my life? I was smouldering with anger, and I did not tell myself: If you come across someone and you do not know what connection there is between you, you should realize that you have not done your duty to him previously and you have both been brought back into the world to put right the wrong you did to your neighbor in another incarnation.

As I sat nursing my anger, Mrs. Klingel said to my wife, "You were away, my dear, and in the meantime your husband spent his nights in pleasure." As she spoke, she shook her finger at me and said, laughingly, "I am not telling your wife that pretty girls came to visit you."

Nothing had been further from my thoughts in those days than pleasure. Even in my dreams there was nothing to give me pleasure, and now this woman tells my wife, "Your husband had visits from pretty girls, your husband took his pleasure with them." I was so furious that my very bones trembled. I jumped up and showered her with abuse. Every opprobrious word I knew I threw in her face. My wife and she looked at me in wonderment. And I wondered at myself too, for after all Mrs. Klingel had only been joking, and why should I flare up and insult her in this way? But I was boiling with anger, and every word I uttered was either a curse or an insult. Finally I took my wife by the arm and left without a farewell.

On my way out I brushed past Mrs. Klingel's three friends, and I believe I heard one saying to the other, "That was a strange joke of Mrs. Klingel's."

My wife trailed along behind me. From her silence it was obvious that she was distressed, not so much because I had shamed Mrs. Klingel but because I had fallen into a rage. But she was silent out of love, and said nothing at all.

So we walked on without uttering a word. We ran into three men. I knew one of them, but not the other two. The one I knew had been a Hebrew teacher, who had gone abroad and come back rich; now he spent his time stuffing the periodicals with his verbiage. These teachers, even if their pupils have grown up, still treat them as schoolmasters do and teach them things of no importance. But in one of his articles I had found a good thing, and now we had met I paid him a compliment. His face lit up and he presented me to his companions, one of whom had been a senator in Poland, while the other was the brother of one of Mrs. Klingel's three friends—or perhaps I am mistaken and she has no brother.

I should have asked the distinguished visitors if they liked the city, and so forth, but my wife was tired from the journey and still distressed, and it was hard to stop. So I cut the conversation short and took my leave.

My wife had already gone off, without waiting for me. I was not angry at her for not waiting. It is hard for a young woman to stand and show herself to people when she is sad and weary.

While I was walking, I put my hand in my pocket and took out an envelope or a letter, and stopped to read: "The main trial of Job was not that of Job, but of the Holy One, blessed be He, as it were, because He had handed over His servant Job to Satan's power. That is, God's trial was greater than Job's: He had a perfect and upright man, and He placed him in the power of Satan." After reading what I had written, I tore up the envelope and the letter, and scattered the pieces to the wind, as I usually do to every letter, sometimes before I read it and sometimes at the time of reading.

After I had done this, I said to myself: I must find my wife. My thoughts had distracted me and I had strayed from the road; I now found myself suddenly standing in a street where I had never been before. It was no different from all the other streets in the city, but I knew I had strayed to a place I did not know. By this time all the shops were locked up, and little lamps shone in the windows among all kinds of commodities. I saw that I had strayed far from home, and I knew I must go by a different road, but I did not know which. I looked at a stairway bounded on both sides by an iron fence and went up until I reached a flower shop. There I found a small group of men standing with their backs to the flowers, and Dr. Rischel standing among them, offering them his new ideas on grammar and language.

I greeted him and asked: "Which way to . . ." but before I could say the name of the street I started to stammer. I had not forgotten the name of the street, but I could not get the words out of my mouth.

It is easy to undersand a man's feelings when he is looking for the place where he lives but, when he is about to ask, cannot pronounce the name. However, I took heart and pretended I was joking. Suddenly I was covered in a cold sweat. What I wanted to conceal I was compelled to reveal. When I asked again where the street was, the same thing happened again.

Dr. Rischel stood there amazed: he was in the midst of expounding his new ideas, and I had come along and interrupted him. Meanwhile, his companions had gone away, looking at me mockingly as they left. I looked this way and that. I tried to remember the name of my street, but could not. Sometimes I thought the name of the street was Humboldt and sometimes that it was West Street. But as soon as I opened my mouth to ask I knew that its name was neither Humboldt nor West. I put my hand in my pocket, hoping to find a letter on which I would see my address. I found two letters I had not yet torn up, but one had been sent to my old home, which I had left, and another was addressed *poste restante*. I had received only one letter in this house where I was living, and I had torn it up a short time before. I started reciting aloud names of towns and villages, kings and nobles, sages and poets, trees and flowers, every kind of street name: perhaps I would remember the name of my street—but I could not recall it.

Dr. Rischel's patience had worn out, and he started scraping the ground with his feet. I am in trouble and he wants to leave me, I said to myself. We are friends, we are human beings, aren't we? How can you leave a man in such distress? Today my wife came back from a journey and I cannot reach her, for the trivial reason that I have forgotten where I live. "Get into a streetcar and come with me," said Dr. Rischel. I wondered why he was giving me such unsuitable advice. He took me by the arm and got in with me.

I rode on against my will, wondering why Rischel had seen fit to drag me into this tramcar. Not only was it not bringing me home, but it was taking me further away from my own street. I remembered that I had seen Rischel in a dream wrestling with me. I jumped off the tramcar and left him.

When I jumped off the car I found myself standing by the post office. An idea came into my head: to ask for my address there. But my head replied: Be careful, the clerk may think you are crazy, for a sane man usually knows where he lives. So I asked a man I found there to ask the clerk.

In came a fat, well-dressed man, an insurance agent, rubbing his hands in pleasure and satisfaction, who buttonholed him and interrupted him with his talk. My blood boiled with indignation. "Have you no manners?" I said to him. "When two people are talking, what right have you to interrupt them?" I knew I was not behaving well, but I was in a temper and completely forgot my manners. The agent looked at me in surprise, as if saying: What have I done to you? Why should you insult me? I knew that if I was silent he would have the best of the argument, so I started shouting again, "I've got to go home, I'm looking for my house, I've forgotten the name of my street, and I don't know how to get to my wife!" He began to snigger, and so did the others who had gathered at the sound of my voice. Meanwhile, the clerk had closed his window and gone away, without my knowing my address.

Opposite the post office stood a coffeehouse. There I saw Mr. Jacob Tzorev. Mr. Jacob Tzorev had been a banker in another city; I had known him before the war. When I went abroad, and he heard I was in difficulties, he had sent me money. Since paying the debt I had never written to him. I used to say: Any day now I will return to the Land of Israel and make it up with him. Meanwhile, twenty years had passed and we had not met. Now that I saw him I rushed into the coffeehouse and gripped both his arms from behind, clinging to them joyfully and calling him by name. He turned his head toward me but said nothing. I wondered why he was silent and showed me no sign of friendship. Didn't he see how much I liked him, how much I loved him?

A young man whispered to me, "Father is blind." I looked and saw that he was blind in both his eyes. It was hard for me not to rejoice in my friend, and hard to rejoice in him, for when I had left him and gone abroad there had been light in his eyes, but now they were blind.

I wanted to ask how he was, and how his wife was. But when I started to speak I spoke about my home. Two wrinkles appeared under his eyes, and it looked as if he were peeping out of them. Suddenly he groped with his hands, turned toward his son, and said, "This gentleman was my friend." I nodded and said, "Yes, that's right, I was your friend and I am your friend." But neither his father's words nor my own made any impression on the son, and he paid no attention to me. After a brief pause, Mr. Tzorev said to his son, "Go and help him find his home."

The young man stood still for a while. It was obvious that he found it hard to leave his father alone. Finally the father opened his eyes and gazed at me. His two beautiful eyes shone, and I saw myself standing beside my home.

Translated by MISHA LOUVISH

A Whole Loaf

1

I HAD NOT tasted anything all day long. I had made no preparations on Sabbath eve, so I had nothing to eat on the Sabbath. At that time I was on my own. My wife and children were abroad, and I had remained all by myself at home; the bother of attending to my food fell upon myself. If I did not prepare my meals or go to hotels and restaurants, I had to put up with hunger inside me. On that particular day, I had intended to eat at a hotel; but the sun had flamed like a furnace, so I decided it was better to go hungry than to walk about in that heat.

In all truth, my dwelling did not keep the heat from me either. The floor was as hot as glowing fire, the roof fevered like piercing fire, the walls simply burned like fire, and all the vessels simply sweated fire, so that it was like fire licking fire, fire of the room licking at the body, and the fire of the body licking against the fire of the room. But when a man is at home, he can soak himself in water if he likes, or take off his clothes when he wants to, so that they do not weigh on him.

Once the greater part of the day had passed, and the sun weakened, I rose and washed myself and dressed, and went off to eat. I was pleased to think that I would be sitting at a well-spread table with a clean tablecloth on it, and waiters and waitresses attending to me while I ate properly prepared food that I had not needed to exhaust myself about. For I was already tired of the poor food I used to prepare for myself at home.

The day was no longer hot, and a gentle breeze was blowing. The streets were filling up. From the Mahneh Yehuda Quarter to the Jaffa Gate or nearby, the old men and women and the lads and girls were stretching their legs all the way. Round fur hats and caps and felt hats and turbans and tarbooshes shook and nodded, on and amid hairy and hairless heads. From time to time fresh faces joined them, coming from Rabbi Kook Street and from the Sukkat Shalom and Even Yisrael and Nahlat Shiva Quarters, and from the Street of the Prophets which people have the bad habit of calling the Street of the Consuls; as well as from all the other streets to which the authorities had not yet managed to give names. All day long they had been imprisoned in their homes by the heat. Now that day was past and the sun was losing its strength, they came out to glean a little of the atmosphere of Sabbath twilight which Jerusalem borrows from the Garden of Eden. I was borne along with them till I came to a solitary path.

2

While I was being carried along, an old man knocked at his window to draw my attention. I turned my head and saw Dr. Yekutiel Ne'eman standing at the window. I hurried over with great pleasure, for he is a great sage, and his words are pleasant. But when I came there, he had vanished. I stood looking into his house until he joined me and greeted me. I greeted him in return, and waited to hear some of those great thoughts we are accustomed to hearing from him.

Dr. Ne'eman asked me how my wife and children were. I sighed and answered, "You have reminded me of my trouble.

They are still abroad and want to come back to the Land of Israel."

"If they want to come back," said he, "why don't they come?"

I sighed and said, "There's some delay."

"Verily the delay comes from a crooked way," said he, rhyming on my word. And he began to scold me. "There's some laziness about you," said he, "so that you have not devoted yourself to bringing them back; and the result for you is that your wife and children are wandering about without father or husband while you are without wife and children."

I looked down at the ground in shame and said nothing. Then I raised my head and turned my eyes to his mouth, in the hope that he would say something consoling. His lips were slightly open, and a kind of choked rebuke hung from them, while his fine, grayshot beard had creased and grown wavy, like the great sea when it rages. I regretted having brought his wrath down on me, and causing him to bother about such trifles. So I took counsel with myself and began to talk about his book.

3

This was a book about which opinions were largely divided. There are some scholars who say that whatever is written in it as from the mouth of the Lord (. . . .) was written by Yekutiel Ne'eman, who neither added nor took away anything from His words. And that is what Yekutiel Ne'eman declares. But there are some who say this is certainly not the case, and that Ne'eman wrote it all himself and ascribed his words to a certain Lord whom no man ever saw.

This is not the place to explain the nature of that book. Yet this I must add, that since it first became known the world has grown slightly better, since a few people have improved their behavior and somewhat changed their natures; and there are some who devote themselves body and soul to doing everything in the manner described there.

In order to make Dr. Ne'eman feel more pleased, I began proclaiming the virtues of his book and said, "Everybody admits that it is a great work and there is nothing like it." Then Yekutiel turned his face from me, let me be, and went his way, I stood eating my heart with grief and remorse for what I had said.

But Dr. Ne'eman did not remain annoyed with me for long. As I was about to go away, he returned with a packet of letters to be taken to the post office and sent by registered mail. I put the letters in my breast pocket and placed my hand on my heart, as a promise that I would perform my mission faithfully.

4

On the way I passed the House of Study and entered to recite the evening prayers. The sun had already set entirely, but the beadle had not yet kindled the light. In view of the mourning of Moses, the congregation did not engage in the study of the Torah, but sat discoursing and singing and taking their time.

Stars could already be seen outside, but complete darkness still held sway within the building. At length the beadle lit a light, and the congregation rose to recite the evening prayers. After the Havdalah ceremony, which brings the Sabbath day to a close, I rose to go to the post office.

All the grocery stores and other shops were open, and people crowded around the kiosks on every side. I also wished to cool myself with a glass of soda water, but since I was in a hurry to send off the letters, I kept my desire in check and did without drinking.

Hunger began to oppress me. I considered whether I should go and eat first. After starting, I changed my mind and said, Let me send off the letters and then I shall eat. On the way I thought to myself, If only Ne'eman knew that I am hungry, he would urge me to eat first. I turned myself about and went toward the restaurant.

Before I had taken more than two or three steps, the power of imagination arrived. What it imagined! What did it not imagine! All of a sudden it brought a sickbed before me. There's a sick man somewhere, I told myself, and Dr. Ne'eman has been told about it and has written down a remedy for him; and now I have to hurry and take the letter containing it to the post office. So I got set to run to the post office.

In the middle of my running I stopped and thought, Is he the only doctor there is? And even if he is, does he promise that his remedy is going to help? And even if it does help, do I really have to put off my meal, when I haven't eaten anything at all the whole day long? My legs grew as heavy as stone. I did not go to eat because of the force of imagination, while I did not go to the post office because of my reasoning.

5

Since I was standing still, I had time to consider my affairs. I began to weigh what I ought to do first and what I ought to do later, and reached the decision to go to an eating place first, since I was hungry. I turned my face at once to the restaurant and marched off as quickly as I could before some other thought should strike me; for a man's thoughts are likely to delay his actions. And in order that my thoughts should not confuse me I gave myself good counsel, picturing all the kinds of good food for which the restaurant was well known. I could already see myself sitting, eating and drinking and enjoying myself. The force of imagination helped me, producing more than an average man can eat or drink, and making good to my taste each article of food and drink. Undoubtedly the intention was for the best, but what pleasure does a hungry man have when he is shown all kinds of food and drink but is given no chance to enjoy them? Maybe he can find satisfaction from this in dream, but it is doubtful if he will do so when awake.

This being the case, I went back toward the restaurant, thinking over what I should eat and drink. At heart I was already happy to be sitting in a pleasant building at a spread table, among fine folk busy eating and drinking. Then maybe I would find a good acquaintance there, and we would spice our repast with pleasant conversation which satisfies the heart and does not weigh on the soul; for I would have you know that Dr. Ne'eman had weighed somewhat on my heart.

Remembering Dr. Ne'eman, I remembered his letters. I began to feel afraid that I might be so carried away by my talk with my friend that I would not send the letters off. So I changed my mind and said, Let us go to the post office first and be done with the job, so that afterwards we can sit comfortably and the letters will not keep on burdening my mind.

6

If only the ground had moved along under me, I would have done my mission at once. But the ground stood still, and the way to the post office is hard on the feet, because the ground is broken and uneven with heaps of earth and stones; while when you do get there the postal clerks are not in the habit of hurrying but keep you hanging about, and by the time they finish whatever it is they are doing, all the food will get cold and you will find no hot dishes so that you are bound to remain hungry. But I gave no thought to this and went to the post office.

It is easy to understand the state of a man who has two courses in front of him: if he takes one, it seems to him that he has to follow the other; and if he takes the other, it seems to him that he ought to go along the first one. At length he takes the course that he ought to take. Now that I was going to the post office, I wondered that I could possibly have had any doubt for a while and wished to give my own trifling affairs precedence over the affairs of Dr. Ne'eman. And within a short while I found myself standing at the post office.

7

I was just about to enter when a carriage came along and I saw a man sitting in it. I stood and stared in astonishment: now, when as much as a horseshoe is not to be found in town, a man comes along in a two-horse carriage. And what was still more surprising, he was mocking the passersby, and driving his horses along the pavement.

I raised my eyes and saw that he was Mr. Gressler. This Mr. Gressler had been the head of an agricultural school abroad, but there he used to ride a horse and here he drove a carriage. When he was abroad he used to joke with the peasants' daughters and the simple folk, and here in the Land of Israel he fooled about with anybody and everybody. Yet he was an intelligent and polite person, and although he was a fleshy fellow, his fleshiness was not noticed by reason of his wide learning.

This Mr. Gressler had something about him that attracted all who saw him. So it is not surprising that I was also affected.

On this occasion Mr. Gressler sat leaning back in his carriage, the reins loose in his hand and dragging below the horses' legs, as he watched with pleasure while people passed on either side and return to the place from which they had run, and jumped about in front of the horses, the dust of their feet mingling with the dust of the horses' hooves; all of them alike as cheerful as though Mr. Gressler were only out to please them.

This Mr. Gressler was my acquaintance, one of my special acquaintances. Since when have I known him? Possibly since the days I reached a maturity of knowledge. Nor do I exaggerate if I say that from the day I met him we have never ceased to have a liking for one another. Now, although all and sundry like him, I can say that he prefers me to all of them, since he has taken the trouble to show me all kinds of pleasures. When I used to tire of them he would amuse me with words of wisdom. Mr. Gressler is gifted with exceptional wisdom, of the kind that undermines all the wisdom you may have learned elsewhere. Never did he ask for any compensation, but he gives of his bounty and is happy to have people accept it. Ah, there were days when I was a lad and he went out of his way to divert me; until the night my house was burned down and all my possessions went up in flames.

The night my house burned, Mr. Gressler sat playing cards with my neighbor. This neighbor, an apostate Jew, was a dealer in textiles. He lived below with his wares, while I lived above with my books. From time to time my neighbor told me that there was no great demand for his goods, that all his textiles were like paper since they were made in wartime; now that the war was over, textiles were being made of proper wool and flax again, and nobody wanted to make a suit out of the substitute stuffs which wear through and tear as soon as they are put on, if he could get himself real material. "Are you insured?" Mr. Gressler asked him. "Insured I am," he answered. While they were talking Mr. Gressler lit a cigar and said, "Drop this match in this rubbish heap and collect your insurance money." He went and set his goods on fire, and the whole house was burned down. That apostate who was insured received the value of his goods, while I, who had not insured my possessions, came out of it in a very bad way. All that I had left after the fire I spent on lawyers, because Mr. Gressler persuaded me to take action against the municipality for not saving my home and, what was more, making the fire worse. That night the firemen had had a party and grown drunk, filling their vessels with brandy and beer, and when they came to put the fire out, they made it burn even more.

For various reasons I kept my distance from Mr. Gressler after that, and it almost seemed to me that I was done with him for good and all, since I bore him a grudge for being the cause of my house burning down, and since I was devoting myself to Yekutiel Ne'eman's book. Those were the days when I was making myself ready to go up to the Land of Israel and neglected all worldly affairs; and since I was neglecting these worldly affairs, Mr. Gressler let me be. But when I set out for the Land of Israel the first person I ran across was Gressler, since he was traveling by the same ship as I was; save that I traveled on the bottom deck like poor folk do, while he traveled on the top deck like the rich.

I cannot say that I was very happy to see Mr. Gressler. On the contrary, I was very sad for fear he would remind me of my one-time deeds. So I pretended not to see him. He noticed this and did not bother me. Then it seemed to me that since our paths did not cross on board ship, they would do so even less on the land. But when the ship reached the port, my belongings were detained at the customs, and Mr. Gressler came and redeemed them. He also made things easier for me in my other affairs until we went up to Jerusalem.

Thenceforward we used to meet one another. Sometimes I visited him and sometimes he visited me, and I don't know who followed the other more. Particularly in those days when my wife was away from the country. I had nothing to do at that time, and he was always available. And when he came he used to spend most of the night with me. His was pleasant company, for he knew all that was going on, and had the inside story even before the things happened. Sometimes my heart misgave me, but I disregarded it.

8

Seeing Mr. Gressler in front of the post office, I signaled and called him by name. He stopped his carriage and helped me up.

I forgot all about the letters and the hunger and went along with him. Or maybe I did not disregard the hunger and the letters, but I put them aside for a little while.

Before I had begun talking to him properly, Mr. Hophni came toward us. I asked Mr. Gressler to turn his horses to one side, because this Hophni is a bothersome fellow, and I am afraid to have too much to do with him. Ever since he invented a new mousetrap, it has been his habit to visit me two or three times a week, to tell me all that is being written about him and his invention. And I am a weak person, I am, who cannot bear to hear the same thing twice. It is true that the mice are a great nuisance, and the mousetrap can greatly correct the evil; but when this Hophni goes gnawing at your brains, it's quite likely that you would prefer the mice to the conversation of the trapmaker.

Mr. Gressler did not turn his horses away, but on the contrary ran the carriage up to Hophni and waved to him to get in. Why did Mr. Gressler think of doing this? Either it was in order to teach me that a man has to be patient, or because he wanted to have some fun. Now I was not at all patient at that time, nor was I in the mood for fun. I stood up, took the reins out of his hands, and turned the horses off in a different direction. Since I am not an expert in steering horses, the carriage turned over on me and Mr. Gressler, and we both rolled into the street. I yelled and shouted, "Take the reins and get me out of this!" But he pretended not to hear and rolled with me, laughing as though it amused him to roll about with me in the muck.

I began to fear that a motorcar might pass and crush our heads. I raised my voice higher, but it could not be heard because of Mr. Gressler's laughter. Woe was me, Mr. Gressler kept on laughing, as though he found pleasure in dusting himself with the dust of the horses' feet and fluttering between life and death. When my distress came to a head, an old carter came along and disentangled us. I rose from the ground and gathered my bones together and tried to stand. My legs were tired and my hands were strained and my bones were broken, and all of my body was full of wounds. With difficulty I pulled myself together and prepared to go off.

Although every part of me was aching, I did not forget my hunger. I entered the first hotel that came my way, and before entering the dining hall I cleaned off all the dirt and wiped my injuries and washed my face and hands.

This hotel has an excellent name throughout the town for its spacious rooms and fine arrangements and polite and quick service and good food and excellent wine and worthy guests. When I entered the dining hall, I found all the tables full, and fine folk sitting, eating and drinking and generally enjoying themselves. The light blinded my eyes and the scent of the good food confused me. I wanted to snatch something from the table in order to stay my heart. Nor is there anything surprising about that, as I had tasted nothing all day long. But when I saw how importantly and gravely everybody was sitting there, I did not have the courage to do it.

I took a chair and sat at a table and waited for the waiter to come. Meantime I took the bill of fare and read it once, twice, and a third time. How many good things there are which a hungry man can eat his fill of, and how long it seems to take until they are brought to him! From time to time I looked up and saw waiters and waitresses passing by, all of them dressed like distinguished people. I began to prepare my heart and soul for them, and started weighing how I should talk to them. Although we are one people, each one of us talks ten languages, and above all in the Land of Israel.

9

After an hour, or maybe a little less, a waiter arrived and bowed and asked: "What would you like, sir?" What would I like and what wouldn't I like! I showed him the bill of fare and told him to fetch me just anything. And in order that he should not think me the kind of boor who eats anything without selecting it, I added to him gravely, "But I want a whole loaf." The waiter nodded his head and said, "I shall fetch it for you at once, I shall fetch it for you at once."

I sat waiting until he came back with it. He returned carrying a serving dish with all kinds of good things. I jumped from my place and wanted to take something. He went and placed the food in front of somebody else, quietly arranged each thing separately in front of him, and chatted and laughed with him, noting on his list all kinds of drinks which the fellow was ordering for his repast. Meanwhile he turned his face toward me and said, "You want a whole loaf, don't you, sir? I'm bringing it at once."

Before long he came back with an even bigger tray than the first one. I understood that it was meant for me and told myself, That's the meaning of the saying: the longer the wait, the greater the reward. As I prepared to take something, the waiter said to me, "Excuse me, sir, I'm bringing you yours at once." And he arranged the food in front of a different guest most carefully, just as he had done before.

I kept myself under control and did not grab anything from others. And since I did not grab anything from others I told myself, Just as I don't grab from others, so others won't grab my share. Nobody touches what's prepared for somebody else. Let's wait a while and we'll get what's coming to us, just like all the other guests who came before me; for it's first come, first served.

The waiter returned. Or maybe it was another waiter and, because I was so hungry, I only thought it was the same one. I jumped from my chair in order to remind him of my presence. He came and stood and bowed to me as though mine were a new face. I began wondering who this waiter could be, a fresh fellow or the one from whom I had ordered my food; for if he were a fresh waiter, I would have to order afresh, and if it were the same one, all I had to do was to remind him. While I was thinking it over, he went his way. A little later he returned, bringing every kind of food and drink, all for the fellows sitting to the right or the left of me.

Meanwhile fresh guests came and sat down and ordered all kinds of food and drink. The waiters ran and brought their orders to them. I began to wonder why they were being served first when I had been there before them. Maybe because I had asked for a whole loaf and you could not get a whole loaf at present, so they were waiting till they could get one from the baker. I began to berate myself for asking for a whole loaf, when I would have been satisfied even with a small slice.

10

What is the use of feeling remorseful after the deed? While I was bothering my heart, I saw a child sitting holding white bread with saffron of the kind that my mother, peace be with her, used to bake us for Purim, and which I can still taste now. I would have given the world for just a mouthful from that bread. My heart was standing still with hunger, and my two eyes were set on that child eating and jumping and scattering crumbs about him.

Once again the waiter brought a full tray. Since I was sure he was bringing it for me, I sat quietly and importantly, like a person who is in no particular hurry about his food. Alas, he did not put the tray in front of me but placed it in front of somebody else.

I began to excuse the waiter with the idea that the baker had not yet brought the whole loaf, and wanted to tell him that I was prepared to do without it. But I could not get a word out of my mouth because of my hunger.

All of a sudden a clock began striking. I took my watch out of my pocket and saw that it was half-past ten. Half-past ten is just a time like any other, but in spite of this I began to shake and tremble. Maybe because I remembered the letters of Dr. Ne'eman which I had not yet sent off. I stood up hastily in order to take the letters to the post office. As I stood up, I bumped against the waiter fetching a tray full of dishes and glasses and flagons and all kinds of food and drink. The waiter staggered and dropped the tray and everything on it fell, food and drink alike; and he also slipped and fell. The guests turned their heads and stared, some of them in alarm and some of them laughing.

The hotel keeper came and calmed me down and led me back to my place, and he asked me to wait a little while until they fetched me a different meal. From his words I understood that the food which had fallen from the waiter's hands had been intended for me, and now they were preparing me another meal.

I possessed my soul in patience and sat waiting. Meanwhile my spirit flew from place to place. Now it flew to the kitchen where they were preparing my meal, and now to the post office from which letters were being sent. By that time the post office doors were already closed, and even if I were to go there it would be no use; but the spirit flew about after its fashion, even to places that the body might not enter.

11

They did not fetch me another meal. Maybe because they had not yet had time to prepare it, or maybe because the waiters were busy making up the accounts of the guests. In any case, some of the diners rose from the table, picking their teeth and yawning on their full stomachs. As they went out, some of them stared at me in astonishment, while others paid me no attention, as though I did not exist. When the last of the guests had left; the attendant came in and turned out the lights, leaving just one light, still burning faintly. I sat at a table full of bones and leavings and empty bottles and a dirty tablecloth and waited for my meal, as the hotel keeper himself had asked me to sit down and wait for it.

While I was sitting there I suddenly began to wonder whether I had lost the letters on the way, while I had been rolling on the ground with Gressler. I felt in my pocket and saw that they were not lost; but they had become dirty with the muck and the mire and the wine.

Once again a clock struck. My eyes were weary and the lamp was smoking and black silence filled the room. In the silence came the sound of a key creaking in the lock, like the sound of a nail being hammered into the flesh. I knew that they had locked me into the room and forgotten about me, and I would not get out until they opened next day. I closed my eyes tight and made an effort to fall asleep.

I made an effort to fall asleep and closed my eyes tight. I heard a kind of rustling and saw that a mouse had jumped onto the table and was picking at the bones. Now, said I to myself, he's busy with the bones. Then he'll gnaw the table-cloth, then he'll gnaw the chair I'm sitting on, and then he'll gnaw at me. First he'll start on my shoes, then on my socks, then on my foot, then on my calf, then on my thigh, then on all my body. I turned my eyes to the wall and saw the clock. I waited for it to strike again and frighten the mouse, so that it would run away before it reached me. A cat came and I said, Here is my salvation. But the mouse paid no attention to the cat and the cat paid no attention to the mouse; and this one stood gnawing and that one stood chewing.

Meanwhile the lamp went out and the cat's eyes shone with a greenish light that filled all the room. I shook and fell. The cat shivered and the mouse jumped and both of them stared at me in alarm, one from one side and the other from the other. Suddenly the sound of trotting hooves and carriage wheels was heard, and I knew that Mr. Gressler was coming back from his drive. I called him, but he did not answer me.

Mr. Gressler did not answer me, and I lay there dozing until I fell asleep. By the time day broke, I was awakened by the sound of cleaners, men and women, coming to clean the building. They saw me and stared at me in astonishment with their brooms in their hands. At length they began laughing and asked, "Who's this fellow lying here?" Then the waiter came and said, "This is the one who was asking for the whole loaf."

I took hold of my bones and rose from the floor. My clothes were dirty, my head was heavy on my shoulders, my legs were heavy under me, my lips were cracked and my throat was dry, while my teeth were on edge with a hunger-sweat. I stood up and went out of the hotel into the street, and from the street into another until I reached my house. All the time my mind was set on the letters that Dr. Ne'eman had handed over for me to send off by post. But that day was Sunday, when the post office was closed for things that the clerk did not consider important.

After washing off the dirt I went out to get myself some food. I was all alone at that time. My wife and children were out of the country, and all the bother of my food fell on me alone.

Translated by I. M. LASK

From Lodging
to Lodging

1

NOT ONE GOOD THING happened all winter. Before I was free
of one illness I was seized by another. The doctor had become
a steady visitor; two or three times a week he came to examine
me. He felt my pulse and wrote out prescriptions, changing
his medicines and his advice. The doctor was always on call,
and the whole house was filled with all kinds of cures whose
smell reminded one of death. My body was weak and my lips
were cracked. My throat was sore, my tongue was coated, and
my vocal cords would produce nothing more than a cough.
I had already given up on myself. But the doctor had not
given up on me. He was constantly piling up pill after pill
and giving new names to my illness. In spite of it all, we
saw no change for the better.

Meanwhile, the cold season passed. The sun began to rise
earlier each day and each day it tarried longer in the sky. The
sky smiled at the earth and the earth smiled at man, putting
forth blossoms and flowers, grasses and thorns. Lambs rol-
licked about and covered the land, children poured from
every house and every shack. A pair of birds came out of the
sky, leaves and stubble in their beaks, and hopped from my
window to a tree and from the tree to my window, chirping
as they built themselves a home. There was a new spirit in

the world, and the world began to heal. My limbs lost their stiffness; they became lithe and limber. Even the doctor's spirit had changed. His instruments seemed to be lighter and he was light-hearted and happy. When he came in he would say, "Well now, spring certainly has arrived," and he would open a window, knocking over two or three bottles of medicine, not caring if they broke. He still would examine me in order to write out prescriptions. At the same time he would write down a woman's name and put it in his jacket or stuff it under the watch strap on his left wrist. After several days, he advised me to change my place of residence for a change of climate, to go down to Tel Aviv, for example, to enjoy the sea air.

When moving time came and I had to leave my lodgings, I decided to go down to Tel Aviv. I said to myself, "He who changes his residence changes his luck. Perhaps the sea will help me get my health back."

The room I rented in Tel Aviv was narrow and low; its windows faced a street filled with people rushing back and forth. There were many shops on this street, dispensing soda and ice cream. And there was one further drawback: the bus station, noisy all day and not resting at night. From five in the morning until after midnight buses came and went, as well as all kinds of two- and four-wheeled vehicles. When this tumult stopped and the soda vendors' kiosks closed, an echo began to resound within my room, as when a stone is thrown against a brass drum, making its sides resound. Often I awoke from my sleep to the sound of clinking glasses and rolling wheels, as if all the soda vendors on the street had gathered within the walls of my house to pour drinks for their customers, and as if all the buses were racing on the roof of the house. Then again, perhaps these sounds were no mere echo but the real sounds of buses and of street cleaners going about their work at night, when people sleep. And as for the pouring of drinks, a neighbor had returned from a meeting and had opened a tap to douse his head in cold water, and it had seemed to me that the soda vendors were pouring drinks. Because of all this, my nights passed without sleep, my mornings without a dream. I gave up on sleep and tried to lie quietly awake, but the city's fish merchants came to shout their wares and the sun came to heat my room like Gehenna.

2

Because of lack of sleep I could not enjoy whatever is available for one to enjoy in Tel Aviv. I betook myself to the sea and took off some of my clothes. Even this exertion tired me, and I could not take off the rest. I took off one shoe; I was unable to take off the other. At times the waves of the sea would come toward me, inviting me in or driving me away. Finally I would return to my room, more weary than when I had left it. And my friends were already warning me, saying, "Leave your lodgings or you will come to a bad end." With fantasy and with words they portrayed all sorts of dangers which were likely to befall a person in such lodgings. Some spoke calmly with me, and some told me of bad things that had befallen them. If I retained any ability to think, I thought that they were right, that I must leave these lodgings. But not every thought leads to action. I remained where I was, until a new trouble appeared. What kind of trouble? The landlord had a child whose frail body was a meeting ground for all kinds of ailments. Before my arrival he had lived with his grandmother; after I arrived, his mother brought him home, because she longed for her son or because my rent enabled her to support the child. I do not know if he was better off with his grandmother; with his mother he was not well off. She was a do-gooder, attending to everyone's affairs with no time to attend to her own son. Each morning she would put him outside with a tomato or a roll in his hand, kiss him on the mouth, tell him what he should and should not do, and leave him. His father, too, was somewhat busy looking for work, and did not have as much free time as he wanted. The child would lie around on the doorstep of the house and lick at dirt or scrape plaster from the wall and eat it. Didn't his mother feed him? But it is human nature to want what we don't have, and it is not human nature to be satisfied with what we do have. Whenever I walked by he would stretch his thin arms and hang on to me, and not let go until I took him in my arms and rocked him back and forth. Why was he attracted to me? I certainly was not attracted to him. I treat children as I treat their parents. If I like them I get closer to them; if I do not like them I keep my distance from them. Humanity has invented many lies, nor am I free of them, but of one thing I can boast: where children are concerned I never lie.

All of this applied to daytime. Nighttime was worse. From the moment they put the child to bed until they wake him he cries and whimpers, stopping only to groan. When he neither cries nor groans it is even worse, for then he seems to be dead, Heaven forbid. I say to myself, Get up and wake his father and mother. Before I can get up I hear the sound of crying and groaning. Like everyone else, I dislike both sounds. But, in this case, the child's cries and groans are dearer to me than all the musical instruments in the world, for then I know that he is alive.

3

In short, this child was attached to me, perhaps because his father and mother did not take care of him and he longed for human companionship, perhaps because I rocked him back and forth. In any case, he would never let me pass the doorstep without taking him in my arms. When I did take him in my arms, he would poke his fingers into my eyes and grin. Throughout the day he smiled only when he stuck his fingernails into my eyes. Often his father and mother would scold him. "Bobby, no! Bobby, no!" But from their manner of scolding it was clear that they were pleased with his cleverness. I, who did not share the joy of his father and mother, could not understand: when flies and mosquitoes crawled over his sores he was too lethargic to chase them away, but whenever he caught sight of my eyes he immediately sprang into action.

I too began to act cleverly. When I had to leave, I checked first to see if Bobby was outside. If he was, I would wait in my room. But since my room was not comfortable to sit in, I would be forced to go out. When I went out, the child would climb on me with a double measure of love, and would not leave me alone until I took him in my arms and rocked him. And, while rocking, he would stick his fingers into my eyes and grin. When I put him down he would shout, "Moo moo, oinkle, moo," which is to say, "More more, uncle, more." Who composed this jingle, the child or a nurseryschool teacher? In any case, the nonsense syllables were something that a nursery teacher would compose. Man's superiority over animals lies in his power of speech, but all of God's works require a process of "redemption" on the part of man, and nurseryschool teachers are the ones who do this. Since he asked for more, I would take him in my arms again and rock him, while he stuck his fingernails into my eyes and shouted, "Bobby! Bobby!" He could see his reflection in my eyes and was trying to snatch it away.

When a man is suffering he should examine his deeds. If he is humble and modest, he blames himself for his misfortunes; if he is neither, he blames others. If he is a man of action, he tries to rid himself of his trouble through action; if he is a man of contemplation, he waits until his trouble ends by itself. Sometimes it goes away, or another trouble appears, causing the first one to be forgotten. I, who have attained neither the passivity of the humble nor the zeal of men of action, would sit and ponder, Why do they make doorsteps for houses? If there were no doorstep, the child would not lie around there and I would not run into him.

I have already mentioned my friends; because of their affection I shall mention them again. At first they warned me. When their predictions came true, they began talking to me as people talk to someone who is sick, and they would say, "The prime need for any man is a place to live in, especially one who has come here to be healed." Since it was difficult for me to change my quarters, I tried to shrug off the matter with a talmudic saying: "A man should never change his quarters." What did my friends say? "In spite of the Talmud we shall rent another room for you." But talk is easier than action, let alone than friendship. This being so, I stayed where I was.

There was one woman who did not argue with me, but took the trouble to find me a pleasant location with a pleasant climate, and she would not desist until I went with her to see it.

She told me that the owner of this house usually did not rent rooms. However, his daughter had gone to a kibbutz, her room remained empty, and he had agreed to rent it. And the rent was no more than what I was paying already. He had explicitly mentioned that "Money is not the main thing; it's the tenant. If a man is looking for rest, I will gladly open my house to him."

4

Among vineyards and orchards rises a hill surrounded on all sides by pleasant trees. On this hill stands a small house. One reaches it by walking up grass-covered steps. And a hedge of fruit trees surrounds the house, shading the house and the grass. One enters a yard wherein is a pool of water with small fish. When I saw the house and the yard, I was glad and I had doubts. I was glad that a man in the Land of

Israel had all this, and I had my doubts that this place was for me.

The lady of the house came out. She greeted us gladly and looked approvingly at me. Then she led us into a pleasant room where the heat of the day was not felt, and brought us cool water to drink. The owner of the house came in, an aging man of about sixty, tall and lean, his head bent slightly to the left. His blue eyes were filled with sadness, but love of humanity shone in them. He greeted me and poured a drink for us. After we drank, he showed me the room I had come to rent.

A pleasant, square room suddenly stood open before me. Its wooden furniture was simple, but every piece appeared indispensable. This was also true of the picture on the wall, painted by the daughter, a picture of a girl alone in a field, looking at the setting sun. Sunset usually brings on sadness, but this one brought on sweet rest. And this was true of the breeze which blew from outside, and it was true of the entire room. After I rented the room, the owner of the house invited us to his garden for a glass of tea. A breeze was blowing from the trees and from the sea, the tea kettle was steaming, and the repose of peace and tranquility hung over the table and the people. As we sat there the lady of the house told us about her daughter who had left every comfort for the kibbutz. She was not complaining, but spoke like a mother who loves to talk about her daughter. The owner of the house was silent. But he looked at us with affection so that he seemed to have joined our conversation.

5

I asked him how he had come here. He answered and said, "I came here as most men in the Land of Israel came here. But some come when they are young; they are happy with the land and the land is happy with them. And some come when they are old; they are happy with the land but the land is not happy with them. I did not have the privilege of coming in my youth, but in my old age I came, even though I had given serious thought to the land before I reached old age. How did this come about? I was a grain merchant and once, in a field, as I walked behind the reapers, I thought about the Land of Israel and the Jews living on their own land, plowing and sowing and reaping. From that time on I could not stop thinking about the Land of Israel. I thought: May I be found worthy of seeing it. I did not intend to settle, but only to see it. During those years I was preoccupied with my business affairs and I had no time to emigrate. Then the war came and closed the road to us.

"When things calmed down and the roads were opened, I sold everything I owned and I came to the Land of Israel, not just to see it but to settle. For in those days, the land in which I had lived had become like Gehenna for Jews, and they could not stand up against their enemies.

"I did not buy land, for most of my life was over and I was not fit to work the land. And I did not want to work through others, since I did not want to be supported by their labors even if the land were mine. I decided to buy some houses, and to support myself from the rent. But I left that enterprise before I scarcely began. Why? The night I reached the Land of Israel I could not sleep. I went outside, to sit at the door of my hotel. The sky was clear and pure, the stars sparkled, and a quiet, secure repose reigned above, but below, on earth, there was neither quiet nor repose. Buses dashed madly about and people rushed in excitement and boys and girls shuffled wearily along, singing, and all kinds of musical instruments screeched from every house, every window.

I considered my surroundings, and I did not know whether to be filled with anger or with pity, for it certainly was possible that they also wanted to sleep, and that their apartments were not made for rest, just as my hotel was not, but since I was an old man, I sat on a bench, while they, being young, milled about in the streets. After several hours, the noises of the city died away, and I thought that I would go to lie down. When I was about to go inside I heard a weary voice. I turned this way and that, but saw no one. The voice seemed to be coming out of the ground, and I was reminded of the followers of Korah who had been swallowed up by the earth. But they are said to sing, while this was a voice of suffering and cursing. I looked again, and saw some light coming up underfoot, and realized that a cellar was there, with people living in it. I thought: Is it possible that in a city in the Land of Israel, built by the great leaders of Israel to enhance the people Israel with grace and greatness in the Land of Israel, people are living in a cellar? I got up and walked away, so that I would not steal any air from them. All that night I could not sleep because of the mosquitoes and because of disturbing thoughts. Finally I reached the conclusion that I could never buy houses in the city, since no one knows what will become of them, for certainly that landlord too had come to Israel out of love and ended up doing what he did.

"I began visiting the outskirts of the city, and I found this hill. But I did not buy it until I had thought about the neighbors first. When I was satisfied that they were not in the class of those who cut up our land like so many olives to make merchandise out of it, I built a house in which my wife, my daughter, and I could live. I planted a garden to appease the land, and the land was appeased, for it gives us fruit and vegetables and flowers."

The lady of the house added, "If people have money they usually travel abroad every year to mend their bodies and to be healed. For this purpose they leave their homes to travel for days by train and by ship. They come to a place with pleasant air, find cramped lodgings which are not pleasant and which have no air. But my husband has made our lodging in a pleasant place with pleasant air, and we do not need to wear ourselves out on the road. We live here in our house, enjoying everything with which the Lord has blessed us."

Before I left, I took out a one-pound note to give to the owner of the house as a deposit. He waved his hand and said, "If you like the room, you will come; but if you do not come, where will I find you to return your money?" I rejoiced that God had brought me to pleasant lodgings and an honest landlord, and I thanked my companion for having brought me here.

In short, I liked the room and the landlord and the location, and the rent was no higher than I was paying the father of the child. I rejoiced over the repose that awaited me in that house and over the sweet sleep in store for me there. Someone who has known neither sleep by night nor repose by day can imagine my joy over that room.

6

It is easier for a man to grow wings and fly from one lodging to another than to tell his landlord, "I am leaving your lodgings." For there is some embarrassment involved, as though it were repugnant for you to live with him—in addition to whatever you make him lose in rent.

Since I was thinking about leaving my lodgings, I paid no attention to the roar of the buses and the tumult of the street. And since I stopped thinking about them, sometimes I even slept. And since I slept, my heart slumbered, free of troubles. I thought to myself: There are people, like those living in cellars, who would be happy in a room like mine, and I didn't need to look for other lodgings. But since I had rented another room I had to move there. But, since I had not yet left my lodgings, perhaps there was no need to leave.

While I was debating whether or not to leave, my eyes

began bothering me. I went to a doctor, and he wrote me a prescription for eyedrops and warned me against touching my eyes with my fingers lest they become worse.

When I am alone I can be careful. But whenever that child sees me he hangs on to me and pokes his fingers into my eyes. And it is not bad enough that his fingers are dirty; his own eyes are diseased. What good is it for a doctor to warn those who take heed if he doesn't warn those who don't?

But Heaven helped me. It so happened that I had to take a trip. Because of this, there was no fear of embarrassing the landlord, since he realized that I was going out of town. I took leave of him and his wife in friendship, and because of their friendship they even let me hold the child in my arms. As I left, they said, "If you should return to Tel Aviv, our house is open to you." I nodded to them, reciting silently, "Praised be He who has rid me of you." From this day on you will not have the privilege of seeing me under your roof.

For eight days I was on the road. I had much trouble and much trouble was caused to me. But since I knew that soon I would move into comfortable lodgings, I accepted all troubles gladly, looking forward to the day of my return to Tel Aviv.

I had much trouble and much trouble was caused to me. But I also took joy in much happiness. I passed through the land and I saw that we had several more villages. Places that had produced only thistles and thorns had become like a garden of God. And like the land, so too the people were happy in their labors and rejoicing in building their land, their sons and daughters healthy and wholesome. Their hands were not soiled, and their eyes were not diseased. It is a pleasure to take a child in your arms. He does not stick his fingers into your eyes, and when he touches you it is as though a pure breeze has blown across your face.

At one kibbutz I met the daughter of my new landlord. Had most of my years not been behind me, and had I not rented lodgings from the parents of this young woman, I might have remained in that kibbutz. I left her as one leaves a friend, happy that he will see him again.

7

I was very happy to return to Tel Aviv, happier than I had been for many years. I could already picture myself living in a pleasant room, in a pleasant climate, with pleasant furniture and pleasant people, and I would come and go with no child to stick his fingers into my eyes. But most important of all would be the sleep, uninterrupted by buses and vendors and crying and groaning. Between you and me, for many years now I have considered man's purpose to be sleep, and whoever has mastered sleep, and knows how to sleep, is as important in my eyes as if he knew why man was created and why man lives. Because of this, it is easy to understand my great joy at coming to occupy lodgings where sleep awaited me.

I do not know if that house is still standing, and, if it is, whether they have not made offices and stores and soda stands out of it, as they have done with most of the houses in Tel Aviv. In those days, it was unique among houses, the pleasantest of houses.

8

When the train arrived in Tel Aviv, my heart began to dance. At last I was entering the city and my room, to sprawl out on the bed for a good sleep. Praised be He who has preserved such satisfaction in His world for His creatures.

I called a porter and he took my baggage. Feeling very expansive, I asked him out of friendliness where he lodged and if he had pleasant lodgings, after the manner of a man whose mind is clear and open enough to ask after the welfare of his neighbor. And I told him all about my new lodgings. Moving from one subject to another, we spoke about the beginning of Tel Aviv, which had been a pleasant place to live. The porter sighed. "We will never be granted peace like the peace we had here at first, until the Messiah comes."

As we spoke we came to the new house. The green hill rose among its stately trees, and lovely flowers put forth their fragrance from every side. The porter stopped and looked around. It was obvious that never in his life had he seen such a pleasant place.

Silently we walked up the grassy steps. A breeze blew in from the garden, and with it every good smell. Small birds were flying swiftly through the air, and fish were swimming below them in the pool, chasing the birds' shadows.

The landlord came out, gave me a warm welcome, and said to the porter, "Bring up the baggage."

Suddenly my heart sank, and I looked at the doorstep of the house. It was clean and scrubbed, and shadows of flowers were playing upon it. But that child was not there and did not climb all over me and did not hang on to me and did not stretch his arms to me. Silently the shadows of the flowers waved upon the doorstep; there was no child there at all. The porter stared at me. Was he waiting for me to tell him to take the baggage elsewhere? The lady of the house came out, affectionately nodded her head to me, and said, "Your room is ready."

I bowed to her and I said something. Or perhaps I said nothing, and I retraced my steps. The porter trailed after me, my baggage on his shoulder.

9

I walked until I came to my first quarters. Truly, this porter be remembered for blessing, for he kept his silence and did not disturb my thoughts. Was he thinking about the peace to come in the days of the Messiah, or did his heart warn him not to disturb a man who returns to the place he has fled?

The child was lying on the doorstep, soiled with sores. His eyelashes were stuck together, covered with some sort of green pus. It would surprise me if eyes like that could see anything.

But he saw me. And when he saw me he stretched his slender fingers and called out, "Oinkle," which is to say, "Uncle." His voice was strained, like that of a cricket whose wings were weak.

I took him in my arms and rocked him up and down, north and south. He hugged my neck and clung to me with all his might. He was lighter than a chick, and his body was very warm. He seemed to be feverish.

For a long time I held him in my arms, and he kicked at my stomach with both of his feet in inexpressible joy. Two or three times I stared at him, to remind him that his reflection was still in my eyes. But he did not stick his hands into my eyes, since during the eight days of our separation his eyes had closed from sobbing so much and he could not see his reflection.

The landlord came out. "Have you come back to us, sir?" And he looked upon himself with great importance. I embraced the child again and said nothing. Finally I put him down, and I paid the porter for his trouble. The child stretched his arms to me and said, "Oinkle, moo." I took him into my arms again. He put his head against my neck and dozed off.

I went into the house and I set him on his bed as his lips

whispered "Moo moo, oinkle, moo," which is to say, "More more, uncle, more."

The child's mother came in. She put down her bag and curled her lips. "So, you have returned to us, sir. Had we known we would have tidied up the room a bit." I nodded to her and went up to my room. There was so much dust there that the real dirt could not be seen.

I took off my clothes and stretched out on my bed. The buses roared in front of my window and sellers of soda poured and shouted. But all of these sounds gradually died away, except for an echo of the child's voice ringing in my ears. I made my ear into a funnel so that I could hear more.

Translated by JULES HARLOW

Metamorphosis

1

SHE WAS WEARING a brown dress, and her warm, brown eyes were moist. As she came out of the rabbi's house with the bill of divorcement in her hand, she found fair-haired Svirsh and Dr. Tenzer waiting for her, two bachelors who had been friendly with her since the first year of her marriage. Through the tears on her lashes, she could see how overjoyed they were: not even in their dreams had they pictured the happy day when Toni Hartmann would be parted from her husband. They both sprang eagerly toward her and clasped her hands. Then Svirsh took the parasol, hung it from her belt, and, taking both her hands in his, swung them affectionately back and forth. Next Tenzer took them in his large, clammy hands and gazed at her with the cold, furtive look of a sensualist who is uncertain of his pleasures. Toni withdrew her tired hands from them both and wiped her eyes.

Svirsh took her arm in his and prepared to accompany her. Tenzer stationed himself on her right and thought: That albino has got in first. But never mind; if it's him today it'll be me tomorrow. And he derived a kind of intellectual satisfaction from the thought that tomorrow he would be walking with Toni, who had been Hartmann's yesterday, and who was Svirsh's today.

As they were about to go, Hartmann emerged from the
rabbi's house. His face was lined and his forehead furrowed.
For a moment he stood there looking about him like someone
who has just come out of the dark and is wondering which
way to go. Catching sight of Toni with the two men, he
looked at her with his hard, tired eyes. "Going with them?"
he asked. Toni lifted her veil to her forehead and said, "Don't
you want me to?" Her voice sent a tremor through him. He
linked his thumbs one in the other and said, "Don't go with
them." Toni crumpled her handkerchief in her hand, raised
her sad eyes, and stood looking at him helplessly. Her entire
appearance seemed to say, "Do I look as if I could go alone?"

He went up to Toni. Svirsh drew back and let her arm fall.
Tenzer, who was taller than Hartmann, drew himself up
bravely to his full height. But he soon lowered his head and
relaxed his posture. He said to himself, "After all, it wasn't
from me that he took her." Waving his hat, he walked off—
as his friend Svirsh had done—humming a little impromptu
tune as he went.

As they went, they looked over their shoulders at the man
who had been Toni's husband. Svirsh mumbled petulantly:
"I've never seen anything like it in my life." Tenzer broke off
his tune and wiped his heavy spectacles. "By the Pope's
slipper," he said, "it's enough to make Mohammed wag his
beard." Svirsh shrugged his shoulders and pursed his lips, but
at Hartmann's anger rather than at Tenzer's levity.

Left alone with Toni, Hartmann made as if to take her arm,
but desisted, so that she should not feel his agitation. For a
moment or two they stood silently together. The whole business of the divorce had suddenly become very real, as if they
were still standing in front of the rabbi, and the old man's
bleating voice were still ringing in their ears. Toni gripped her
handkerchief tightly and checked her tears with an effort.
Hartmann removed his hat for relief. Why are we standing
here? he asked himself. Once again he heard bleating in his
ears—not the rabbi's voice, but that of the scribe who had

read out the bill of divorce, and he thought there was a mistake in it. Why was the wretched man in such a hurry? Because Toni and I . . . The whole thing was so strange. But as Hartmann could not define exactly what it was that was so strange, he became confused. He felt he must do something. He crumpled his hat and waved it about. Then he smoothed out the creases, crumpled it again, put his hat back on his head, and passed his hands over his face, from temples to chin. He could feel the stubble on his face: in his preoccupation with the divorce, he had forgotten to shave. What a disgusting sight I must look to Toni, he thought. *Ausgerechnet heute*—today of all days, he muttered between his teeth. He consoled himself with the thought that, although the greater part of the day was over, his beard was not yet noticeable. At the same time he was dissatisfied with himself for seeking lame excuses for his negligence. "Let's go," he said to Toni. "Let's go," he repeated, not certain whether he had uttered the words the first time or, if so, whether she had heard them.

The sun betook itself elsewhere. A spirit of gloom brooded over the street, and a harsh melancholy groaned among the paving stones. The windows looked out from the walls of the houses, strangers to themselves and to the houses. Hartmann fixed his gaze on a window being opened across the way, trying to remember what it was he had wanted to say. He saw a woman peeping out. That's not what I meant, he thought, and he began talking, not about what he'd been thinking, but about something quite different. And after every two or three words he waved his hand despairingly at the things that were coming into his mouth and that he was laying before Toni. Toni fixed her eyes on his mouth and thought: What is he trying to say? Her gaze followed his hand as she tried to fathom his meaning. His conversation was generally not beyond her understanding; if only he would speak coherently and calmly, she would understand everything. Her mouth quivered. The new crease on her upper lip, near the right hand corner, twitched involuntarily. As she smoothed it with her tongue she thought: God in Heaven, how sad he is. Perhaps he has reminded himself of his daughters.

Hartmann had indeed reminded himself of his daughters: they had not been out of his thoughts all day. Although he had not mentioned them to Toni, not even indirectly, he was constantly thinking of them, now of the two of them together, now of each one separately. Beate, the elder, was nine, and she was old enough to realize that Daddy and Mummy were angry with one another. But Renate, who was only seven, had not yet noticed anything. When the atmosphere at home had become too strained, Toni's aunt had come and taken the children to live with her in the country, and they didn't know that Daddy and Mummy . . . Before Hartmann could pursue his thought to the end, he saw Beate's eyes, the way they had looked when she had seen Daddy and Mummy quarreling for the first time. Her childish curiosity had been mingled with dull surprise at the sight of grownups quarreling. Hartmann had hung his head before his daughter's eyes as they grew dark with sorrow and her mouth assumed an expression of voiceless anguish. Then she had lowered her eyelashes and gone out.

Once again Hartmann felt the need to do something. Not knowing what to do, he removed his hat, mopped his brow, wiped the leather band inside his hat, and put it back on his head. Toni grew sad: she felt as if she were responsible for all his troubles. She took the parasol which Svirsh had hung from her belt and toyed with it. Meanwhile Hartmann had begun talking again. He made no reference whatever to the day's events, but they were all reflected in his voice. Toni answered him vaguely. If she were aware of what she was saying, she would have noticed that she, too, was talking to no particular purpose. But Hartmann accepted her replies as if they were to the point.

A little girl approached them and held out a bunch of asters to Hartmann. Perceiving her intention, he took out his purse and threw her a silver coin. The child put the coin in her mouth but did not move. Hartmann looked at Toni inquiringly: What could the child be wanting now? Toni stretched out her hand and took the flowers, inhaled their scent, and said, "Thank you, my dear." The girl twisted one leg around the other, rocked back and forth, and then went away. Toni looked affectionately at her retreating figure, a sad smile on her lips. "Ah," said Hartmann smiling, "she's an honest little trader. If she gets money, she has to give goods in exchange. Well, this is one transaction I've emerged from safely."

Toni thought: He says, this is one transaction he's emerged from safely; that means there was another transaction he didn't emerge from safely. She raised her eyes to him, even though she knew that he was not in the habit of talking to her about his business affairs. But this time he opened his heart, and without any prompting began discussing business. He was involved in transactions he had entered into unwillingly, and now he could not extricate himself. These had led to disputes, quarrels and fights with partners and agents, who had bought merchandise with his money and, on seeing they were likely to incur a loss, had debited the amount to him.

Hartmann had started in the middle, like one who is preoccupied and talks of the things that are weighing on his mind. A person unfamiliar with the world of commerce could not have made head or tail of what he was saying, and Toni certainly knew nothing about business. But he ignored this and went on talking. The more he talked, the more confused he made matters sound, until his patience gave way completely, and he began to vent his anger on his agents, on whom he had relied as he relied on himself and who had betrayed his trust, causing him financial loss and involving him in degrading fights and disputes. He still didn't know how to get rid of them.

Realizing that Toni was listening now, he went back and began from the beginning, carefully explaining each point to her. He now clarified what he had left unexplained in the first telling, and what he did not explain as he went along, he made clear later. Toni began to get the drift of his story, and what she did not grasp with her mind, her heart understood. She looked at him with concern, and wondered how he could bear so many worries without anyone to share them. Hartmann became conscious of her gaze and recounted the entire story in brief. Suddenly he realized that he was seeing his affairs in a new light. Although he had not intentionally set out to prove himself in the right, matters now seemed clearer to him, and he saw that the problem was after all not so insoluble as he had thought.

Toni listened attentively to all he said and realized that his angry mood had been due entirely to his business worries. She applied her new knowledge to the other matter, to the divorce. It was as if he had said, "Now you know why I have been so short-tempered, now you know why we have come to this, to getting divorced, I mean."

Toni was thinking about the divorce and the period leading up to it, but she did not divert her attention from what he was saying. She lifted her brown eyes, which were full of trust and confidence, and said, "Michael, I'm sure you'll find a suitable way out of it." She looked at him again, trusting and submissive, as if it were not he but she who was in trouble, and as if it were she who was seeking help from him. He looked at her as he had not looked at her for a long time past, and he beheld her as he had not beheld her for a long time past. She was a head shorter than he. Her shoulders had grown so thin that they stuck out. She was wearing a smooth brown dress, open at the shoulders but fastened with rings of brown silk through which two white spots were visible. With difficulty he kept himself from caressing her.

2

Hartmann had not been in the habit of talking to his wife much, least of all about business. From the day he had built his house he had tried to keep home and office completely separate. But business has a way of not letting itself be shaken off. Sometimes he would enter the house looking worried. At first, when their love was still strong, he would fob Toni off with a kiss when she asked him to tell her what was worrying him. At a later stage, he would change the subject. Later still, he would scold her: "Isn't it bad enough that I have worries outside? Do you have to go and drag them into the house? When a man's at home he wants to take his mind off business worries."

But a man cannot control his thoughts, and they would come crowding in on him, turning his home into a branch of his shop. The difference was that when he was in the shop, his business affairs got the better of his thoughts, while at home his thoughts got the better of him. His father had not left him any inheritance, nor had his wife brought him a dowry; whatever he had acquired had been the result of his own exertions. He applied himself to business and kept away from other matters. That is how it had been both before and after his marriage. While still a bachelor he had thought: I'll get married, build a home, and find contentment there; but when he did get married and built a home, he found himself stripped of all his expectations. At first he had solaced himself with hope, but now even that was gone. True, his wife did her best to please him, and the daughters she had borne him were growing up. On the face of it, he had no complaints against his home; the trouble was that he did not know what to do with himself there. At first he had numerous friends, but as time went on he had lost interest in them: it seemed to him that they only came on Toni's account. At first he used to look at the books Toni read and tried to keep up with them. But after reading three or four books, he stopped: the love affairs, dresses, plots, and sentiment with which they were filled—what need had an intelligent man to know of such matters? Would I care to hob-nob with such characters?

From the books he drew inferences about Toni, and from Toni about the whole house. Since he knew only his shop and was not in the habit of frequenting clubs, he had no recourse after locking up his shop but to return home. And since, once at home, he did not know what to do, he grew disgusted with himself. He began to find solace in smoking. At first he smoked in order to smother his thoughts; and he went on smoking because they were smothered. He began with cigarettes, and went on to cigars. At first he smoked in moderation, but later took to smoking continuously, until the whole house was filled with the smell of tobacco. He did not consider that he was in any way harming himself; on the contrary, he congratulated himself on the fact that he was sitting quietly by himself and not demanding anything of others. Every man has his form of pleasure: I derive mine from smoking, she derives hers from other sources. And since he didn't trouble to discover what her form of pleasure was, and he failed to find satisfaction in his own, he became troubled at heart and began to be jealous on her account of every man, woman, and child —in fact, of everything. If he saw her talking to a man or chatting with a woman or playing with a child, he would say: Has she no husband or children of her own that she has to chase about after others?

Michael Hartmann was a merchant, and he sold his goods by weight and by measure: he knew that to waste a measure meant losing it. Eventually he reconciled himself to the situation, not because he condoned her activities, but because she had come to assume less importance in his eyes.

3

The sun was about to set. In the fields the wheat swayed silently, and the sunflowers gazed one-eyed out of their darkening yellow faces. Hartmann stretched his hand out into the vacant air and caressed Toni's shadow.

All around him the silence was complete. Toni took the

parasol and poked at the ground in front of her. Her action seemed devoid of both purpose and grace, and that bothered him. Once again he extended his hand and caressed the air. By now the sun had ended its course and the sky had become dulled. The countryside took on an appearance of desolation, and the trees in the field grew dark. The air began to grow cool, and the cucumber beds were fragrant. High up in the sky was a tiny star, the size of a pinhead. Behind it another star made its way through the clouds and began shining, and other stars followed.

The houses and barns stood in comfortable silence, and the smell of burnt weeds and of cattle rose from the pasture. Michael and Toni walked along silently. A boy and a girl sat with their arms twined about each other, talking; then their voices broke off abruptly, and the scent of hidden desire hung in the air. A light breeze sprang up, but no sound was heard. A little boy ran past holding a burning torch. He too had run like that in his childhood once, when his mother had found herself without matches and had sent him over to the neighbor's to fetch a light. He took out a cigarette and was about to light it; but the scent of the fields took away his desire to smoke. He crumbled the cigarette between his fingers and threw it away. He smelled his fingers and wrinkled his nose.

Toni opened her handbag, took out a bottle of scent, and sprinkled her hands with it. The scent reached his nostrils and put him in a good mood. So, so, he said to himself, by way of assent or as a question.

After his talk with Toni, in which he had told her all about that business, he began chiding himself for never, in all those years, discussing his affairs with her. If he had not snapped at her every time she wanted to know something about his doings, perhaps her interests would have grown closer to his, and they would not have come to regard themselves as such strangers to one another. This lesson was good for him at the moment, since it enabled him to blame himself and to justify Toni.

Again he folded his thumbs together and said, "I can't stand that Svirsh."

Toni hung her head and said nothing.

Hartmann repeated: "I simply can't stand him."

"And Dr. Tenzer?" Toni asked softly.

"Dr. Ten-zer?" said Hartmann angrily, stressing each syllable of the name. "I hate all the Tenzers of this world. They never seem to try and get anything for themselves. All they ever do is lie in wait for things meant for other people. I know what that fellow Svirsh is after. Whenever I see those pink eyes of his and his manicured nails, I know at once what he wants. But with Tenzer you never know where you are. He makes himself out to be in love with the whole world, but in reality he doesn't love anything. He runs after women, but he doesn't love any woman for herself, because she's pretty, or because she's this or that, but because she's another man's wife. The very fact that someone else has an interest in her makes her desirable to Tenzer."

Toni lifted her face toward Michael. It was night, and he could not see her eyes, but he felt that they were thanking him, as if he had taught her things she could never have learned by herself. Hartmann, who had been angry with himself for mentioning Svirsh and Tenzer, now experienced a feeling of relief, and he looked about him with a sense of freedom and happiness. He saw a light glimmering in the darkness. He stretched out his arm and, beckoning Toni with his finger, said: "Do you see the light?" Toni looked and said: "Where?" "Really, really, I can see the glimmer of a light over there," he said. "It's the lamp of an inn." "Is that so," Toni replied, "I thought it was a firefly."

A slight shudder ran through Toni, giving her a mysteriously pleasant sensation. Hartmann's saying it was the lamp of an inn and not a firefly suddenly set her musing about the first firefly she had ever seen. She had been on a visit to her aunt's in the country. It was Sabbath, and she was sitting in the garden at dusk. A spark darted through the gloom and settled on her aunt's hat. Not knowing it was a firefly, she thought it was fire and became frightened. How old had she been at the time? About seven. Now Beate and Renate were at her aunt's, and she, Toni, was here walking with their father.

"We can rest there and have something to eat," Hartmann said. "You must be hungry: you had no lunch. We won't get roast duck there, but at least we can have a meal and rest."

Toni nodded in agreement. She was thinking, When did I recollect the firefly: when Michael pointed to the light, or when I said I thought it was a firefly? But she felt she must have been thinking about the firefly before, as she had been thinking about her daughters in the country. She shivered, as if the incident had taken place only now.

The road twisted and turned, now to the right, now to the left. The inn lamp kept on vanishing and reappearing. A moist smell rose from the earth. Toni shivered a little, though she did not actually feel cold. She gazed silently into the darkness which was shrouding both her and Michael. Once more the inn lamp came into view, only to disappear a moment later. Toni drew in her shoulders, and a breeze passed across her body.

"Cold?" Hartmann asked solicitously.

"I think I see people coming."

"There is no one here, but perhaps . . ."

"I've never seen such a tall person before," said Toni. "Do look." A man with a ladder came toward them. Placing the ladder on the ground, he climbed it and lit a lamp. Toni blinked her eyes and drew in her breath. "Was there something you wanted to say?" Michael asked her. She looked down and said: "I didn't say anything."

Hartmann smiled. "That's strange, I fancied you wanted to say something."

Toni blushed. "Did I want to say something?" She looked at her shadow in silence.

Hartmann smiled again: "So you didn't want to say anything. But I thought you did."

Toni walked on silently at Michael's side.

Two shadows became visible. The head of one of them was close to Toni's, while the other was close to Hartmann's. Two young people came in sight, a boy and a girl. The whole air became charged with their unfulfilled desires. Hartmann looked at them, and they at him. Toni lowered her head and looked at her wedding ring.

4

A little later they came to a garden fenced on three sides. The gate was open, and to the right of it shone a lamp. Some smaller lanterns, in the shape of apples and pears, hung from the trees in the garden. Hartman looked at the sign and said: "I wasn't mistaken, this is a restaurant. We'll get something to eat here." Taking Toni by the arm, he walked in with her.

A plump, loose-limbed girl was sitting in front of the house, cleaning vegetables and occupying half the width of the bottom step. She greeted them in a loud voice and lowered her skirt. Hartmann thought: She's red-haired and freckled. Although I can't see her in the dark, I've a feeling that's the type she is.—Toni shook her head at him. He gazed at her in astonishment. Could she possibly have sensed what I was thinking? He took her parasol and laid it on a chair, and placed his hat on top of it. "Let's sit in the garden," he said, "or would you prefer to eat indoors?" "No," Toni replied, "let's eat out here."

A waiter came up, wiped the top of the table, spread a cloth on it, and handed them a menu. Then he fetched a glass of water and put the flowers in it, and stood waiting until they were ready with their order. Hartmann saw that most of the dishes listed in the menu had been struck out. He grumbled: "Most of the dishes have already been eaten up." Looking over Hartmann's shoulder, the waiter said: "I'll bring you some others immediately." "You're hiding your wares under a bushel," said Hartmann. The waiter bent down and said: "The dishes we have struck out have all been eaten. Others have been cooked instead, but we haven't had time to enter them in the menu." "In that case," observed Hartmann, "we ought to be glad that we shall be getting fresh dishes." "Your pleasure is our happiness," the waiter replied. "Will you have brown bread or white?" "When you eat in the country," Toni said, "you must have brown bread." "And what wines do you care for, sir?" the waiter asked. "Wine," exclaimed Hartmann happily, as if rejoiced to discover that such a thing still existed for people's delectation. He studied the wine list and placed his order.

"We're in luck," he said to Toni. "This is far better than we expected." Toni smoothed the crease on her upper lip with her tongue, either because she was hungry or maybe because she could think of nothing to say in reply. The waiter returned with their order. Michael and Toni drew up their chairs and began eating. Toni was ashamed to eat too heartily, but her bashfulness failed to blunt her appetite.

The potatoes, spinach, eggs, meat, turnips, and other things that the waiter brought them were all excellently prepared. Toni ate with relish. The stars winked at them from the sauce, and from the bough of a tree came the song of a bird. Hartmann covered his knees with his napkin and listened to the bird.

The girl they had seen on their arrival passed by. She gave them a glance of recognition. Hartmann looked at her and said, "Didn't I say she was a red-head with freckles?" though in fact he did not manage to see whether she had freckles or not.

Toni lifted the glass with the flowers, looked at them and then smelled them. She had always been particularly fond of asters, they were so modest and lovely. She had planted some on her mother's grave, and those asters, not particular about growing in the best soil necessarily, would look at her gratefully when she came for a visit.

Again the girl passed by, this time carrying a basket of plums with both hands. The juice of the overripe plums gave off an odor of cloying sweetness.

5

Taking his wineglass in his hand, Hartmann mused: Since the day I married her I never behaved so decently toward her as when I gave her the divorce. Unconsciously raising his glass higher, he continued: If a man quarrels with a woman, he has no right to live with her. Marriage without love is no marriage at all. Divorce is preferable to a quarrelsome marriage. He put down the glass, moved the cruet-stand, and selected a toothpick. Following the same trend of thought, he reflected: If a man marries a woman and does not love her, he has to give her a divorce. If he doesn't divorce her, he has to love her. And that love has to undergo constant renewal. "Did you say anything?" Toni stretched out her hand, pointed to the tree, and said: "A bird."

Hartmann looked at the tree.

"Is that the one that was singing," Toni asked, "or was it another one?"

"Of course it was," Hartmann replied with great animation, although his certainty rested upon insecure ground.

Toni leaned her head on her left shoulder and thought to herself, That little creature sits hidden in a tree, and its voice brings a thrill to one's heart.

Hartmann clenched his fingers and looked at Toni as she sat with her head resting on her shoulder. Her shoulders seemed to him to be hidden, and two white specks peeped at him through the openings in her dress where her blouse had slipped down, exposing one shoulder. Now, Hartmann thought, we shall see the other one. Unconsciously he rapped on the table. The waiter heard and came up to them. Once he had come,

Hartmann took out his purse, paid the bill and tipped him. The waiter thanked him and bowed profusely: either he was drunk, or else the tip was larger than he had anticipated.

The meal had been a good one, and it had cost Hartmann less than he had expected. He sat with a feeling of contentment and ordered a quarter-bottle of brandy for himself and a sweet liqueur for Toni. He took out a cigar and trimmed it with his knife. Then he offered his cigarette case to Toni. They sat opposite one another, the smoke from the cigar and cigarette mingling. Above them shone the little lanterns, and above the lanterns shone the stars. Toni parted the smoke with her fingers and went on smoking tranquilly. Hartmann looked at her and said: "Listen, Toni." Toni raised her eyes to him. Hartmann put down his cigar and said: "I had a dream."

"A dream?" Toni closed her eyes as if dreaming herself.

"Are you listening?" Hartmann asked. She opened her eyes, looked at him, and closed them again.

"I don't remember whether I had this dream last night or the night before," he went on. "But I remember every detail of it, as if I were dreaming it now. Are you listening, Toni?" She nodded her head.

"In this dream I was living in Berlin. Suessenschein came to visit me. You remember Suessenschein? At the time he had just returned from Africa. I'm always glad to see him, for he brings with him an atmosphere of the far-off places I used to dream of in my childhood. But that day I wasn't glad. Perhaps it was because he came in the morning, when I like to sit by myself. Perhaps it was because in dreams we aren't always happy to be with the people we enjoy when we're awake. He had someone else with him, a young man to whom I took a violent dislike the instant he walked in. He acted as if he had wearied himself with Suessenschein on all his travels. But for Suessenschein's sake I treated him civilly. Are you listening?"

"I'm listening," Toni whispered, as if afraid that the sound of her voice would interrupt his story. Hartmann continued:

"Suessenschein looked around at my flat and said: If I found a flat like yours, I'd take it; I want to stay here awhile, and I'm tired of hotels. I replied: I've heard of a very nice flat that's going in Charlottenburg. To which he rejoined: All right, let's go there. Wait, I suggested, let me phone up first. No, he said, we'll go there straight away. I went along with him."

Toni nodded, and Hartmann went on:

"When we got there, the landlady was nowhere to be seen. I wanted to tell him off for being so impulsive, but I stopped myself, as my temper was very frayed, and I felt I was in danger of going too far. His companion urged the maid to go and call the landlady. The maid looked at him suspiciously, or maybe she just looked at him without any particular expression, but I hated him so much that I thought she looked at him with suspicion. As she went, the landlady came in. She was dark, neither young nor old, on the short side, eyes a trifle filmy, and one leg shorter than the other, though this did not seem like a blemish in her. On the contrary, she seemed to dance along rather than walk. A secret joy twinkled on her lips, a hidden, yearning joy, a virginal joy."

Although Hartmann was aware that Toni was listening with interest, he nevertheless asked, "Are you listening, Toni?" and went on.

"The rooms she showed us were very nice. But Suessenschein turned away from them and said: I wouldn't advise you to take this flat. Winter is approaching, and there is no stove. I gazed at him in astonishment: Who was it that wanted to rent a flat, I or he? I have a fine one of my own; I'm very pleased with it, and I have no intention of exchanging it for another. Suessenschein repeated: A place without a stove, a place without a stove, if I were you I wouldn't take it. Here the landlady put in: But there is a stove. But Suessenschein interrupted her: Where is the stove? In the bedroom. But the study, madam, is all of glass. Are you looking for somewhere to live, or for an observatory from which to view the frozen birds? His words depressed me so much that I began to feel cold. I looked around and saw that the study did indeed consist more of windows than walls. I nodded and said: That's so. The landlady looked at me with her filmy but charming eyes, and straightened herself with a caper. I turned away from her and thought, How shall I ever get away from this cold? My skin was already clinging to my bones. I woke up and found that the blanket had slipped off my bed."

After Hartmann had finished, he had a feeling that perhaps he ought not to have recounted his dream; and yet at the same time he experienced a sense of relief. In order, therefore, to give expression to both emotions, he assumed a tone of banter and said: "That was a fine story I told you. The whole thing really wasn't worth telling." Toni licked her lips, and her eyes grew moist. He looked at her involuntarily, and it seemed to him that it was with just such eyes that the landlady had looked at him. Now there was nothing wrong with her, except . . . except for something whose meaning he did not understand, but he felt that if Toni were to get up, she, too, would turn out to be lame. However, since that would not seem like a blemish—as he knew from the woman in the dream— it followed that even if Toni were lame, she would not seem crippled to him. He got up, took his hat, and said: "Let's go."

6

Toni stood up, removed her flowers from the glass, shook the moisture off them, and wrapped them in paper. She inhaled their scent and paused a moment or two in the hope that Michael might sit down again: she was afraid lest on the way back something should happen to disturb their atmosphere of calm. The waiter came up, handed Toni her parasol, bowed them out, and followed them until they were out of the garden. When they had gone, he extinguished the lanterns.

The garden and its surroundings became dark. A frog jumped in the grass. Toni dropped her flowers in alarm.

The croaking of frogs rose from the banks of the stream. The electric wires were giving off sparks: something had obviously gone wrong with them. After a few paces the wires and poles disappeared from view, and other sparks could be seen: they were the fireflies, which dappled the darkness with their glitter.

Hartmann stood wondering. What has happened here? he asked himself. His mind was tranquil, as if his question had furnished the answer.

Gradually they reached the stream. It lay there in its bed, its waters gently rocking. The stars cast their reflection upon its formless ripples, and the moon floated on the surface. The cry of a bird of prey was heard in the distance, and its echo pierced the air.

Toni crossed her feet and leaned on her parasol. She lowered her eyelids and drowsed. The waves raised themselves up and fell back exhausted. The frogs croaked, and the river plants exuded a tepid smell.

Toni was tired, and her eyes dropped. The river willows whispered, and the waters of the stream undulated languidly. Toni was no longer able to control her eyes, and they began to close of their own accord. But Michael was awake.

Never in his life had he been so wide awake. The tiniest movement set his mind working, and he looked about him searchingly, lest anything of what was happening should escape him. It was good, he felt, that Toni existed for him in this world and at that hour. But what was good for him was not good for her. She was exhausted, and her legs were incapable of supporting her body.

"Tired?" he asked her. "I'm not tired," she replied; but her voice belied her words.

Michael laughed, and Toni looked at him in surprise. He laughed again and said: "One day I was out walking with the

girls. I asked them if they were tired, and Renate answered:
'I'm not tired, but my legs are.' "

"The sweet chick," said Toni with a sigh.

Hartmann was sorry he had mentioned the girls. He looked
around to see if he could find a conveyance to take them back
to town. But the earth was silent: no sound of a carriage wheel
or motor. He looked in all four directions, to see if he could
discover a telephone booth. He was filled with pity for this
small woman who had not the strength to walk. Once or
twice he supported her with his arm. Her dress was damp from
the moist air, and she shivered a little. If he did not get her
under a roof, she would certainly catch cold.

But the city was far away, and the air was dank. He wanted
to take off his jacket and wrap it around Toni. But he was
afraid she might refuse; and he did not want to do anything
that would evoke her refusal.

Perhaps, Michael thought, there would be a bed for her at
the inn where they had eaten. Taking her arm, he said: "Let's
go back to the inn." Toni dragged after him, bereft of strength.

7

They took the same road by which they had come and found
their way back to the garden. Hartmann shoved the gate open,
and they went up the stone steps. The house was silent. The
waiter was not to be seen, neither was the girl. Obviously the
household was asleep, and no guests were expected. Every step
they took cried out at the intrusion.

Hartmann opened the door to the house and stepped inside.
He spoke a greeting into the room, but there was no reply.
He found an old man sitting bent over a table, pipe in mouth,
an expression of annoyance on his face.

"Is there any room to sleep here?" Hartmann asked. The old
man looked at him and at the woman by his side. It was clear

from the old man's expression that he was not pleased to see a couple who had turned up after midnight to seek a haven of love. He took his pipe from his mouth, laid it on the table, and, giving them a look of annoyance, said severely: "We have one room vacant." Toni blushed. Hartmann crumpled his hat and said nothing. The landlord took his pipe, turned it upside down, knocked it against the table, and removed the ash. Putting aside the ash and the burnt shreds, he gathered the remnants of tobacco and put them back in the pipe. Pressing them down with his thumb, he said: "We'll prepare the room for the lady." Finally, raising his eyes, he said: "We'll find a place for the gentleman as well. When we're full we usually make up a bed on the billiard table."

Toni inclined her head toward the landlord and said: "Thank you very much indeed." Said Hartmann: "Would you show us the room?"

The landlord got up and lit a candle. Opening a door for them, he followed them into a spacious room in which there were three beds, one of them made up. There was a washstand with two basins and two jugs filled with water, and a large decanter half-full of water covered with an inverted tumbler. Above the made-up bed hung a broken horn with a bridal wreath on it, and a ram's head and the head of a wild boar with eyes of red glass hung upon the walls. The innkeeper took the tumbler, examined it, stood it upside down, and waited for Hartmann to leave.

Hartmann put out his hand to test the mattress. Seeing him do so, the innkeeper said: "No one has yet complained of not getting a good night's sleep in this house." Hartmann paled, and his hand remained dangling. The innkeeper placed the candle next to the made-up bed and said: "Now sir, if you'll come with me, I'll make your bed for you." And he waited for his guest to accompany him.

Finally Hartmann grasped the innkeeper's intention. Taking Toni's hand, he wished her goodnight. Her hand clung to his, and her eyes enfolded his heart.

A few moments later the innkeeper was making up Hartmann's bed on the billiard table and chatting to him as he
did so. His annoyance gave way to affability. Now that the
guest was without the woman, he considered him respectable.
He asked his guest how many pillows he liked to sleep on,
and whether he preferred a heavy blanket or a light one, and
did he wish to take anything to drink before he retired for the
night. Finally he gave him a lighted candle and a box of
matches and left the room. A few moments later, Hartmann
went out into the garden.

The lanterns had gone out, but a light from heaven illuminated the darkness. The grass and the mandrakes gave off a
damp, refreshing scent. A chestnut dropped from a tree and
burst. Another chestnut fell sharply and burst.

Hartmann stood reviewing the night's events. After a brief
pause he went across to the table at which he had dined with
Toni. The chairs had been leaned against it, and the dew
glistened on the bare tabletop. Underneath the table lay a
thick cigar. It was the cigar that he had put down on the table
when he began telling Toni his dream.

"Now we'll have a smoke," he said. But before he could
take out a cigar he had forgotten what it was he had meant
to do.

8

"What was I góing to do?" he asked himself. "To get up
on this little mound in front of me." He had not really intended to do so, but once he had told himself, he went and
did it.

The mound was dome-shaped, wide at the base and narrow
at the top and not far across, and it was surrounded by bushes.
He drew in his breath and considered: I expect each thorn
and thistle has a different name. How many names of thorns

do I know? More than I thought. I wonder if the gardener doesn't lavish more care on the thorns than on the flowers. Those gardeners destroy the thorns where they normally grow and plant them in the wrong places. Perhaps the names I know are the names of the thorns growing here . . . Suddenly he smiled: That innkeeper doesn't know what Toni and I are to one another. How annoyed he was when we asked for somewhere to sleep. Now let me see what's here.

He looked down on the mound and recalled an incident of his childhood. He had gone for a walk with some friends, and, seeing a mound, he had climbed it, then slipped and slid down to the bottom. He imagined himself back in the same situation, and began to be afraid he would fall; no, it was rather a wonder he had not already slipped to the bottom. And if he had not already slipped and fallen, he was bound to do so; although there was no real danger of his falling, his fear itself would make him fall; though he was still on his feet, his legs were beginning to give way and to slip, he would roll down, his bones would get broken.

He took heart and climbed down. When he reached the bottom he was amazed. How high was the mound, a foot or eighteen inches? Yet how it had frightened him! He closed his eyes and said, "I'm tired," and returned to the inn.

An air of calm pervaded the entire house. The innkeeper sat by himself in a little room, rubbing his ankles together and drinking a beverage to help him sleep. Hartmann slipped in quietly, undressed, stretched out on the billiard table, covered himself, and looked at the wall.

Strange, he thought, all while I stood on the mound, I was thinking only about myself, as if I were alone in the world, as if I did not have two daughters; as if I did not have —a wife.

Hartmann loved his daughters the way a father does. But, like any other father, he did not forego his own interests for the sake of his children. The incident of the mound had opened his heart. He was both ashamed and surprised. And he proceeded once more to occupy his thoughts with himself.

What had happened to him on the mound? Actually, nothing. He had got onto the top of the mound and imagined he was slipping down. And what if he had fallen? He would have lain on the ground and picked himself up again. He stretched out on the bed and thought, smiling: How ridiculous Tenzer looked when I took Toni away from that albino! There are still things left in the world to make one laugh. But let me get back: What happened on the mound? Not the one I was standing on just now, but the one I fell from. One day I went for a walk with my friends. I climbed onto the top of the mound, and suddenly I found myself lying in the ditch. He did not remember himself actually falling, only that he was lying in the ditch. Something sweet was trickling into his mouth, his lips were cut, his tongue swollen, and his entire body bruised. But his limbs felt relaxed, like those of a man who stretches himself after throwing off a heavy burden. He had often fallen since then, but he had never experienced such a feeling of tranquility in any other fall. It seems that one does not have to taste such an experience more than once in a lifetime.

9

He extinguished the candle, closed his eyes, and sought to recollect the event. The details of it were confused, as in a dream. From the walls of the house a cricket sounded, then stopped, and the silence became twice as intense. His limbs relaxed, and his mind grew tranquil. Once more the cricket chirped. What I want to know, said Hartmann to himself, is how long he's going to go on chirping. As he framed the question, he began thinking of Toni. He could see her face, and her movements, and also the two white spots where her skin showed through the brown dress . . . There's no doubt about it, she isn't young. Even if her hair hasn't turned gray, she has many more wrinkles. The worst of them all is that crease in her upper lip. Has she a tooth missing?

He still thought of Toni critically, as he always had, but now he felt that all those shortcomings in no way detracted from her. With a sweet feeling of adoration he summoned up her face, that wonderful face; but then it began to fade away from him, against his will. How thin her shoulders were, but her figure was that of a pretty girl. Hartmann embraced the air with his arm and felt himself blushing. As he was talking to himself he heard a sort of moan. Since he was thinking about his wife, it seemed to him that the sound came from her room. He opened his eyes and, lifting his head, listened intently. Help me, O Lord, help me. Has anything happened? In reality he could have heard nothing, for there was a thick wall between them. Nor was it a moan of distress he had heard. Nevertheless, he sat upright on his bed in case he should hear anything, in case anything of her vital being should reach his ears. Perhaps he might be able to help her.

Once again she appeared before him the way she had looked that day—lifting her veil onto her forehead, raising the asters to her face, digging her parasol into the ground, parting the cigarette smoke with her fingers. Gradually the parasol vanished, the smoke dispersed, and the asters grew more numerous, until they covered the whole mound. Astonished and puzzled, he gazed in front of him. As he did so his eyes closed, his head dropped on the pillow, his soul fell asleep, and his spirit began to hover in the world of dreams, where no partition separated them.

Translated by I. SCHEN

The Doctor's Divorce

1

WHEN I JOINED THE STAFF of the hospital, I discovered there
a blonde nurse who was loved by everyone and whose praise
was on the lips of all the patients. As soon as they heard her
footsteps, they would sit up in bed and stretch their arms
out toward her as an only son reaches for his mother, and each
one of them would call, "Nurse, nurse, come to me." Even
the ill-tempered kind who find all the world provoking—as
soon as she appeared, the frown-lines in their faces faded, their
anger dissolved, and they were ready to do whatever she
ordered. Not that it was her way to give orders: the smile
that illuminated her face was enough to make patients obey
her. In addition to her smile, there were her eyes, a kind of
blue-black; everyone she looked at felt as if he were the most
important thing in the world. Once I asked myself where such
power comes from. From the moment I saw her eyes, I was
just like the rest of the patients. And she had no special
intentions toward me, nor toward anybody in particular. That
smile on her lips, however, and that blue-black in her eyes had
the further distinction of doing on their own more than their
mistress intended.

One indication of the degree of affection in which she was
generally held was the fact that even her fellow nurses liked
her and were friendly toward her. And the head nurse, a
woman of about forty, well born, thin and wan as vinegar, who

hated everyone, patients and doctors alike, with the possible exception of black coffee and salted cakes and her lap dog— even she was favorably disposed in this case. Such a woman, who couldn't look at a girl without imagining her half wasted away, showed special kindness to this nurse. And one hardly need mention my fellow doctors. Every doctor with whom she happened to work thanked his stars. Even our professor, accustomed as he was to concern himself less with the suffering of the sick than with the orderliness of their beds, made no fuss if he found her sitting on a patient's bed. This old man, the master of so many disciples and the discoverer of cures for several diseases, died in a concentration camp where a Nazi trooper tormented him daily by forcing him to go through exercises. One day the trooper ordered him to lie flat on his belly with arms and legs outstretched, and as soon as he was down, he was commanded to get up. As he was not quick about it, the trooper trampled him with his cleated boots until the old man's thumbnails were mutilated. He contracted blood poisoning and died.

What more can I say? I took a liking to this girl just as everyone else did. But I can add that she also took a liking to me. And though any man could say as much, others did not dare while I dared, and so I married her.

2

This is how it came about. One afternoon, as I was leaving the dining hall, I ran into Dinah. I said to her, "Are you busy, nurse?"

"No, I'm not busy."

"What makes today so special?"

"Today is my day off from the hospital."

"And how are you celebrating your day off?"

"I haven't yet considered the matter."

"Would you allow me to give you some advice?"

"Please do, doctor."

"But only if I am paid for the advice. Nowadays you don't get something for nothing."

She looked at me and laughed. I continued, "I have one good piece of advice which is actually two—that we go to the Prater and that we go to the opera. And if we hurry, we can stop first at a cafe. Do you agree, nurse?" She nodded yes good-humoredly.

"When shall we go?" I asked.

"Whenever the doctor wants."

"I'll take care of what I have to as soon as possible and I'll be right over."

"Whenever you come, you'll find me ready."

She went to her room and I to my responsibilities. A little while later, when I arrived to pick her up, I discovered that she had changed clothes. All at once she seemed a new person to me, and with the metamorphosis her charm was doubled, for she had both the charm I felt in her when she was in uniform and that which was lent her by the new clothes. I sat in her room and looked at the flowers on the table and by the bed, and after asking her whether she knew their names, I recited the name of each flower, in German and in Latin. But I quickly became apprehensive that a serious patient might be brought in and I would be paged. I got up from my seat and urged that we leave at once. I saw she was disturbed.

"Is something bothering you?" I asked.

"I thought you'd have something to eat."

"Right now, let's go, and if you are still so kindly disposed toward me, I'll come back to enjoy everything you give me, and I'll even ask for more."

"May I count on that?"

"I've already given you my word. Not only that, but, as I said, I'll ask for more."

As we left the hospital court, I said to the doorman, "You see this nurse? I'm taking her away from here." The doorman looked at us benevolently and said, "More power to you, doctor. More power to you, nurse."

We walked to the trolley stop. A trolley came along, but turned out to be full. The next one that arrived we thought we would be able to take. Dinah got onto the car. When I tried to climb up after her, the conductor called out, "No more room." She came down and waited with me for another car. At that point I commented to myself, Some people say that one shouldn't worry about a trolley or a girl that has gone because others will soon come along. But those who think that are fools. As far as the girl is concerned, can one find another girl like Dinah? And as to the trolley, I regretted every delay.

Along came a suburban trolley. Since its cars were new and spacious and empty of passengers, we got on. Suddenly (or, according to the clock, after a while), the trolley reached the end of the line and we found ourselves standing in a lovely place filled with gardens, where the houses were few.

We crossed the street talking about the hospital and the patients and the head nurse and the professor, who had instituted a fast once a week for all patients with kidney ailments because someone with kidney pains had fasted on the Day of Atonement and afterward there was no albumen in his urine. Then we mentioned all the cripples the war had produced, and we were pleased by the setting for our walk because there were no cripples around. I threw up my arms suddenly and said, "Let's forget about the hospital and cripples and speak about more pleasant things." She agreed with me, even though from her expression one could tell she was concerned that we might not find any other subject for conversation.

Children were playing. They saw us and began to whisper to each other. "Do you know, Fräulein," I asked Dinah, "what the children are talking about? They are talking about us." —"Perhaps." "Do you know what they're saying?" I went on. "They're saying, 'The two of them are bride and groom.'"

Her face reddened as she answered, "Perhaps that's what they are saying."

"You mean you don't object to it?"

"To what?"

"To what the children are saying."

"Why should I care?"

"And if it were true, what would you say?"

"If what were true?"

I summoned my courage and answered, "If what the children say were true, I mean, that you and I belong together." She laughed and looked at me. I took her hand and said, "Give me the other one, too." She gave me her hand. I bent over and kissed both her hands, then looked at her. Her face became still redder. "There is a proverb," I told her, "that truth is with children and fools. We've already heard what the children say, and now listen to what a fool has to say, I mean, myself, for I have been touched with wisdom."

I stuttered and went on, "Listen, Dinah . . ." I had hardly begun to say all that was in my heart before I found myself a man more fortunate than all others.

3

Never was there a better time in my life than the period of our engagement. If it had been my opinion that marriage exists only because a man needs a woman and a woman a man, I now came to realize that there is no higher need than that one. At the same time, I began to understand why the poets felt it necessary to write love poems, despite the fact that I would have no part of them or their poems, because they wrote about other women and not about Dinah. Often I would sit and wonder, How many nurses there are in the hospital; how many women in the world; and I am concerned with one girl alone, who absorbs all my thoughts. As soon as

I saw her again, I would say to myself, The doctor must have lost his wits to put her in the same category as other women. And my feelings toward her were reciprocated. But that blue-black in her eyes darkened like a cloud about to burst.

Once I asked her. She fixed her eyes on me without answering. I repeated my question. She pressed against me and said, "You don't know how precious you are to me and how much I love you." And a smile spread across her melancholy lips, that smile which drove me wild with its sweetness and its sorrow.

I asked myself, If she loves me, what reason could there be for this sadness? Perhaps her family is poor. But she said they were well-to-do. Perhaps she had promised to marry someone else. But she told me she was completely free. I began to pester her about it. She showed me still more affection, and she remained silent.

Nevertheless, I began to investigate her relatives. Perhaps they were rich but had been impoverished and she felt bad about them. I discovered that some of them were industrialists and some were people of distinction in other fields, and they all made comfortable livings.

I grew proud. I, a poor boy, the son of a lowly tinsmith, became fastidious about my dress, even though she paid no attention to clothes, unless I asked her to look at them. My love for her grew still greater. This was beyond all logic, for, to begin with, I had given her all my love. And she, too, gave me all her love. But her love had a touch of sadness in it which injected into my happiness a drop of gall.

This drop worked its way into all my limbs. I would ponder, What is this sadness? Is that what love is supposed to be like? I continued to beleaguer her with questions. She promised an answer but persisted in her evasiveness. When I reminded her of her promise, she took my hand in hers and said, "Let's be happy, darling, let's be happy and not disturb our happiness." And she sighed in a way that broke my heart. I asked her, "Dinah, what are you sighing about?" She smiled and answered through her tears, "Please, darling, don't say anything more." I was silent and asked no more questions. But my mind was not at ease. And I still awaited the time when she would agree to tell me what it was all about.

4

One afternoon I stopped in to see her. At that hour she was free from her work with the patients and she was sitting in her room sewing a new dress. I took the dress by the hem and let my hand glide over it. Then I lifted my eyes toward her. She looked straight into my eyes and said, "I was once involved with somebody else." She saw that I didn't realize what she meant, so she made her meaning more explicit. A chill ran through me and I went weak inside. I sat without saying a word. After a few moments I told her, "Such a thing would have never even occurred to me." Once I had spoken, I sat wondering and amazed, wondering over my own calmness and amazed at her for having done a thing so much beneath her. Nevertheless, I treated her just as before, as though she had in no way fallen in esteem. And, in fact, at that moment she had not fallen in my esteem and was as dear to me as always. Once she saw that, a smile appeared on her lips again. But her eyes were veiled, like someone moving out of one darkness into another.

I asked her, "Who was this fellow who left you without marrying you?" She evaded the question. "Don't you see, Dinah," I pursued, "that I bear no ill feelings toward you. It's only curiosity that leads me to ask such a question. So tell me, darling, who was he?" "What difference does it make to you what his name is?" Dinah asked. "Even so," I persisted, "I would like to know." She told me his name. "Is he a lecturer or a professor?" I asked. Dinah said, "He is an official." I reflected silently that important officials worked for her relatives, men of knowledge and scholars and inventors. Undoubtedly it was to the most important of them that she gave her heart. Actually, it made no difference who the man was to whom this woman more dear to me than all the world gave her love, but to delude myself I imagined that he was a great man, superior to all his fellows. "He's an official?" I said to her. "What is his job?" Dinah answered, "He is a clerk in the legislature." "I am amazed at you, Dinah," I told her, "that a minor official, a clerk, was able to sweep you off your feet like that. And, besides, he left you, which goes to show that he wasn't good enough for you in the first place." She lowered her eyes and was silent.

From then on I did not remind her of her past, just as I would not have reminded her what dress she had worn the day before. And if I thought of it, I banished the thought from my mind. And so we were married.

5

Our wedding was like most weddings in these times, private, without pomp and ceremony. For I had no family, with the possible exception of the relative who once hit my father in the eye. And Dinah, ever since she became close to me, had grown away from her relatives. During that period, moreover, it was not customary to have parties and public rejoicing. Governments came and governments went, and between one and the next there was panic and confusion, turmoil and dismay. People who one day were rulers the next day were chained in prisons or hiding in exile.

And so our wedding took place with neither relatives nor invited guests, except for a bare quorum summoned by the beadle, miserable creatures who an hour or two ago were called for a funeral and now were summoned for my wedding. How pitiful were their borrowed clothes, how comic their towering high hats, how audacious their greedy eyes that looked forward to the conclusion of the ceremony when they could go into a bar with the money they had gotten through my wedding. I was in high spirits, and as strange as the thing seemed to me, my joy was not diminished. Let others be led under the bridal canopy by renowned and wealthy wedding guests. I would be married in the presence of poor people who, with what they would earn for their trouble, could buy bread. The children we would have wouldn't ask me, "Father, who was at your wedding?" just as I never asked my father who was at his wedding.

I put my hand in my pocket and pulled out several shillings which I handed to the beadle to give to the men over and above the agreed price. The beadle took the money and said nothing. I was afraid they would overwhelm me with thanks and praise, and I prepared myself to demur modestly. But not one of them came up to me. Instead, one fellow bent over, leaning on his cane, another stretched himself in order to appear tall, and a third looked at the bride in a way that was not decent. I asked the beadle about him. "*That* one," the beadle replied, and he bore down emphatically on the "th"-sound, "that one was an official who got fired." I nodded and said, "Well, well," as though with two well's I had concluded all the fellow's affairs. Meanwhile, the beadle chose four of his quorum, put a pole in the hand of each of the four, stretched a canopy over the poles, and, in doing that, pushed one man who bent forward and thus brought the canopy tumbling down.

Afterward, while standing under the bridal canopy, I recalled the story of a man whose mistress forced him to marry her. He went and gathered for the ceremony all her lovers who had lived with her before her marriage, both to remind her of her shame and to punish himself for agreeing to marry such a woman. What a contemptible fellow and what a contemptible act! Yet I found that man to my liking, and I thought well of what he had done. And when the rabbi stood and read the marriage contract, I looked at the wedding guests and tried to imagine what the woman was like and what her lovers were like at that moment. And in the same way, just before, when my wife put out her finger for the wedding ring and I said to her, "Behold thou art consecrated unto me," I knew without anyone's telling me what that man was like at that moment.

6

After the wedding we left for a certain village to spend our honeymoon. I won't tell you everything that happened to us on the way and in the station and on the train; and, accordingly, I won't describe every mountain and hill we saw, nor the brooks and springs in the valleys and mountains, as tellers of tales are accustomed to do when they set about describing the trip of a bride and groom. Undoubtedly there were mountains and hills and springs and brooks, and several things did happen to us on the way, but everything else has escaped me and been forgotten because of one incident which occurred on the first night. If you're not tired yet, I'll tell you about it.

We arrived at the village and registered at a little hotel situated among gardens and surrounded by mountains and rivers. We had supper and went up to the room that the hotel had set aside for us, for I had telegraphed our reservation before the wedding. Examining the room, my wife let her eyes dwell on the red roses that had been put there. "Who was so nice," I said jokingly, "to send us these lovely roses?" "Who?" asked my wife with genuine wonder, as though she thought there were someone here beside the hotel people who knew about us. "In any case," I said, "I'm taking them away, because their fragrance will make it hard to sleep. Or perhaps we should leave them in honor of the occasion." "Oh, yes," my wife answered after me in the voice of a person who speaks without hearing his own words. I said to her, "And don't you want to smell them?"—"Oh, yes, I want to." But she forgot to smell them. This forgetfulness was strange for Dinah, who loved flowers so much. I reminded her that she hadn't yet smelled the flowers. She bent her head over them. "Why are you bending down," I asked her, "when you can hold them up to you?" She looked at me as though she had just heard something novel. The blue-black in her eyes darkened, and she said, "You are very observant, my darling." I gave her a long kiss; then with closed eyes I said to her, "Now, Dinah, we are alone."

She stood up and took off her clothes with great deliberation, and began to fix her hair. As she was doing that, she sat down, bending her head over the table. I leaned over to see why she was taking so long, and I saw that she was reading a little pamphlet of the kind one finds in Catholic villages. The title was "Wait for Your Lord in Every Hour That He May Come."

I took her chin in my hand and said to her, "You don't have to wait, your lord has already come," and I pressed my mouth against hers. She lifted her eyes sadly and laid the pamphlet aside. I took her in my arms, put her in bed, and turned the lamp-wick down.

The flowers gave off their fragrance and a sweet stillness surrounded me. Suddenly I heard the sound of footsteps in the room next to ours. I forced the sound out of my mind and refused to pay attention to it, for what difference did it make to me whether or not there was someone there. I didn't know him and he didn't know us. And if he did know us, we had a wedding and were properly married. I embraced my wife with great love and was happy beyond limit with her, for I knew she was entirely mine.

With Dinah still in my arms, I strained attentively to make out whether that fellow's footsteps had stopped, but I heard him still pacing back and forth. His footsteps drove me to distraction: a strange idea now occurred to me, that this was the clerk my wife had known before her marriage. I was horror-stricken at the thought, and I had to bite my lip to prevent myself from cursing out loud. My wife took notice.

"What's wrong, sweetheart?"

"Nothing, nothing."

"I see something's troubling you."

"I've already told you nothing is."

"Then I must have been mistaken."

I lost my head and said to her, "You were not mistaken."

"What is it, then?"

I told her.

She began to sob.

"Why are you crying?" I said.

She swallowed her tears and answered, "Open the door and the windows and tell the whole world of my depravity."

I was ashamed of what I had said, and I tried to mollify her. She listened to me and we made peace.

7

From then on that man was never out of my sight, whether my wife was present or not. If I sat by myself, I thought about him, and if I talked with my wife, I mentioned him. If I saw a flower, I was reminded of the red roses, and if I saw a red rose, I was reminded of him, suspecting that was the kind he used to give my wife. This, then, was the reason she refused to smell the roses on the first night, because she was ashamed in her husband's presence to smell the same kind of flowers that her lover used to bring her. When she cried, I would console her. But in the kiss of reconciliation I heard the echo of another kiss which someone else had given her. We are enlightened individuals, modern people, we seek freedom for ourselves and for all humanity, and in point of fact we are worse than the most diehard reactionaries.

Thus passed the first year. When I wanted to be happy with my wife, I would remember the one who had spoiled my happiness, and I would sink into gloom. If she was happy, I told myself, What makes her so happy? She must be thinking of that louse. As soon as I mentioned him to her, she would burst into tears. "What are you crying for?" I would say. "Is it so difficult for you to hear me talk against that louse?"

I knew that she had long since put all thought of him out of her mind, and if she thought of him at all, it was only negatively, for she had never really loved him. It was only his supreme audacity together with a transient moment of weakness in her that had led her to lose control and listen to his demands. But my understanding of the matter brought me no equanimity. I wanted to grasp his nature, what it was in him that had attracted this modest girl raised in a good family.

I began to search through her books in the hope of finding some sort of letter from him, for Dinah was in the habit of using her letters as bookmarks. I found nothing, however. Perhaps, I thought, she has deliberately hidden them somewhere else, inasmuch as I have already searched all her books and found nothing. I could not bring myself to examine her private things. And that made me still angrier, for I was pretending to be decent while my thoughts were contemptible. Since I had spoken with no one else about her past, I sought counsel in books and began to read love stories in order to understand the nature of women and their lovers. But the novels bored me, so I took to reading criminal documents. My friends noticed and jokingly asked me if I were planning to join the detective squad.

The second year brought no mitigation or relief. If a day passed without my mentioning him, I spoke about him twice as much on the following day. From all the anguish I caused her, my wife fell sick. I healed her with medicines and battered her heart with words. I would tell her, "All your illness comes to you only because of the man who ruined your life. Right now he's playing around with other women, and me he has left with an invalid wife to take care of." A thousand kinds of remorse would sting me for every single word, and a thousand times I repeated those words.

At that time I began visiting my wife's relatives together with her. And here a strange thing occurred. I've already mentioned that Dinah came of good family and that her relatives were distinguished people. In consequence, they and their homes gratified me, and I began to show favor to my wife because of her relatives. These people, the grandchildren of ghetto dwellers, had achieved wealth and honor: their wealth was an ornament to their honor and their honor an ornament to their wealth. For even during the war, when the great figures of the nation made money out of people's hunger, they kept their hands clean of all money coming from an evil source, and, accordingly, they refused to stuff themselves with food and accepted only their legitimate rations. Among their number were the kind of imposing men we used to imagine but never really saw with our own eyes. And then there were the women. You don't know Vienna, and if you know it, you know the sort of Jewish women the gentiles wag their tongues over. If they could only see the women I saw, they would stop up their own mouths. Not that I care what the non-Jewish peoples say about us, for there is no hope that we'll ever please them, but inasmuch as I have mentioned their censure of us, I also mention their praise, because there is no higher praise for a brother than that which he receives from his sisters, through whom he is commended and extolled.

Before long I thought of my wife's relatives without connecting them with her, as though I and not she were their relation. I would think to myself, If they only knew how miserable I make her. And I was just about ready to unlock my lips and to open my heart to them. When I realized that my heart was urging me to talk, I stayed away from them, and they quite naturally stayed away from me. It's a big city and people are busy. If someone avoids his friends, they don't go hunting after him.

The third year my wife adopted a new mode of behavior. If I mentioned him, she ignored what I said, and if I connected his name with hers, she kept silent and didn't answer me, as though I weren't speaking about her. Infuriated, I would comment to myself, What a miserable woman not to take notice!

8

One summer day at twilight she and I were sitting at supper. It hadn't rained for a number of days, and the city was seething with heat. The water of the Danube showed green, and a dull odor floated over the city. The windows in our glass-enclosed porch gave off a sultry heat that exhausted body and soul. Since the day before, my shoulders had been aching, and now the pain was more intense. My head was heavy, my hair was dry. I ran my hand over my head and said to myself, I need a haircut. I looked across at my wife and saw that she was letting her hair grow long. Yet ever since women adopted men's haircuts, she always wore her hair close-cropped. I said to myself, My own head can't bear the weight of the little hair it has, and she's growing herself plumes like a peacock without even asking me if it looks nice that way. As a matter of fact, her hair looked lovely, but there was nothing lovely about my state of mind. I shoved my chair back from the table as though it were pushing against my stomach, and I ripped a piece of bread from the middle of the loaf and chewed it. It had been several days since I last mentioned him to her, and I hardly have to say that she made no mention of him to me. At that time, I was accustomed to saying very little to her, and when I did speak to her, I spoke without anger.

All at once I said to her, "There's something I've been thinking about."

She nodded her head. "Oh, yes," she said, "I feel the same way."

"So you know what is in the secret corners of my heart. Then, go ahead, tell me what I was thinking of."

In a whisper, she said, "Divorce."

As she spoke, she lifted her face to me and looked at me sadly. My heart was torn from its moorings, and I felt weak inside. I thought to myself, What a pitiful creature you are to treat your wife this way and cause her such pain. I lowered my voice and asked, "How do you know what is in my heart?"

"And what do you think I do with all my time? I sit and think about you, my dear."

The words leaped out of my mouth: I said to her, "Then you agree?"

She lifted her eyes to me. "You mean the divorce?"

I lowered my eyes and nodded in affirmation.

"Whether I want to or not," she said, "I agree to do whatever you ask, if it will only relieve your suffering."

"Even a divorce?"

"Even a divorce."

I was aware of all that I was losing. But the statement had already been made, and the desire to turn my wrath against myself drove me beyond reason. I clenched both hands and said angrily, "Well and good."

Several days passed, and I mentioned to her neither the divorce nor the one who had brought down ruin upon us. I told myself, Three years have passed since she became my wife. Perhaps the time has come to wipe out the memory of that affair. If she had been a widow or a divorcee when I married her, would there be anything I could have held against her? As things are, then, let me consider her as though she were a widow or a divorcee when I took her to be my wife.

And having reached this conclusion, I upbraided myself for every single day I had tormented her, and I resolved to be good to my wife. During that period I became a completely new person, and I began to feel an awakening of love as on the day I first met her. I was soon ready to conclude that everything is the result of man's will and desire: if he so wills it, he can introduce anger and hatred into his heart; if he wills it, he can live in peace with everyone. If this is so, I reasoned, what cause is there to stir up anger and bring evil upon ourselves when we are capable of doing good for ourselves and being happy? So I reasoned, that is, until something happened to me which set things back right where they were before.

9

What happened was this. One day a patient was brought to the hospital. I examined him and left him with the nurses to be washed and put to bed. In the evening I entered the ward to make my rounds. When I came to his bed, I saw his name on the card over his head, and I realized who he was.

What could I do? I'm a doctor, and I treated him. As a matter of fact, I gave him an extraordinary amount of care, so that all the other patients grew jealous of him and called him doctor's pet. And he really deserved the name, for whether he needed it or not, I treated him. I told the nurses that I had discovered in him a disease which hadn't been adequately studied yet, and that I wanted to investigate it myself. I left instructions for them to give him good food, and sometimes to add a glass of wine, so that he would get a little enjoyment out of his hospital stay. Further, I asked the nurses not to be too strict with him if he took certain liberties and didn't follow all the hospital regulations.

He lay in his hospital bed eating and drinking and enjoying all sorts of luxuries. And I came in to visit him and examine him again and again, asking him if he had a good night's sleep and if he was given all the food he wanted. I would order medication for him and praise his body to him, telling him that it would in all probability last to a ripe old age. He on his part listened with enjoyment and basked in pleasure before me like a worm. I told him, "If you're used to smoking, go ahead and smoke. I myself don't smoke, and if you ask me whether smoking is a good thing, I'll tell you it's bad and harmful to the body. But if you're used to smoking, I won't stop you." And in this way I gave him various special privileges, just so he would feel completely comfortable. At the same time I reflected, Over a man for whom I wouldn't waste so much as a word I am going to all this trouble, and it's all because of that business which is difficult to speak of and difficult to forget. Not only that, but I watch him and study him as though I could learn what rubbed off on him from Dinah and what rubbed off on her from him—and from devoting so much attention to him, I was acquiring some of his gestures.

At first I kept the whole matter secret from my wife. But it burst forth when I tried to suppress it, and it told itself. My wife listened without the slightest sign of interest. On the surface, one would have thought that this was just what I wanted, but I was not satisfied, even though I realized that if she had responded differently I would certainly not have been pleased.

After some while he was cured and had recuperated, and it was high time for him to leave the hospital. I kept him day after day and ordered the nurses to give him the best of treatment, so that he would not be anxious to leave. And that was the period right after the war, when it was hard to get provisions for the sick, not to speak of the convalescent, and certainly not to speak of the healthy, so I gave him from my own food which the farmers used to bring me. He sat in the hospital eating and drinking and gladdening his heart, reading newspapers and strolling in the garden, playing with the patients and laughing with the nurses. He put on some weight and was healthier than the people who took care of him, so that it became impossible to keep him any longer in the hospital. I gave instructions that a proper final dinner be prepared for him, and I discharged him.

After the dinner, he came to say goodbye to me. I looked at the double chin he had developed. His eyes were embedded in fat, like those of a woman who has given up everything for the sake of eating and drinking. I stood by my desk rummaging through the papers on it as though I were looking for something I had lost. Then I took a stethoscope to examine him. As I was trying to appear busy, two nurses came in, one to ask me something and one to say goodbye to the doctor's pet. I pulled my head back suddenly, as though I had been reminded that someone was waiting for me, and I let out a brief exclamation of surprise, the way Dinah does when she sees that someone has been waiting for her. As I did that, I looked at the healthy patient with his double chin and I said to myself, You don't know who I am, but I know who you are. You are the man who brought ruin down on me and wrecked my wife's life. Anger surged within me, and I became so furious that my eyes ached.

He extended his hand to me in special deference and began to stutter words of thanks about my saving him from death and restoring him to life. I offered him my fingertips to shake, in an impolite and deprecatory manner, and immediately I wiped them on my white coat, as though I had touched a dead reptile. Then I turned my face away from him as from some disgusting thing, and I walked away. I sensed that the nurses were looking at me and knew the reason for my behavior, even though there were no grounds for such apprehension.

After a little while I went back to work, but my head and heart were not with me. I went up to the doctors' lounge and looked for a friend to take my place. I told him that I had been summoned to court to give testimony about a certain criminal, and that it was impossible to postpone the case. A nurse came and asked whether she should order a cab. "Certainly, nurse, certainly," I answered. While she went to the switchboard to telephone, I ran out of the hospital like someone who had gone berserk.

I passed by a bar and considered going in to drown my sorrows in drink, as embittered men are accustomed to say. I grew a bit calmer and told myself, Troubles come and go, your troubles will also pass. But I had only grown calm temporarily, and only to lose control again. I began walking. After an hour or so, I stopped and saw that I had gone all around myself and completed a circle around the same spot.

10

I came home and told my wife. She listened and said nothing. I was infuriated that she should sit there in silence, as if she had heard nothing of significance. I bowed my head over my chest the way he did when he stood before me to thank me, and, imitating his voice, I said, "I wish to thank you, doctor, for saving me from death and restoring me to life." And I told my wife, "That's the way his voice sounds and that's the way he stands," in order to show her how low he was, what a pitiful creature was the man whom she had preferred to me and to whom she had given her love before she knew me. My wife looked up at me as though the whole thing were not worth her while to care about. Rising, I scrutinized her face in the hope of finding some indication of joy over that good-for-nothing's recovery, but just as I had seen no signs of sorrow when I told her he was sick, I saw now not the slightest sign of joy over his recovery.

After two or three days, the experience lost its sting and no longer disturbed me. I treated patients, talked much with the nurses, and immediately after work went home to my wife. Sometimes I would ask her to read to me from one of her books, and she would agree. She read while I sat looking at her, thinking, This is the face that had the power to drive away the frowns and dissipate the anger of whoever saw it. And I would run my hand over my face in gratification as I continued to look at her. Sometimes we had a friend over for coffee or for supper. And once again we talked about everything people talk about, and once again I realized that there were things in the world other than woman-trouble. Often now I climbed into bed at night with a feeling of contentment and gratification.

One night this fellow came to me in a dream: his face was sickly and yet just a little—just a little—likable. I was ashamed of myself for thinking evil of him, and I resolved to put an end to my anger against him. He bent down and said, "What do you want from me? Is the fact that she raped me any reason for you to have it in for me?"

The next night we had as dinner guests two of our friends, a married couple, whom we both particularly liked—him because of his admirable qualities, her because of her blue eyes filled with radiance, and because of her high forehead which deceived the eye into thinking that she was unusually intelligent, and because of the golden curls trembling on her head, and also because of her voice, the voice of a woman who suppresses her longings within her. We sat together some three hours without being aware of the time. He discussed the questions of the day, and she helped him with the radiance from her eyes.

After they left, I said to my wife, "Let me tell you a dream."

"A dream?" cried my wife in surprise, and fixed her eyes on me sorrowfully and repeated in a whisper, "A dream." For it was not my way to tell dreams, and it seems to me that all those years I had not dreamed at all.

"I had a dream," I told her. And as I said it, my heart suddenly quaked.

My wife sat down and looked into my face intently. I proceeded to tell her my dream. Her shoulders shook and her body began to tremble. She stretched out her arms all of a sudden and, placing them around my neck, she embraced me. I returned her embrace and we stood clinging together in love and affection and pity, while all that time, this fellow never left my sight, and I could hear him saying, "Is the fact that she raped me any reason for you to have it in for me?"

I pushed my wife's arms away from my neck, and a terrible sadness welled up within me. I got into bed and thought over the whole affair quietly and calmly until I fell asleep.

The next day we got up and ate breakfast together. I looked over at my wife and saw that her face was the same as always. I thanked her in my heart for bearing no grudge against me over the night before. At that moment, I recalled all the trouble and suffering I had caused her since the day she married me, how time after time I drained her lifeblood and insulted her in every possible way, while she took everything in silence. My heart swelled with love and tenderness for this miserable soul whom I had tortured so much, and I resolved to be good to her. And so I was for one day, for two days, for three days.

11

And I was quite prepared to conclude that everything was being set right. In point of fact, nothing had been set right. From the very day I made peace with myself, that peace was robbed from me through another means. My wife treated me as though I had become a stranger to her. Yet all the efforts I was making with her were for her sake. How this woman failed to take notice! But she did notice.

One day she said to me, "What a good thing it would be if I were dead!"

"Why do you say that?"

"Why, you ask?" And in the wrinkles around her lips there was visible a sort of smile which made my heart jump.

"Don't be a fool," I scolded her.

She sighed. "Ah, my dear, I am not a fool."

"Then I am a fool."

"No, you're not a fool either."

I raised my voice and challenged her. "Then what do you want from me?"

"What do I want?" she answered. "I want the same thing you want."

I brushed one palm off with the other and said, "There's nothing at all I want."

She looked into my face intently. "There's nothing at all you want. Then everything must be all right."

"All right?" I laughed scornfully.

"You see, my dear," she said, "that laugh does not sit well with me."

"What am I supposed to do, then?"

"Do what you've been wanting to do."

"Namely?"

"Namely, why should I repeat something you yourself know?"

"I'm afraid I don't know what that something is. But since you know, you can tell me."

She pronounced in a whisper, "Divorce."

I raised my voice as I answered. "You want to force me into giving you a divorce."

She nodded. "If you think it's proper for you to put it that way and say that I want to force you, then I agree."

"Meaning what?" I asked.

"Why do we have to repeat things when there's no call for it? Let us do what is written for us above."

In anger, I mocked her. "Even Heaven is an open book for

you, as you know what's written there. I am a doctor and I can only go by what my eyes see, while you, madam, you know what is written on high. Where did you pick up such knowledge, maybe from that louse?"

"Be still!" Dinah cried. "Please, be still!"

"You don't have to get so angry," I told her. "After all, what did I say?"

She rose, went to her room, and locked the door behind her.

I came to the door and asked her to open it for me, but she refused. "Look, I'm leaving," I said to her. "The whole house is yours, and you don't have to lock the door." When she still did not answer, I began to be afraid that she had taken sleeping pills and, God forbid, committed suicide. I began to beg and plead for her to open the door, but still she did not open. I peeked through the keyhole, my heart pounding me blow after blow, as though I were a murderer. Thus I stood before the locked door until evening came on and the walls darkened.

With darkness, she came out of her room, pale as a corpse. When I took her hands in mine, a deathly chill flowed out of them that made my own hands cold. She made no effort to pull her hands away from me, as though she had no feeling left in them.

I laid her down on her bed and calmed her with sedatives, nor did I move from her until she had dozed off. I looked at her face, a face innocent of any flaw, without the slightest blemish, and I said to myself, What a lovely world in which such a woman exists, and what difficult lives we have to live! I bent down in order to kiss her. She turned her head in sign of refusal. "Did you say something?" I asked. "No," she said, and I couldn't tell whether she was conscious of me or simply was talking in her sleep. Thoroughly disconcerted, I kept my distance from her. But I sat there all night long.

The next day I went to work and came back at noon. Whether out of prudence or for some other reason, I made no mention to her of what had happened the day before. She on her part did not speak of it either. So it was on the second day, so again on the third day. I was ready to conclude that matters were returning to their previous state. Yet I knew that though I might try to forget, she would not forget.

During that period her appearance became more vigorous and she changed some of her habits. Where she was accustomed to greet me as I came in the door, she no longer greeted me. Sometimes she would leave me and go off somewhere, and there were times when I came home and did not find her.

The anniversary of our engagement fell at that time. I said to her, "Let's celebrate and take a trip to the place we went to when we were first married."

"That's impossible."

"Why?"

"Because I have to go somewhere else."

"Pardon me, but where is it you are going?"

"There's a patient I'm taking care of."

"Why this all of a sudden?"

"Not everything a person does is all of a sudden. For a long time now I've felt that I ought to work and do something."

"And isn't it enough for you that I am working and doing something?"

"Once that was enough for me. Now it's not enough."

"Why not?"

"Why not? If you yourself don't know, I can't explain it to you."

"Is it such a complicated issue that it's difficult to explain?"

"It's not hard to explain, but I doubt if you would want to understand."

"Why are you doing it?"

"Because I want to earn my own living."

"Do you think you're not supported adequately in your own home, that you have to go look for a living elsewhere."

"Right now I'm being supported. Who knows what will be tomorrow?"

"Why all of a sudden such ideas?"

"I already told you that nothing happens all of a sudden."

"I don't know what you're talking about."

"You understand, all right, but you prefer to say, 'I don't understand.' "

I nodded my head in despair and said, "That's how it is, then."

"Really, that's how it is."

"This whole dialectic is beyond me."

"It's beyond you, and it's not particularly close to me. So it would be better if we kept still. You do what you have to do, and I'll do what I have to."

"What I do, I know. But I have no idea what it is you want to do."

"If you don't know now, you'll soon find out."

But her efforts did not succeed. And however they may have succeeded, she failed to make a penny out of them. She was caring for a paralyzed girl, the daughter of a poor widow, and she received no payment for her work. On the contrary, she helped the widow financially, and she even brought her flowers. At that time Dinah's strength drained from her as though she were sick, and she herself needed someone to take care of her instead of her caring for others. Once I asked her, "How long are you going to continue working with that sick girl?" She fixed her eyes on me and said, "Are you asking me as a doctor?"

"What difference does it make whether I ask as a doctor or as your husband?"

"If you ask as a doctor, I don't know what to tell you, and if you ask for other reasons, I see no need to answer."

I tried to act as if she were joking with me, so I laughed. She averted her face from me, and, leaving me where I was, went off. The laughter immediately died on my lips, nor has it yet returned.

It's just a mood, I told myself, and I can put up with it. Yet I knew that all my optimism was completely baseless. I recalled the first time she spoke to me about a divorce, and I remembered what she said: "Whether I want it or not, I am prepared to do whatever you ask, if only it will relieve your suffering—even a divorce." Now I thought, However you look at it, there's no way out for us except a divorce. As soon as this idea occurred to me, I dismissed it, as a man will dismiss something painful from his thoughts. But Dinah was right when she said we had to do what was written for us above. Before long I saw with my own eyes and I grasped with my own understanding what at first I had not seen and I had not grasped. At once I decided that I would grant Dinah the divorce. We had no children, for I had been apprehensive about begetting children for fear they would look like him. I arranged our affairs and gave her the divorce.

And so we parted from one another, the way people will part outwardly. But in my heart, my friend, the smile on her lips is still locked up, and that blue-black in her eyes, as on the day I first saw her. Sometimes at night I sit up in bed like those patients she used to take care of, and I stretch out both hands and call, "Nurse, nurse, come to me."

Translated by ROBERT ALTER

The Face and the Image

NAOMI HAD WASHED the floor, arranged the furniture, watered the flowers, and wiped the inkwells; and the room was filled with peace. I waited for Naomi to finish all her work, and then I would sit down to do mine. For it was a great work I wanted to do, to write down in a book my thoughts about polished mirrors. This device, which shows you whatever you show it, aroused my wonder even in childhood, perhaps more than the thing itself. And now that I have grown old, and seen the deeds that pass, and some of the deeds that last, I have continued to ponder on the qualities of mirrors. They are flat, and thin, and smooth as ice, and there is nothing inside them. But they store up whatever you put before them, and before them there is no cheating, or partiality, or injustice, or deceit. Whatever you show them, they show you. They do not expunge or amplify, add on or take away—like the truth, which neither adds nor takes away. Therefore I said: I will tell of their virtues and their perfect rectitude.

"Finished," said Naomi, and a smile of satisfaction seemed to play on her chaste lips. Naomi was really entitled to be satisfied with her work, and I should have been satisfied too, but for a sudden sadness that enfolded my heart.

But I took no notice of this sadness, though it was heavier today than it had been yesterday, for that is how it goes: anything that lives continues to grow. So I took a chair to sit down and begin my work. A paper fell off the chair, and I saw it was a telegram. I looked at Naomi. "When they brought the telegram I was busy wiping the table," she said, "and I left it on the chair so it wouldn't get soiled."

For tidiness' sake I took the telegram and laid it on the table. Then I took a knife to open it. At that moment there appeared before me the image of my grandfather, my mother's father, in the year he died, lying in his bed and reading his will all night. His beard was bluish silver and the hair of his beard was not wavy but straight, every single hair hanging by itself and not mingling with the next, but their perfect rectitude uniting them all. I began to calculate how old my grandfather had been when I was born, and how old my mother had been when she bore me, and it turned out that her age today was the same as my grandfather's age at that time, and my age was the same as hers when I was born.

Many other thoughts passed through my mind, but I set them aside and went back to the telegram. I opened the telegram and read: "Mother sick, awaiting you." Mother sick, waiting for me. Taking the plain sense of the words, they meant: Mother is on the point of death; or perhaps she was already dead and they were waiting for me before burying her.

I quickly took my traveling kit and put it in my valise; I gazed at the room, and at the table where a few moments before I had longed to do my work. I stood there all alone with myself, like a man who is shown a clenched hand and thinks that what he wants is inside, but when the hand is opened it turns out to be empty.

"Naomi," I said to her, "I am going away, and I do not know how long I shall stay. Close up the house behind me, lock it up thoroughly, and take the key with you until I come back."

Naomi nodded her head with its two plaits and looked at me. I saw from the look in her eyes that she disapproved of a man going to see his mother in the patched trousers in which he was in the habit of doing his work; it was not respectful to his family to come to them like that. What would people say? How many years he has spent in the world, and he has not managed to buy a whole garment!

I closed my eyes to Naomi's apprehensions. When Mother might be on the point of death, could I worry about my dress? By the time I took off my old clothes and put on new, Mother might have breathed her last. I waved my hand deprecatingly and said, "No, I am going as I am. In any case, I shall take another pair of trousers with me." But the valise was small and did not hold much. And my other valise was in the attic, and to get up there I needed a ladder, and if I found a ladder and climbed up, the valise might well be locked, and if it was locked, I might not find the key. So, since there were more doubts than certainties, I took my little valise in my hand and went out, dressed as I was in my patched trousers.

Thinking about the way ahead, I said to myself: I am going to my mother and I do not know whether she is alive or dead, for when I last left her she was sick, and she cried and said, "My heart tells me that I shall never see you again." And it is known that the sick see with a third eye, which the Angel of Death lends them.

I took a short cut through a certain old courtyard, like the one where I used to play hide-and-seek in my childhood. The same sensation I felt in my head during this game came back to me. Picture to yourselves a large, old courtyard, full of many corners, and every corner full of corners, besides various articles and bits and pieces deposited by their owners in case they might need them. The owners are dead, the articles are rusty, and the rust glows with a kind of damp light which terrifies but does not illuminate. And as I am a little child with my little friends, I hide from them and they hide from me. We stand and wait, and none of us knows whether he wants to be found or not. Finally, none of us looks for the others. We run about looking for a secret corner more secluded than the first, and my head goes around and around, and the rust that glimmers from the junk makes my flesh creep.

They were taking a body out of the yard, and a man I knew was carrying the bier, exerting all his strength and pushing his feet into the ground until they were getting flattened with the weight. The very nails of his hands and toes cried: Come and carry with me. His eyes were weary; he seemed to be carrying them on his shoulders, from which they were looking out in entreaty. I began to worry in case he told me with his mouth what his eyes were entreating, when I was hurrying to Mother. I slipped through into a cranny, and from there to another, from there to the street and then to the railroad station, and from the station into a carriage.

Thank Heaven I had reached the train and got my ticket, and no longer had to push and be pushed, but could sit and leave my time at the disposal of the train, which knew when to depart and when to arrive. And since I was always engrossed in my work and had no time to look at myself, I thought: Now that I have set aside all my affairs, let me think about myself a little. It is good for a man to think about himself a little and not think what he is always thinking. I looked at myself and saw myself standing in the station on the carriage step. The station was full of people and luggage, some carrying their belongings in their hands and some pulling at the porters to carry their luggage. The guard was waving his flag and all of them were slipping from their places, some this way and some that, returning as they ran to the place they had come from.

Suddenly, I felt eyes staring at this man who is already taking his place in the train. I began to be afraid they might give me the evil eye. I turned my head toward the wall and found a notice there, stating that every traveler to this place needed a travel permit. I realized that this place where I was going was in a military area, and I had left my travel permit at home. This place where I was born, and where my mother was dying, was in a military area, and I had to go there, and I did not have my travel permit with me.

What was to be done? There was nothing to be done but to go back home, get my travel permit, and set off on tomorrow's train, for the guard was already blowing his whistle and the train was on the point of departure. I hastily jumped out of the carriage. Those who had come to see travelers off looked at me, startled, and those who had come to travel and had not arrived in time began to run in haste and confusion, as if I had left a place vacant for them. I held up my hands, as if begging their pardon, and felt that my hands were empty, for my valise was still in the compartment.

I fixed my eyes on the train, which had set out on a long journey and taken my valise with it. The train chugged on, emitting a heavy trail of smoke. My eyes were smothered in the smoke and covered with the smoke, and out of the smoke slipped the man who had been carrying the bier. Strange to say, he was no longer carrying his eyes on his shoulders, but his eyes were in his head, and his hands were empty, and on his lips there was a kind of smile. "Where are you going?" he said to me. "Home," I said to him. He passed his hand over his beard, blew a hair at me, and said, "Home?" And again he was looking at me from between his shoulders. How people can change! A short time before, he had been looking at me face to face, and a short time later he was looking at me from the back of his neck.

I took no short cuts on my way back, for you did not know what was hidden in that courtyard and what lay in store for you there. When I reached my house, I found it locked; the key was still in my valise, and my valise was still in the railway carriage. There was one more key, and Naomi had it. And You, O God, made me send Naomi on leave until my return.

I went to Naomi's house but did not find her. Where was Naomi? Naomi had gone to visit her uncle. Which uncle? Some of the neighbors said her uncle on her father's side, and some said her uncle on her mother's side. If she had gone to her father's brother, he lived in Shaarayim; if to her mother's brother, he lived in Sdeh Shalom. If I went one way, it would take half a day; if I went the other way, it would take half a day; if I did not find her and had to go after her again, that would be a day gone, and I would be late for tomorrow's train. And after all, I could not tear myself in two—sending one part this way and one the other. Whether I liked it or not, I must go one way or the other. And my heart was pulling away from me, wanting to go to Mother; and it was right, for all the trouble I had taken had only been for Mother's sake, and if I did not hurry and set off at once, I might never find my mother and reach her before her burial.

Suddenly an idea came into my mind: perhaps Naomi had not gone away, and if she had not gone away she was still in the city, and if she was in the city, she might have gone to one of her relatives. I must go there and find her. It is a happy man who finds a new idea when all his ideas are exhausted. I began to inquire which of her relatives here Naomi was in the habit of visiting, and they told me: She has one relative here, a carpenter; perhaps she has gone to him.

I went to the carpenter and found him on his knees fitting a mirror into the door of a wardrobe. I greeted him and he returned my greeting from between his knees, without raising his head an inch for my sake. Almost certainly he had looked in the mirror and seen that my trousers were old, and he had understood in his own way that a man like this was not worth troubling his head over. "Is Naomi here?" I asked him; but he did not reply. "Where is Naomi?" I asked again. He looked at me over his shoulder and replied angrily, "What do you want of Naomi?" "Naomi works for me," I said, "and I need her."

When he heard I was Naomi's master, he stood up and started to treat me with deference. He snatched a chair and then another, set them before me and asked me to sit down, and began to say how fond of me Naomi's family were. And, since he was a relative of Naomi's and now had the privilege of seeing me in his home, I must eat something to bring a blessing on his house. So he called his wife and told her to bring refreshments. His wife came and brought some sweet-meats. She spread her hands in front of her eyes and kissed the tips of her fingers, as simple women do when the scroll of the law is taken out of the Ark. So sacred was the virtue of hospitality in her eyes. She started persuading me to eat and drink, while her husband begged me to drink and eat, she on one side and he on the other.

My lips were sealed and my hands were numb; they would not obey me and take some food or drink. I overcame them and replied in speech and gesture: "Impossible, I am in a hurry. I cannot stay here. I have to rush away." But Naomi's relatives turned a deaf ear, repeating their invitation over and over again. So I took something of what they offered me.

So there I sat against my will, eating and drinking what-ever Naomi's relatives gave me. At first I ate and drank against my will, without enjoyment, and then willingly, for hunger had begun to torment me. My house was locked, the key in the valise, the valise in the railway carriage, and the carriage on the way to its destination, and all my thoughts were with my mother; perhaps while I was filling my gullet they were sealing her grave. I turned my head aside so as not to look at what I saw. My image rose before me from the mirror in the wardrobe, which the carpenter had been fixing an hour before. The mirror stared at me face to face, reflect-ing back every movement of the hand and quiver of the lips, like all polished mirrors, which show you whatever you show them, without partiality or deceit. And it, namely, the reve-lation of the thing, surprised me more than the thing itself, perhaps more than it had surprised me in my childhood, perhaps more than it had ever surprised me before.

Translated by Misha Louvish

The Lady
and the Pedlar

THERE WAS A Jewish pedlar who walked his rounds in townlets and villages. One day he happened upon a clearing in a forest, far from any settlement. He saw a house that stood there alone. He went up to it and cried out his goods at the door. Out came a lady and said: "What do you want here, Jew?" He bowed, greeted her, and said: "Perhaps you need some of the nice things that I have." He put his pack down from his shoulders and offered her all kinds of goods. She said: "I need neither you nor your goods." He said: "Have a look, perhaps, nevertheless? Here are loops, here are rings, here are scarves, here are sheets and soap and all kinds of scent that the noblewomen are using." She looked a little at his chest, turned her eyes away from his, and said: "There is nothing here. Go away." Again he bowed before her and took things out of his chest and offered them to her and said: "Look here, my lady, and don't say there is nothing here. Perhaps this here is desirable to you, or perhaps you will like that nice thing. Please, lady, look again." She bowed over the chest and rummaged a little here and there. She saw a hunter's knife, gave him its price, and went back into her house. He took his pack and went away.

At that hour the sun had already set, and he lost his way. He walked for an hour and for another hour. He entered among the trees and walked out of them and entered again among the trees. Darkness covered the land and the moon did not shine in the sky. He looked around himself and began to be afraid. He saw a light that was burning. He walked toward the light and came to a house. He knocked at the door. The mistress looked at him and called, "Again you are here? What do you want, Jew?" He said: "From the time I left here, I have been going astray in the dark and cannot reach a settled place." She said to him: "So what do you want?" He said to her: "Please, my lady, give me leave to stay here until the moon comes out and I can see my way, so that I can go." She looked at him with angry eyes and permitted him to sleep in an old cowshed in her courtyard. He lay down on the straw and fell asleep.

During the night much rain came down. When the pedlar got up in the morning, he saw that all the land had become a morass. He knew that this lady was a hard woman. He said to himself: I shall put myself in the hands of Heaven and not ask favors from niggardly people. He took his pack and was about to go. At that moment the lady looked out at him and said: "I believe the roof has cracked, can you repair something there?" The pedlar put his pack down and said: "I'll climb up at once." She gave him a ladder, and he climbed up on the roof. He found roof tiles that the wind had shaken out of position. He put them back in their places and did not care that his clothes were dripping with water and that his shoes were like two pails. He told himself: What does it matter, whether I stand on top of this roof or walk in the forest? Here it is raining and there it is raining. Perhaps, if I am useful to her, she will bear with me and let me stay in her house until the rain stops.

After he had arranged the tiles and filled up the chinks of the roof, he climbed down and said to her: "I am sure that from now on the rain will no longer come into the house." She told him: "You are a craftsman; tell me your wage and I shall pay you." He put his hand on his heart and said: "By no means shall I take a penny from milady. I am not used to being paid for anything that is not part of my trade, and especially not after the lady did me a favor and let me spend the night in her house." She looked at him suspiciously, as she believed that he talked thus in order to endear himself to her, so that she would pay him a higher wage. Finally she said: "Sit down, I shall make you breakfast." He stood and wrung his clothes and poured the water out of his shoes and looked around. From the many antlers that were hanging on the walls, it seemed to be a hunter's house. Or perhaps it was not a hunter's house, and the antlers were hanging there only as decoration, as forest dwellers are wont to do, who adorn their houses with antlers of deer.

While he stood and looked, the lady of the house returned and brought him warm beer and some food. After he had eaten and drunk, he told her: "Perhaps there is something else here that needs repair? I am ready to do whatever the lady will tell me." She looked around the house and said: "Look for yourself." The pedlar was pleased that he had been given permission to stay in the house, until the rains would have stopped. He got to work and repaired things here and there, and did not ask for pay. In the evening she prepared dinner for him and made up his bed in a room where old things were lying around that were no longer in use. The pedlar thanked the lady of the house for her favor and swore that he would never forget her kindness.

Next morning new rains began to pour down. The pedlar looked outside and looked at the face of the lady of the house, to see who would have pity on him first. The lady of the house sat drawn in upon herself and kept silent, and a great boredom emanated from the furniture. The antlers on the walls were clouded by steam, and a smell like the smell of living flesh floated from them. Whether she wished to relieve the boredom in her heart or whether she took pity on the fellow who had to walk through rain and in the morass, whatever it was, the lady began to speak to him. What didn't she speak about: about the rains that do not stop, about the winds that blow endlessly, about the roads that get worse and worse, and about the grain that is likely to rot, and about similar matters. The pedlar thanked her in his heart for each speech, for each speech gave him a foothold in her house, so that he did not have to take to the roads and walk in the rain and in the cold and in the storm. And she, too, was satisfied that there was a living soul with her. She took her knitting things and told him to sit down. He sat down in front of her and told her things about noblemen and noblewomen, about gentlemen and gentlewomen, everything he knew and everything she liked to hear. By and by they came closer to each other. He said to her: "My lady lives here alone, has she no husband or friend? Certainly there are here many honorable noblemen who crave the company of a fine lady such as you." She said: "I did have a husband." Sighed the pedlar and said: "And he died." She said to him: "No, he was killed." Sighed the pedlar for her husband that was killed and asked, "How was he killed?" Said she: "If the police do not know, you want to know? What matter is it to you, whether a wild beast has eaten him or whether he was slaughtered with a knife. Why, you too are selling knives with which one can slaughter a man."

The pedlar saw that the lady was not in a mind to tell what happened to her husband, and he ceased to speak. And she too was silent. After a little while the pedlar spoke again and said: "Grant God that the murderers of your husband will be found and revenge be taken on them." She said: "They won't find them, they won't find them. Not every murderer lets himself be caught." The pedlar lowered his eyes and said: "I regret, my lady, that I reminded you of your sorrow. If I would know how I could please your heart, I would give half of my life." The lady looked at him and smiled a strange smile, contemptuous or pleased, or just a smile that a person smiles and his fellow interprets in his own manner, and if he is a guileless man, he interprets it in his own favor. The pedlar, who was a guileless man, interpreted the smile that this woman smiled in his favor and for his enjoyment. And as he was sorry for this woman who by her age and by the measure of her beauty deserved that decent people should court her, he suddenly saw himself as one of them. He began to speak to her words that the ear of a single woman loves to hear. God knows from where this simple pedlar took such words. She did not scold him and did not rebuff him. On the contrary, she was lief to hear more. So he took heart and began to speak words of love. And although she was a lady and he a simple pedlar, she accepted his words and showed him kindness. And also after the rains had stopped and the roads had dried they did not part from each other.

And the pedlar stayed with the lady. Not in the old cow-shed and not in the room of the old things that were no longer in use, but in the room of the lady he lived and in the bed of her husband he slept, and she served him, as if he were her lord. Every day she prepared him a meal of every-thing she had in the house and in the fields, every good bird and every fat bird. And if she roasted him meat in butter, he did not turn away from it. At first he shuddered, when he saw her wring the head of a bird, then he ate and even sucked the bones, in the manner of frivolous people who in the beginning do not intend to commit any offense and then commit every offense in the world with pleasure. Wife and children he did not have, and he had nobody to long for, and so he stayed with the woman. He took off the pedlar's clothes and wore the clothes of a man of leisure and associated with the local people until he became like one of them. The lady did not let him exert himself in the house or in the fields; on the contrary, she took upon herself every work and pampered him with food and drink, and if she scolded him during the day, she showed him kindness in the night, in the manner of women who are sometimes this way and some-times that way. So passed a month and another month, until he began to forget that he was a poor pedlar and she a lady. And she, too, forgot that he was a Jew and all the rest.

And so they lived together in one house under the same roof, and he ate and drank and enjoyed himself and slept in a made bed and seemingly did not lack a thing. But there was one thing that made him wonder: in all these days he never saw her eat or drink. At first he had thought that it was beneath her to eat with him. After he got used to her and forgot that she was a lady and he a Jew, he wondered more and more.

Once he said to her: "What is this, Helene? These several months I live with you and I do not see you eat or drink. Did you make yourself a larder in your bowels?" Said she to him: "What matter is it to you whether I eat or drink or whether I do not eat and drink? It should be enough for you that you lack nothing with me and that you get your food at any time." He said to her: "It is true that I eat and drink and my food is more plentiful than ever, but all the same I am eager to know how you manage and on what you feed yourself. At the same table with me you do not dine, and also elsewhere I have not seen you eat or drink; is it possible to subsist without eating and drinking?" Helene smiled and said: "You want to know what I eat and drink. Human blood I drink and human flesh I eat." And while she spoke, she embraced him with all her might and put her lips on his lips and sucked and said, "I never imagined that the flesh of a Jew is so sweet. Kiss me, my raven. Kiss me, my eagle, your kisses are sweeter than all the kisses in the world." He kissed her and thought in his heart, These are poetical expressions, such as noblewomen are wont to use when they give pleasure to their husbands. And she, too, kissed him again and said, "Joseph, when you first showed yourself to me, I wanted to set my bitch on you, and now I am myself biting you like a mad bitch, in such manner that I fear you will not get away alive out of my hands, oh my sweet carcass mine!" So they were passing their days in love and endearments, and nothing in the world disturbed their doings.

But this one thing plucked at the pedlar's heart. They lived together in one house in one room and her bed was next to his bed, and all she had she gave to him, except that she did not eat bread with him at one table. To such an extent that she did not taste any of the dishes she prepared for him. As this one thing plucked at his heart, he asked her again. Said she, "He who keeps asking for it, deepens his own pit. Rejoice, my sweet carcass, with all that is given to you, and don't ask questions for which there is no answer." Thought the Jew in his heart: Perhaps she is really right and I am wrong. What matters it to me whether she eats and drinks with me or whether she feeds herself and quenches her thirst from somewhere else. Isn't she healthy and her face beautiful, and I lack nothing while I am with her. So he resolved to keep silent. He stayed with her and enjoyed himself at her table and all the rest. He did not nag her with his questions and did not bother her with superfluous talk, but doubled his love for her, perhaps because he really loved her or because of that riddle without solution.

He who has dealings with women knows that every love that is not unconditional must come to naught in the end. And even a man who loves a woman as Samson loved Delilah —in the end she makes fun of him, in the end she annoys him until his soul is weary to death. So it was with the pedlar. After some time she began to make fun of him, then she began to annoy him, in the end his soul was weary to death. All the same he did not leave her. And she, too, did not tell him: Go away! He stayed with her another month and another month, quarreling and making up, making up and quarreling, and he did not know why they quarreled and why they made up. Yet he thought in his heart: We are so near, we are so close to each other, we do not ever leave one another, and all the same I do not know about her today more than I knew about her yesterday, and yesterday I did not know more about her than I knew on the day on which I came to her the first time, when she bought the knife from me. As long as they were at peace with one another he did not ask her much, and when he asked, she silenced him with kisses. As their peace had departed, he began to think more and more, until he said to himself, I shall not give her rest until she tells me.

One night he said to her: "Many times did I ask you about your husband and you did not tell me anything." Said she to him: "About which one did you ask?" Said he: "Is it that you had two husbands? Didn't you mention only the one that was killed?" Said she to him: "What matter is it to you, whether they were two or three?" Said he to her: "So I am your fourth husband?" Said she: "My fourth husband?" Said he: "So it appears from your words. Isn't it so, Helene?" Said she to him: "Wait until I count them all." She stretched out her right hand and began to count her fingers, one, two, three, four, five. When she had counted all the fingers on her right hand, she stretched out her left hand and went on counting. Said he to her: "And where are they?" Said she: "Did I not tell you, he who keeps asking for it, deepens his own pit?" Said he: "You must tell me." She stroked her belly and said: "Perhaps some of them are here." Said he: "What does this mean?" She looked askance and smiled. Then she looked at him a while and said: "And if I tell you will you understand? Mother of God, look what a face this carcass has got!"

Already, when she began to count her fingers, his mind had left him, and all he had asked, he had asked unconsciously. Now also the power of speech was taken from him. He sat and was silent. Said she to him: "My darling, do you believe in God?" He sighed and said: "Is it possible, not to believe in God?" Said she to him: "Aren't you a Jew?" He sighed and said: "Yes, I am a Jew." Said she: "But the Jews don't believe in God, for if they had believed in him, they would not have killed him. But if you believe, pray for yourself that your end will not be as theirs." "The end of whom?"—"As the end of those you asked about."—"Of your husbands?"—"Of my husbands."—"What was their end?" Answered Helene and said: "If you don't understand, it's no use to talk to you." While she spoke, she looked at his throat, and her blue eyes shone as the blade of a new knife. He looked at her and trembled. She, too, looked at him and said: "Why did your face grow pale?" He touched his face and said: "Did my face grow pale?" Said she: "And the hair on your head rose up like hog's bristles." He touched his head and said, "My hair bristles?" Said she: "And the roots of your beard got like goose skin. Phew, how ugly are the faces of cowards!" She spat at him and went away. While she walked away, she turned her face back and said to him: "Take care of your Adam's apple. Mother of God, doesn't it tremble, as if it saw the knife. Don't get upset, little dear. I won't bite you yet."

The pedlar remained sitting. Intermittently he touched his face and his beard. The hair on his head had calmed down again and was lying as before, one part here and one part there and a parting in the middle, and he was cold, as if ice had been placed on him. From the other room Helene's steps could be heard. At this hour he did not love her and did not hate her. His limbs were numb, as if they had lost their strength; his mind worked with increasing intensity. He told himself: I must get up and take my pack and go away. As he wanted to go, his legs grew limp again. Again Helene's footsteps could be heard. When her steps ceased, the clatter of pots was heard and the smell of cooking was noticeable. Again the pedlar began to think: I must get away from here, if not now, then tomorrow morning. How glad he had been on the day she let him pass the night in the cold cowshed, now even the bed that is made for him cries out: Take your legs from here and flee! At that hour it had already grown dark. Against his will he reconciled himself to spending the night in this house, yet not in his wife's room in the bed of her husbands that had been killed, but in the cowshed or in some other room, until he would leave at the dawn of day.

Helene entered and said, "You look as if I had swallowed you already." She took him by his arm to the dining room, made him sit at the table, and told him to eat. He lifted up his eyes and looked at her. Again she said, "Eat!" He took a morsel and swallowed it whole. Said Helene: "I see you need to have your bread chewed for you." He withdrew his hands from the bread and got up. Helene said, "Wait, I shall go with you." She put on a coat of lamb's skin and went out with him.

On their way they spoke neither words of friendship nor of enmity, but just made conversation like people who are vexed and wish to distract themselves. While they walked, they came upon a stone marker. Helene stopped and made the sign of the cross over her heart and stood still and prayed a short prayer. Then she took Joseph by his arm and walked with him to their house.

In the night Joseph awoke from his sleep in a fright and cried out aloud. It seemed to him that a knife had been plunged into his heart—no, not into his heart but into that stone marker—no, not into that stone marker, but into another marker, made of ice, as the Christians make it by the rivers on their holy days. And although the knife had not wounded him, he felt a pain in his heart. He turned about and sighed. Then sleep overpowered him and he dropped off. He heard a noise and saw that the bitch had freed herself of the chain around her neck. He closed his eyes and did not pay attention. She jumped up and came on him. She dug her teeth into his throat. His throat began to bleed and she licked his blood. He cried out aloud and turned about violently. Helene woke up and shouted, "Why do you wake up the house and not let me sleep." He pulled himself together on his pillows and featherbeds and lay without moving until the dawn of the day.

In the morning Joseph said to Helene, "I disturbed your sleep." Said Helene, "I don't know what you are talking about." He said to her, "But you shouted that I don't let you sleep." "I shouted?" Said Joseph, "In that case you talked in your sleep." She grew pale and asked, "What did I say?"

When night came, he took his bedding into the room of the old things that were no longer in use. Helene saw it and said nothing. When bedtime had arrived he said to her, "I do not sleep and I keep turning about, and I am afraid that I disturb your sleep. Therefore I took my bed to another room." Helene nodded approvingly and said, "Do whatever is good for you." Said Joseph, "That's what I did." Said Helene, "It is all right then."

From now on they talked no more. Joseph forgot that he was just a guest and behaved as it pleased him. Every day he intended to leave her house and do without her favors. A day passed, a week, without his leaving her house. She, too, did not tell him to get out. One night he sat down to dinner. Helene brought him his meal. At that moment came from her mouth the breath of a hungry person. He twisted his mouth. She noticed it and asked him, "Why do you twist your mouth?" Said he, "I did not twist my mouth." She smiled strangely and said, "Perhaps you smelled my breath." He said, "Take a piece of bread and eat." Said she, "Don't worry about me, I shall not go hungry." And again the strange smile appeared on her face, more unpleasant than the first time.

After he ate and drank, he departed into his room and made his bed. Suddenly it came into his head to recite the bedtime prayer. As a crucifix was hanging on the wall, he left the house to pray outside.

It was a winter night. The ground was covered with snow and the sky was overcast and dark. He looked at the sky and did not see a glimmer of light, he looked at the ground and could not make out his own feet. Suddenly he saw himself as imprisoned in the forest clearing in this snow which is being covered by new snow. And he himself is being covered by the snow more and more. He pulled his legs out of the snow and started to run. He came upon a stone marker that stood in the snow. "God in Heaven," cried Joseph, "how far have I gone!

If I do not return at once, I am lost." He looked around, until he noticed the direction of the winds. He turned in the direction of that house and went there.

Utter quiet was all about. Nothing was to be heard but the muffled sound of his legs as they sank in the snow and struggled to get out. His shoulders were very heavy, as if he carried his heavy pack. After a little time he reached his house.

The house stood in darkness. No light shone in its rooms. "She sleeps," Joseph whispered and stopped, his teeth locked in hatred. He closed his eyes and entered his room.

When he entered, it seemed to him that Helene was in the room. He hid his hatred from her. Quickly he got out of his clothes and groped in the pillows and the featherbeds. In a whisper he called, "Helene," and was not answered. Again he called and received no answer. He got up and lighted a candle. He noticed that his bedclothes were full of holes. What had happened here? What had happened here? When he had left his room they had been whole, and now they were punctured all over. No doubt these holes were made by somebody, but for what purpose? He looked around and saw a spot of blood. He looked at the blood and wondered.

Now he heard the sound of a sigh. He looked and saw Helene thrown on the ground and a knife in her hand. It was the knife she had bought from him on the day he had come here. He took the knife out of her hand, lifted her up from the ground, and laid her on his bed. Helene opened her eyes and looked at him. While she looked at him, she opened her mouth so that her teeth shone.

Joseph asked Helene, "Do you wish to say something?" And she said nothing. He bent down toward her. All of a sudden she raised herself up and dug her teeth into his throat and began to bite and to suck. Then she pushed him away and cried, "Phew, how cold you are! Your blood is not blood, but icewater."

The pedlar nursed the lady a day and two and another day.

He dressed the wounds which she had inflicted on herself when she had come in the night to slaughter him. He also cooked for her. But she vomited all food he put into her mouth, for she had unlearned the art of eating as humans eat, because she had become used to eating the flesh of her husbands, whom she had slaughtered, eaten, and drunk their blood as she had intended to do with him.

On the fifth day she gave up the ghost and died. Joseph went to look for a priest and did not find one. He made her a coffin and a shroud and dug in the snow to bury her. As the ground was frozen, he could not dig her a grave. He took her corpse and put it into the coffin and climbed on the top of the roof and buried the coffin in the snow. The birds smelled her corpse. They came and pecked at the coffin and broke it and divided among themselves the corpse of the lady. And the pedlar took his pack and resumed his rounds from place to place and again cried out his goods.

Translated by GERSHOM SCHOCKEN

On the Road

THE TRAIN WAS LOST among the mountains and could not find its way. All the travelers who were with me had got out. I remained alone. Apart from the guard and the driver of the train, not a soul was left. Suddenly the train had stopped and stood still, and I knew that I was done with the train and would have to go on foot among strange places and alien people whose language I did not know and with whose customs I was not familiar. Another day I would have had no regrets. On the contrary, I would have been pleased at the unexpected opportunity for a pleasant stroll. But that evening I was not pleased. It was the evening of the penitential hymn "Remember the Covenant," and next day was the New Year. How should I spend this sacred festival without public prayer and hearing the ram's horn? I got up and looked outside. The hills were silent, and all around was an awesome darkness.

The guard came up and said, "Yes, sir, the train has stopped and can't move." Seeing my distress, he took my satchel, put it on the seat, and went on, "Lay your head on your satchel, sir, and perhaps you will fall asleep and gather strength, for you have a long way ahead." I nodded and said, "Many thanks, sir." I stretched myself out on the seat and laid my head on my satchel.

Before daybreak the guard came back. He scratched his temples and said, "We're far from any inhabited place, so I have to wake you, sir, for if you want to get human company before nightfall you'll have to hurry." I got up and took my staff and satchel, he showing me whither to turn and where to go.

The dawn had risen and the stars had set. The mountains were beginning to doff the covering of night, and the springs gleamed as they emerged. The mountains raised their heads and narrow paths wound their way among them. The dew rested on them and the birds pecked at the morning dew. I looked this way and that. Far and near, mountains and rocks; near and far, not a place of habitation. The road was long, and my feet were heavy, and the day was short, and the hour was pressing. God knew when I would reach an inhabited town and whether I would see a human face that day.

I do not know whether I followed the road the guard showed me or strayed from it. In any case, the day passed and the sun soon set. The mountains darkened, and awesome forms took shape in the space of the world. There was still a trace of day, but night was drawing on: the day that belonged to a year that had passed and the night that belonged to a new year. And between day and night, between one year and the next, far from man and town, I stood, a wayfarer, with my staff and my satchel, not knowing where to go and where I would lay my head.

The night was overcast and the moon did not shine. The springs still gleamed a little, but they too began to be covered. I looked this way and that. The whole land was like one block of darkness. I went into a cleft in the rock and laid myself down to sleep. The birds of heaven nested above my head, and all around were the beasts of the earth. The birds were already asleep and the beasts had not yet come out. Silence reigned, the silence of mountain rocks at night. From far and near came the sound of the spring waters, flowing as in a land at peace.

I lie on the ground and look at the dark skies. This is the

night of the New Year, when all the multitudes of Israel stand in prayer, and the women have already lit candles before nightfall in honor of the day, so that they should enter the new year with light and joy. And here I lie in a dark country among the beasts of the earth, and if I reach an inhabited place tomorrow, I doubt if I will find a Jew there. Israel is like scattered sheep; wherever a Jew goes he finds Jews; but here all the communities have been destroyed and the Jews have not returned.

So I lay in the cleft of the rock and waited for morning. My feet moved off on their own and started walking. I reached a great park full of fine trees. I wanted to enter, but was afraid I might be rebuked by the wardens, who look askance at wayfarers. I entered—I do not know how—and they did not say a word. I walked from tree to tree and from flower bed to flower bed, until I was tired out, and fell down from the effort. Oh, those beautiful parks we see in dreams. They are larger than any parks in the world, and their fragrance is sweeter than all the sweet odors, and we walk in them without end or limit. What is the purpose of our walking in these parks? Only that in the end we should collapse in exhaustion? But the fragrance that clings to us is worth all that effort. This is the fragrance that refreshes our souls when we merely mention it.

The sound of my fall woke me, and I heard a man's voice. Since I knew that I was far from any inhabited place, I said to myself: I am dreaming; but since I longed to see a man I said to myself: Perhaps, after all, I am awake. I raised my eyes and saw two men, and then, behind them, two women. The morning mists hung below the mountains and the men and women were walking above the hills, above the mist.

I got up and went to meet them. Two more came and another two: those from behind the mountain and these from the lower slopes. And their wives came after them, two on this side and two on that, joining up and going on together, two by two. Their clothes were modest; they wore white gowns over their clothes, and white caps on their heads, with a band of silver, two fingers broad, surrounding the cap and tied at the back, and prayer shawls hanging over their shoulders, and belts over their clothes; they were distinguished by beard and sidelocks, and they had old, black books, festival or weekday prayerbooks, in their hands. Like the men, the women were clad in modest, humble clothes. Their heads were covered with white coifs, shaped like the Hebrew letter *kaf*, covering the head and the forehead and partially surrounding face and chin. I greeted them and they returned my greeting.

"Where do you come from, brothers, and where are you going?" I asked them. They pointed to the mountains and said, "We are going to the House of God," they said, pointing to the mountains. "And are there Jews here?" I said to them. "In days gone by," they replied, "all these places here were covered with sacred congregations, but because of our manifold sins and the malice of the gentiles, all the congregations were burned and killed and destroyed and laid waste, and none were left but one Jew here and one there. On the three Pilgrim Festivals, on the New Year and the Day of Atonement, and also at the New Moon of Sivan, which was the day of the great slaughter, we assemble and make a quorum, and recite the congregational prayers." They spoke an antique German, but the voice of Jacob somewhat sweetened the language. And their beautiful dark eyes gazed in grief and concern, like men who stand at sunset awaiting a tenth for the quorum.

We reached a ruined building of great stones. On the walls inside, there were visible signs of congealed blood, from the blood of the martyrs who slaughtered themselves, their wives and their sons and daughters, to prevent their falling into the hands of the accursed ones. And the smell of burning emanated from the ruin, for after the martyrs had slaughtered themselves, the accursed ones set fire to the synagogue over them. Above the sanctuary hung a heavy curtain. Once it was white, but now it was black. And marks of congealed blood were visible upon it: the blood of the martyrs.

When we entered, we found three men who had come before us. Among them was an old man, standing bowed, with his head resting on the old black festival prayerbook which lay on the lectern. He was clad like the other people of the place, but they wore gray trousers, while his were white. He had the small fringed garment over his clothes, with a mantle over it and his prayer shawl drawn up over his cap. Because of the sanctity of the day and the sanctity of the place, they did not speak, either in the profane or in the holy tongue.

The old man raised his head from the lectern and looked into the House of Prayer. He rapped on the prayerbook and said, "People, we now have a quorum. Let us pray." They replied, "Samuel Levi has not yet come." "Why does he not come," said the old man, "and why is he holding up the prayer?" One of them pricked up his ears and said, "I hear the sound of footsteps, here he comes." But no, those were not his footsteps. An old gentile woman came in and asked, "Who is the gravedigger here?" One of them removed the prayer shawl from his face and asked her, "What do you want?" "The Jew Levi is about to die," she said, "and perhaps he is already dead. He sent me to tell you to come and see to his burial." The whole congregation sighed deeply, and looked at each other, as people look at a little orphan who has suddenly lost his parents. And each and every one of them looked as if he had been bereaved and he was the orphan.

"People, what does the gentile woman want in the holy place?" the old man asked. They told him. "He was a good Jew," he said with a sigh. "Alas that he is dead, alas that he is dead." Then the old man looked at me and said, "Blessed be

the Almighty who has brought you here. Surely He has brought
you to complete the quorum." He rapped on the prayerbook
and said, "The dead praise not the Lord, neither any that
go down into silence. People, we have a quorum, praise the
Lord. Let us rise and pray." He let down his prayer shawl
over his face and began to recite the blessings. Immediately
they all raised their prayer shawls and covered their heads.
They recited the blessings, the hallelujahs, the "Bless ye" and
the hymns. They recited the "Hear, O Israel" and then the
Prayer of Benedictions. They took out the scrolls from the
sanctuary and read the Torah. And I, Samuel Joseph, son of
Rabbi Shalom Mordecai the Levite, went up to the lectern
for the reading of the Torah in place of Samuel Levi, who
had passed away. After the blowing of the ram's horn and
the Additional Service, we went down to accompany our
friend to his last resting place.

So that they should not be deprived of congregational
prayer on the Day of Atonement, I postponed my departure
until after the Day. Since I was idle and free to my own
devices, I walked about during the intervening days from
house to house and from man to man. Their houses were
small, and as low as the stature of an ordinary man; each
consisted of a small room with a courtyard surrounded by a
stone wall. Attached to the room was a wooden hut, which
they called the summer house all the year around and
sanctified to serve as a festival booth at the Festival of Booths,
but they had to rebuild it every year, for the winds sent the
boards flying a Sabbath day's journey and more. The doors
of their houses were all made in the same measure and of
the same width, for their fathers, when they built the houses,
used to make the doorways the width of a bier, so that
when they brought them out on the way to their last resting
place, they should be able to take them out without trouble.
Every householder had a milk goat, and four or five fowls,
and plant-pots in which they grew onions to flavor their

bread and sweeten the Sabbath stew. Because of scanty re-
sources and the pangs of poverty, the sons went out to the
big cities and drew their sisters after them, and sent for the
parents to come to their weddings. Some of the parents
agreed and went, but immediately after the wedding they
would leave quietly and go back home on foot. Old Mrs.
Zukmantel told me, "At my son's wedding banquet, which
was held with great splendor, I went outside for a breath
of air. I saw my husband sitting on the steps with his head
resting on his knees. 'Is that the way to sit at your son's
wedding?' I said to him. 'I can't stand all that noise,' he
replied. 'In that case,' I said, 'let us go back home.' 'Let us go,'
he said, sitting up. So we got up straightway and set off.
We walked all night, and in the morning our feet were
standing on the ground of our house." A similar tale I heard
from Mistress Yettlein, the wife of Mr. Koschmann, son-in-
law of Mr. Anschel Duesterberg, nephew of old Rabbi Anschel,
who was cantor and ritual slaughterer, as well as rabbi.

To fulfill the precept of hospitality, which they had not
been privileged to carry out for many years because they got
no visitors, they took much trouble with me, and everyone
devoted himself to me in love and affection and honor. Since
they do little work on the Ten Days of Penitence, which
they treat, as far as work is concerned, exactly like the inter-
mediate festival days, they were all free to their own devices
and free for me. They went out with me to some of their
holy places, where they have a tradition that the bones of the
martyrs who were slaughtered and killed and burned are
interred. Most of the graves have no stones upon them, but
only signs to warn the descendants of the priestly family to
keep away. On the other hand, there are tombstones and
fragments of stones without any inscription on them strewn
all over the hills and valleys. On one of them I found the
inscription: "My beloved is gone down into his garden," on
another: "Glorious is the king's daughter," and on another I
found the inscription,

"They slandered the Jew,
And vilely slew
Numbers untold,
Both young and [old].
On every hill
Our blood they [spill]."

Among the fragments I saw the fragments of one gravestone
bearing a verse from the Song of Songs: "Thou that dwellest
in the gardens, the companions hearken to thy voice." They
told me that there was a certain distinguished woman, Mistress
Buna, who composed hymns for women, and they have a
tradition that this was the tombstone of Mistress Buna. She
died a year before the massacre, and after her death she
would come in a dream to the leaders of the community and
sing, "Flee, my beloved . . ." and the rest of the verse. They
did not know what she meant, until the unbelievers came
and slaughtered most of the communities, and those who were
not slaughtered by the unbelievers slaughtered themselves so
that they should not fall into their hands. And those who
did not succeed in taking their own lives went to the stake
with gladness and song, and sanctified the Heavenly Name
in the sight of the gentiles, so that the uncircumcised were
astonished when they saw it, and some of them cried, "These
are not sons of man, but angels of God."

On account of the massacres they have special customs.
They do not recite the hymn "It is for us to praise" after
the prayers, whether individual or congregational. And if a
man longs to recite it, he covers his face and says it in a
whisper, because with this song of praise their martyred forefathers went to the stake, singing the praises of the Holy
One, blessed be He, out of the fire. It is their custom to
recite the prayer in memory of the slaughtered communities
every Sabbath, even when there is a wedding. And they recite
the Supplication in the month of Nisan, from the day after
Passover. They fast on the New Moon of Sivan until after

the Afternoon Service, and recite penitential prayers and the Song of Praise, and visit the tombs of the martyrs. At the Afternoon Prayer they recite the Supplication of Moses, because on that day the entire community was killed, and before the open scroll they pray for the souls of the martyrs who were killed and slaughtered and burned alive in those evil days. Another custom they once had: in the first day of the Feast of Weeks, before the reading of the Torah, one of the young men would lay himself on the floor of the synagogue and pretend to be dead, in memory of the Giving of the Law, of which it is said, "My soul failed when He spake." They would say to him, "What aileth thee? Fear not. The statutes of the Lord are right, rejoicing the heart." Immediately the young man opened his eyes, like a man who has come back to life, and there was great rejoicing; they surrounded him, dancing and singing and crying, "He liveth forever, awesome, exalted and holy!" This custom has been abolished, for once a certain illustrious scholar, Rabbi Israel Isserlin, who wrote a famous book, happened to visit them; he rebuked them angrily and said, "Pfui, ye shall not walk in their ordinances, neither shall ye do after the doings of the gentiles." For the gentiles used to behave in this way for several years after the disappearance of the sickness called the Black Death: they used to gather together and eat and drink until they were intoxicated; then they would choose one of their young men and lay him on the ground, and little girls and old women would dance around him, and they would sniff at each other, and say, "Death is dead, death is dead!" Then they would take a girl and lay her down, and old men and boys would surround her, knock their heads together, and dance around her, screeching, "Death is dead, death is dead!" so as to notify the Black Death that it was dead, for in those days there was a spirit of madness abroad, and people did strange things.

Blessed be He that distinguishes Israel from the gentiles. Let us return to the Jewish customs. They do not perform the ceremony of casting away sins either at rivers or at wells, because the gentiles used to say that the Jews dropped poison into the water and polluted it; but anyone who has a well in his yard recites the prayer beside the well. And although the suspicion has disappeared, the custom has not been changed. And it was an ancient custom among them to recite the blessing "Who hast not made me a gentile" twice. They have evening hymns and morning hymns and hymns of redemption and penitential hymns that are not in our festival prayerbook. The melodies of their prayers resemble ours, but ours are according to the taste of this generation, while theirs are as they have inherited them from their fathers, may they rest in peace. Sometimes their voices are terrifying, and sometimes a cry, as of a man whose soul struggles to escape, is wrenched from them. But when they stand up to pray, they recite in a sweet voice: "O my dove, that art in the clefts of the rock . . ." and so forth; "My dove, my undefiled is but one . . ." and so forth; "She is the choice one of her that bore her." Never in my life have I heard a melody so sweet. And I saw an excellent custom that they observed on the Day of Atonement: they do not leave the House of Prayer, or speak, from the approach of night until the end of the Day of Atonement, either in the secular or in the sacred tongue, and even the women are very careful in this. And they do not interrupt the reading of the Torah to pronounce a blessing on those who are called up for the reading, but after it is over the reader blesses them all together. On festivals when they read the passage "Every firstborn," the leader of the congregation rises after the last reader has finished the final blessing, goes up to each one, carrying a scroll of the Torah, and blesses him, saying, "He that blessed our forefathers, etc., may He bless thee for giving a donation in honor of the Almighty, etc.," and the people contribute voluntarily to the cost of wine for the sanctification and lamps for the lighting and other needs of the congregation. Their scrolls of the law are tall; when they elevate the scroll they spread it out as far as their arms can reach. You have never seen a finer sight than a broad scroll held by tall Jews, for all of them are stalwart and powerful men. The one who elevates the scroll holds in firmly, while everyone looks at the Torah and puts together, from it, the letters of his name. Their ram's horns are kept in their cases. On some of the cases, beautiful shapes are engraved, and on others verses of the services connected with the sounding of the horn are written. They have no particular melody for reading the Scroll of Esther, but the reader reads it like an ordinary story. And when Master Moses Molin, the son-in-law of Reb Jacob Slitz-stat, was good enough to read me a few verses, I felt as if I were hearing the story of Esther for the first time.

It is their way to mingle words of the holy tongue in their conversation. When it is warm they say *hamima* and when it is cold they say *karira*. They do not say *Soehne*, but *banim*, and not *Toechter*, but *banot*. But in the singular, they say *Sohn* and *Tochter*. When I asked them the reason, they could not answer, and I quoted to them in jest, "Ye are sons (*banim*) to the Lord your God." As for the daughters, I quoted, "Many daughters (*banot*) have done worthily." Most of the names of their articles of food and drink are in the holy tongue, such as *lehem*—bread, *basar*—meat, *dagim*—fish, *yayin*—wine, and *mayim*—water. A dish which is neither meat nor of milk, they call *lavlah*, from the initials of *lo vasar lo halav*. I found several beautiful words in use among them, which I have not found in our dictionaries, and no doubt they come from the festival prayerbook, for they often recite the hymns. And most of the names of animals are in the holy tongue, except the calf, which they call *Kalb*, so as not to recall the sin of the Golden Calf. And if a man calls someone a calf, he makes his life a misery.

Their favorite entertainment at festival meals is to ask riddles about the laws, such as, "How can we prove so-and-so?" Another hallowed custom they have is to assemble in the synagogue on the Seventh of Adar and spend the day in fasting and prayer and the reading of the Torah, and I do not remember if they told me that they read the Supplication of Moses or "And Moses went up . . ." from the end of Deuteronomy. They recite the Memorial for the Departed, and everyone kindles lights in memory of his relatives who have died, as on a *Yahrzeit*, because no one can go to the synagogue all winter because of the tempests and snowfalls, so they decided to assemble on the Seventh of Adar, the day of the passing of Moses, our Teacher, blessed be his memory. At night, after midnight, they hold a meal, and all eat together, and they have special penitential hymns for that day and special songs for that meal, which they sing to special melodies, and afterwards they go home in peace. They also have several other customs. Happy is the man that follows them.

In the morning of the day after the Day of Atonement I went on my way. When I left, the entire community came out to see me on my road, standing on the hilltops. Five or six times I turned my head to look back at them, until they were swallowed in the blue mists. I kept to the road and walked on until I reached the railroad, which had been repaired in the meantime by craftsmen brought for the purpose. I traveled by rail to the port, and from there I traveled by ship to the haven of my desire, the Land of Israel. Blessed be the Almighty who has restored me to my place.

Translated by MISHA LOUVISH

The Orchestra

1

I HAD BEEN BUSY that entire year. Every day, from morning until midnight, I would sit at my table and write—at times out of habit, and at times stimulated by the pen. We sometimes dare to call this divine inspiration. I therefore became oblivious to all other affairs; and I would recall them only to postpone them. But on the eve of Rosh ha-Shanah I said to myself: A new year is approaching, and I have left many letters unattended. Let me sit down and reply to them, and enter the new year without obligaions.

I proceeded on that day as on every other, save that I am regularly accustomed to arise at dawn, and that day I arose three hours earlier. For this is a night when one arises especially early for penitential prayers on the theme of "Remember the Covenant."

Before I sat down to take care of the letters, I reflected: A new year is approaching, and one ought to enter it clean, but if time does not permit me to go and bathe in the river, because of these letters, I will take a hot bath.

At that moment Charni happened to be visiting us. The same old Charni who usually boasts to me that she served in my grandfather's house long before I was born. Charni said: "Your wife is busy with holiday preparations, and you are placing extra burdens upon her. Come to our house and I will prepare you a hot bath." I liked her suggestion; after all, I needed a haircut in honor of the Rosh ha-Shanah festival, and on the way to the barber I would stop off and bathe.

I examined the letters and weighed which of them ought to be answered first. Since they were many and the time was short, it was impossible to answer in one day all that many men had written to me in the course of an entire year, and I decided to pick out the most important ones, then to deal with those of middling importance, and afterwards with the least important. While I stood deliberating, it occurred to me that I should get rid of the trivial letters first, in order to be free for the more important ones.

Trivia tend to be frustrating. Because a matter is trivial and has no substance, it is difficult to handle. If there is a trace of substance, it lies in what the author of the letter had in mind and what answer he expected. As much as I knew that I had nothing to say in reply, my desire to answer increased, for if I left them unattended, they would trouble me. Their very existence is a burden, for I remember them and come to trivial thoughts.

I picked up a pen to write, but my mind was blank. How strange! The entire year I write effortlessly, and now that I have to write two or three inconsequential lines, my pen refuses to cooperate. I put that letter down and picked up another.

This letter was no letter, but a ticket to a concert conducted by the king of musicians. I have heard that the minds of those who hear him are transformed. There actually was a man who used to go to all the concerts but got nothing out of them; he used to think that he did not appreciate music until he chanced upon a concert of this conductor. He said afterward: "Now I know that I do understand music, but that all musicians whom I have heard until now do not know what music is." I took the concert ticket and put it in my pocket.

2

The days before a holiday are brief—some of them because sundown is early and others because holiday preparations are heavy. All the more so the day before Rosh ha-Shanah, which is short in itself and is sped by preparations for the Day of Judgment. By noon I hadn't managed to answer so much as a single letter. I put the letters aside and said to myself that what I had not managed to do before Rosh ha-Shanah I would do in the days between Rosh ha-Shanah and the Day of Atonement. It would have been good to enter a new year free of obligations, but what was I to do when trivial letters did not instruct me how they were to be answered.

I got up and went to my grandfather's house to bathe before the holiday, for Charni had prepared me there a hot bath. But when I got to the house, I found the door locked. I walked around and around the house, and each time I reached the door, I stopped and knocked. A neighbor peeked out from behind her curtains and said: "Are you looking for Charni? Charni went to the market to buy fruit for the holiday benediction." I continued walking around the house until Charni arrived.

By rights the old lady should have apologized for making me wait and robbing me of my time. But not only didn't she excuse herself, she stood and chattered. If I remember correctly, she told about finding a pomegranate which was partly squashed, yet its seeds had not separated.

Suddenly three sounds were heard from the tower of the Council house. I looked at my watch and saw that it was already three o'clock. My watch is always in dispute with the tower of the Council house, and today it made peace with it. And it seemed that the Heavens were agreeing with them. Had I tarried so long on the way, and been detained walking around the house? In any case, three hours had passed and scarcely two and a half remained before the New Year's festival began. And this old woman was standing and chattering about a pomegranate that was squashed and about its seeds that had not separated.

I interrupted her and asked: "Have you prepared the bath for me, and is the water heated?" Charni set down her basket and exclaimed: "God in Heaven, I had intended to prepare a bath for you!" I said: "And you haven't done it?" She replied: "Not yet, but I will do it right away." I urged: "Hurry, Charni, hurry. The day doesn't stand still." She picked between her teeth with her finger and said: "You don't have to rush me. I know that time doesn't stand still, and neither will I. Look, I am already on my way in to make the fire and warm up some water. You practically have your hot bath." I took a walk in front of the house while waiting for the water to heat.

The old judge passed by me. I remembered a question that I had meant to ask him, but I was afraid to get involved with him and so not manage to cleanse myself for the holiday; for this judge, once you turn to him, will not let you go. I postponed my question for another time, and did not turn to him. In order to occupy myself, I took out the ticket and noticed that the concert was for the eve of Rosh ha-Shanah. Isn't it strange that I, who am not a concert-goer, should be invited to a concert on the eve of Rosh ha-Shanah!

I put the ticket back in my pocket, and resumed pacing in front of the house.

Ora, my little relative, came by, whose voice was as sweet as the sound of the violin, and who looked like a violin which the musician had leaned against an unstable wall, and the wall collapsed upon it. I looked closely at her and saw that she was depressed. I asked her: "What have you been doing, Ora? You look like a little fawn that went to the fountain and found no water." Ora said: "I'm leaving here." I asked: "Why are you leaving? What's your reason? You have always wanted to see this magnificent conductor, and now that he has come to conduct our orchestra, you are leaving." Ora burst into tears and said: "Uncle, I don't have a ticket." I laughed good-heartedly and said to her: "Let me wipe away your tears." I looked at her affectionately, and thought how lucky I was to be able to gratify this dear child, who found music more delightful than all the delights in the world, and was most enthralled with the famous conductor who was this evening conducting the great chorus. I put my hand in my pocket to take out the ticket and give it to Ora. And again I smiled good-heartedly, like one who has the power to do good. But Ora, who did not know my generous intentions, threw herself about my neck and kissed me goodbye. I became distracted, forgot what I was about, and didn't give Ora the ticket. And while I was standing there, bewildered, Charni came and called me.

The oven was flaming, the bath clean and clear, and the bath water leaped and rose to meet me. But I hadn't the strength to bathe. Even my time was not with me. I said to my brother: You bathe, for I am a weak person, and if I bathe in hot water, I have to rest afterwards, and there isn't enough time. I left the bath and went home. In order to be more comfortable, I removed my hat from my head and carried it in my hand. A passing wind mussed my hair. Where were my brains? For in the hour that I stood and waited for the bath, I could have gone to the barber's. I lifted my eyes and looked up at the sky. The sun was already about to set. I went home with a heavy heart. My daughter came out to meet me, dressed in her holiday best. She pointed her finger into space and said: "Light." I thought to myself: What is she saying? The sun has already set, and hasn't left a trace of light behind. Or perhaps she meant the candle that was kindled in honor of the festival. I looked at the candles and realized that the festival had already begun, and I had better run to the House of Prayer. My daughter stared at my old clothes and put her little hands on her new dress to cover it, so as not to shame her father in his old garments. And her eyes were on the verge of tears, both for herself who wore a new dress when her father was dressed in old clothes, and for her father who wore old clothes at a time when the New Year had arrived.

3

After dinner I went outside. The heavens were black, but many stars glittered in them and lit up their darkness. Not a man was outdoors, and all the houses were sunk in sleep. And I too started to doze off. But this sleep was not really sleep, for I could feel that my feet were walking. And I kept walking and walking like this until I arrived at a certain place and heard the sound of music, and I knew I had reached the concert hall. I took out my ticket and entered.

The hall was full. Men and women violinists, men and women drummers, trumpeters, and players of a variety of instruments all stood, dressed in black, and played incessantly. The great conductor was not to be seen in the hall, but the musicians played as if someone were standing over them and waving his baton. And all the men and women musicians were my friends and acquaintances, whom I knew from all the places I had ever lived. How did it happen that all my acquaintances came together in one place and in one chorus?

I came upon a place, sat down, and concentrated. Each man and woman was playing for himself. However, all the melodies joined to form a single song. And every man and woman was bound to his instrument, and the instruments were fastened to the floor, and each one thought that he alone was bound, and was ashamed to ask his neighbor to release him. Or perhaps the players knew that they were fastened to their instruments, and their instruments fastened to the floor, but thought that it was by their free choice that they and their instruments were so bound, and it was by their free choice that they played. One thing was clear, that though their eyes were on their instruments, their eyes did not see what their hands were doing, for all alike were blind. And I fear that perhaps even their ears did not hear what they were playing, and that from much playing they had grown deaf.

I slid out of my seat and crept toward the door. The door was open, and a man whom I had not noticed upon entering was standing at the entrance. He was like all other door-keepers; but there was about him something like the air of that same old judge, who, once you have turned to him, does not let you go.

I said to him: "I would like to leave." He plucked the word out of my mouth and replied in my voice: "To leave? What for?" I said to him: "I have prepared myself a bath, and am in a hurry lest it grow cold." He replied in a voice that would have terrified even a man stronger than I, and said to me: "It's flaming. It's flaming. Your brother has already been scalded by it." I replied, apologetically: "I was occupied with correspondence, and didn't have time to take my bath." He asked: "With what letters were you occupied?" I took out a letter and showed him. He bent over me and said: "But I wrote that letter." I replied: "I intended to answer you." He looked at me and asked: "What did you intend to answer?" My words hid because of his voice, and my eyes closed, and I began to grope with my hands. Suddenly I found myself standing before my house.

My daughter came out and said: "Let me bring you a candle." I answered her: "Do you really think the candle will light my darkness?" By the time she had gone to bring it, the fire escaped from the furnace and blazed around about. And some woman stood before the furnace heaping wood on the fire. Because of the fire and the smoke, I could not look on. And I didn't see if it was old Charni who stood before the furnace, or if it was my young relative Ora who heaped up the fire.

A terror descended upon me, and I stood as if fixed to the earth. My spirit grew despondent within me that, at the time when all who sleep were sleeping, I should be so awake. In truth, not I alone was awake, but also the stars in heaven were awake with me. And by the light of the stars of heaven I saw what I saw. And because my spirit was lowly, my words hid in my mouth.

Translated by JUDAH STAMPFER

The Letter

1

ALL THAT DAY I was busy writing a letter of condolence to
the relatives of Mr. Gedaliah Klein. Mr. Gedaliah Klein had
been one of the most prominent men in our city, well-born
and wealthy like his fathers before him, liked by the authorities and respected by the community, blessed with a long
life and a full one. He had married his daughters to the most
learned men of his time; he had taken wealthy wives for his
sons; and he had lived to see them producing shrewd and
gifted sons and daughters, fit for anything the country needed.
In short, he had achieved in this world every temporal success,
and no doubt all good things awaited him in the world to
come, through legacies he had left behind for works of charity
and mercy.

When good men are successful in life, it is good for them
and good for the world; moreover, they provide convincing
testimony that virtue pays, for everyone can see that a man
does not toil for nothing or waste his strength in vain. The
whole world, therefore, mourns the passing of successful men.
Relatives and friends, companies and charities, banks and
business firms, managers and administrators, householders and
craftsmen, speculators and agents, authors and teachers—all
proclaimed their grief in public: in the press and on every

wall. The newspapers also praised him at great length, and
if they exaggerated, the exaggeration itself showed that the
deceased was a great man, for if anyone is praised, he must
be praiseworthy.

I too put aside my work to sympathize with his relatives
and write them a few words of condolence, for I had been
his friend and acquaintance for thirty years. It started when
I arrived in the Land of Israel with nothing in my possession
but love of the land and love of labor. I went to Mr. Klein
to ask his advice, because I had heard that he was an amiable
man and one could get advice and assistance from him; but
since he had his hands full with the general good, he could
not manage to deal with each individual, and he put me
off time and again. Several years later, when I had married
into a good family and become a family man, he took notice
of me and showed me affection and friendship, as if we had
been friends all the time. He honored me in the presence of
my neighbors and visited me at home; and he used to rebuke
me, saying: "I was the first you came to, as soon as you
arrived in the country, and now you do not show me your
face." He remembered that I had waited at his door, but
forgot that he had put me off. Because he was a great doer
and was always doing good to people, he thought he had
done good to me as well, like all the public benefactors, who
feel as if they have worked for each and every man. I, too,
felt as if I had benefited from him. Anyone who has asked
another man for a favor, even if it is not granted, feels in
his bones an attachment to him, as if he had received a
benefit from him.

At the time when Mr. Klein was friendly to me, he had
given up all his business and was busy only with his body,
treating it with baths and medicines and taking a walk every
day. But even during his walks he did not ignore the public
needs, like a man of property who surveys his possessions to
learn what they require. And during his walks he would call
over anyone he met by the way, like those who are accus-

tomed to company and do not like to walk alone. Often he
would summon me and walk with me. It is not my way to
boast, but I may be permitted to boast of this, because it
shows Mr. Klein's affection, for he took the trouble to tell
me all that had been done in Jerusalem during the years of
his life. Sometimes he repeated himself, like an old man who
is fond of his memories, and sometimes he changed a little,
according to the needs of the time and the place.

We used to stroll in the streets and neighborhoods of
Jerusalem, Mr. Klein straight as a cedar and I swaying like
a reed. As he walked, he would lift his stick and point to a
house or a ruin, and tell me how much money had been
sunk in the ruin, or how often the house had passed from
hand to hand, from bank to bank, from speculator to speculator, from creditor to creditor, and it was still doubtful
whether the creditor had acquired permanent possession, for
one of the ten things said of Jerusalem is that no house can
be held in absolute ownership there. So in every neighborhood he used to tell me how many lives had been spent
there and how much Jewish money had gone down the drain.
This is how it used to happen: When a Jew wanted a plot
of land, the speculators would immediately raise the price.
But Jews are stubborn by nature, and stubborn by heredity;
they say that real estate can never be overvalued. So they
go to the owner of the land and raise their bid. But the
trouble is that the speculators are also Jews, stubborn by
nature and heredity; so they raise their bids too, until a speck
of dust costs a golden pound. Humble people have no option
but to withdraw from the deal in disappointment, and but
for him there would be no neighborhood here, not even a
house. But this is a story within a story, and every story is
longer than the earth—and any one of them would take a
thousand and one nights to tell. And as he told me about
the building of Jerusalem, so he would talk to me about the
land and its worthies. Mr. Klein used to say that by the
nature of things every great man was small to begin with,

so small that he needed a godfather at his circumcision, and he had been privileged to be godfather to most of the leaders.

During the year in which Mr. Gedaliah Klein died, and half a year before as well, I had been separated from him somewhat by reason of distance, because he lived in town and I had gone out to live in a distant neighborhood, and when I came to town I did not happen to see him. Now that he had passed away I said to myself: I will write a letter of condolence to his relatives.

2

When I sat down to write I did not know whom to write to, for of all his household I knew only one daughter, and she had no great respect or regard for me, for she remembered the early days when I would shuffle my feet on the threshold of her father's house and he would pay me no attention, though she did not know that in the meantime Mr. Klein had changed his attitude to me. So I girded up my intellectual loins, as the literary men say, wrote a few words of condolence, and put the letter aside till the next day to check it.

I felt depressed and sad. I always feel sad whenever I am distracted from my work. Some people can do many things at a time without worrying, but as soon as I interrupt my work my heart feels sad, like a bookcase empty of books, or a field riddled by ants. For a year and a half I had set aside every other occupation to study the works of our later sages. I gave up the pleasures of the time and cut down my sleep, but not all dreamers see in sleep the good dreams I saw in waking. Days gone by and communities uprooted would come and appear before me, as at the time when Israel clung to the fear of God and were deeply in love with the wisdom of the Torah. And sometimes I was privileged to see

the great men of Israel, the princes of the Torah in that
generation; to perceive, if not the depths of their words, at
least the fragrance of their teaching. There were times and
periods when we had patriarchs and elders, judges and kings,
heroes and men of war, seers and prophets, men of the Great
Synagogue and Hasmoneans, sages of the Mishnah and the
Talmud, scholars and eminences, nobles and princes, rabbis
and codifiers, hymnalists and poets, who exalted the glory
of Israel and sanctified the Divine Name in the world. But
I love our later sages. Like a child in the darkening Sabbath,
who comforts himself with the thought that the Sabbath
still delays its departure, so I would comfort myself with the
words of our later sages, which showed that there was still
a little left of the Torah. For love of the Torah I would sit
and study until the second watch of the night, and if I
went to bed I would rely on the Divine Mercy to raise me up
in the morning so that I could go back to my studies. Until the
affair of that letter, when I put aside my studies.

I took a book, to restore my equanimity with the study of
the Torah. The book slipped and fell out of my hand. I
picked it up and opened it, but forgot what I had opened
it for. When I remembered and looked into it, the letters
skipped about in confusion and did not combine to make any
sense. And I, too, skipped from one subject to another until
I returned to the subject of Mr. Klein. The image of Mr.
Klein rose before me, as when he and I used to stroll in the
streets and neighborhoods of Jerusalem. I said to myself: I
will go out and stroll a little, and recover my peace of mind.

3

I had not managed to cross the road before Mr. Gedaliah
Klein tapped me on the shoulder and asked, "Where have
you been and where are you going?" "I am having a stroll,"

I replied. Mr. Klein stroked his handsome beard and said, "I only came out to stroll too. So let us stroll together."

The sunny days had passed; and a cold wind was blowing. No rain had fallen as yet, but clustering clouds in the sky foreboded the approach of winter. Mr. Klein was dressed in a fine fur coat, with a collar of silver fox over his shoulders and around his neck, and a fine cane with a silver knob in his hand. The white hair of his head and his white beard gleamed like the silver knob in his hand, and his face gleamed out of the collar of his coat like polished copper.

I began to apologize for not having come to see him for several days. He held up his hand to my mouth, as a person does who wants to speak and bids his companion be silent. And immediately he started talking and talking. Even if a bird had come from Paradise to teach us its talk, he would not have stopped his. Many things Mr. Klein told me on that occasion, and more than he told he hinted. From all he said I understood that, had he not raised up Jerusalem out of the dust, nothing worth a row of buttons would have been done.

The sun stood on the tops of the hills and enveloped the rocks with clouds of gold. Mr. Gedaliah Klein's beard glowed even more than that gold, and so did the silver knob in his hand.

So we strolled. He talked and I listened. The streets darkened, and the houses hid in their shadows. Old men and women ran by, as they do close to the time of the afternoon prayer. As they passed, they looked at Mr. Klein in wonderment and moved their lips. I looked after them in surprise, for they and their clothes were different from those of the other old people of Jerusalem.

After we had made the rounds of several places we came back to my house.

I began to be afraid that Mr. Klein might want to go up to my room—and the letter of condolence I had written to his daughter lay open on my table.

I began to shiver.

"Are you worried about anything?" he said. I was silent and did not answer. "I see you are shivering," he said. I thought it would not be polite to tell him what I was worried about, so I said to him, "Yesterday my grandfather appeared to me in a dream." "Is your grandfather dead?" said he. I nodded in assent. "Well?" he said. "I will go and kindle a light in the House of Study," I replied. He put his hand to his forehead and said, "You have reminded me where I was going." He stretched out his cane, made a kind of circle in the air, and whispered, "I am going to the House of Study too."

I said to myself: What will he do when the Divine Name is uttered during the prayers and in answering *Amen*? Is he not afraid they might realize that he is dead, and he will be put to shame? As in the case of the dead cantor, who used to slur over the Name when he prayed, because the dead cannot utter the Heavenly Name. Once a sage happened to be there, who sensed that the cantor was dead—and it is said: "The dead shall not praise the Lord." He examined him and found that the Sanctified Name was sewn into his wrist. So he took a scalpel, cut into his flesh, and took out the Name —and immediately the body collapsed, and they saw that the flesh was already decomposed.

Mr. Klein did not perceive what I was thinking, and walked on. This is the greatness of Mr. Klein: if he decides to act, he pays no attention to anyone.

I dragged my feet and stopped at every step; perhaps the Almighty would find him some other topic on the way and distract his mind from the House of Study. He saw that I was lingering, and said with a smile: "If you had not told me your grandfather was dead, I would have thought I was walking with him." I wanted to answer, but did not know what to say. To tell him the truth was impossible, but nothing else came into my mind.

The streetlamps had been lit, and the lights peered out feebly from the latticed windows. I breathed deeply and said, "It is late for the afternoon prayer." He breathed deeply too,

and said, "I feel warm—no, but . . . " He wrapped himself
up better and began to fumble with his cane like a blind
man, saying, "Do me a favor, see if there is not a House of
Study here. Yes, there is one here."

The worshippers stood bowed with their faces toward the
wall. Mr. Klein went up to the most prominent place, and I
remained standing by the door. Wherever they go, people like
Mr. Klein find their places at the top. One old man turned
his head from the wall and fixed his eyes on me. Mr. Klein
gripped his cane. The cane trembled, and so did his hand.
He was old, and his hands quivered.

A dim light shone from the four or five candelabra, of copper, of tin, of iron, and of clay. A peace not of this world pervaded the room. The worshippers finished their prayer and took
two steps backwards, but the cantor still delayed the recitation
of the final kaddish until the last of them should finish.

I looked around to see whom he was waiting for, and saw
an old man standing in the southeastern corner, wrapped in
his prayer shawl, covered in a fur coat up to above his neck.
I did not see his face because it was turned toward the wall,
but I saw his weary shoulders, those shoulders which the Holy
One, blessed be He, has chosen to bear the burden of His
Torah. My heart began to throb and fill with sweetness. The
Almighty has still left us men who fill the heart with sweetness when we see them.

The old man turned his face, and I saw he was one of the
princes of the Torah whose books I had been studying. I
rushed forward and stood beside him. I knew that this was
not a courteous thing to do, but I could not control myself.
And I still wonder where I took the strength to do it.

Mr. Klein tapped me on the shoulder, took me by the hand,
and said, "Come." I looked at that illustrious scholar and
went with Mr. Klein.

Mr. Klein noticed the president of the House of Study. So
he left me and went up to him.

That illustrious scholar left the House of Study. As was

always his way, so he behaved at that moment, not looking beyond the four cubits, either in front of him or behind him. Devoted as he was to the Torah, he saw nothing but the affairs of the Torah. As I looked at him, I saw that a deep hole was open at his feet. While he had been engrossed in prayer and study, a band of children, playing in front of the House of Study, had dug the hole and left it uncovered. I ran up and bowed before him, so that he should lean on me and pass over the hole.

But he, in his deep devotion to the Torah and the fear of God, saw neither the hole nor me, who had come to save him from it. I did not have the heart to raise my voice and warn him against the danger, in case I might distract him from his thoughts. I stood still, making myself like a staff, a stick, a block of wood, a lifeless object. The Almighty put it into the saint's mind to lean on me. His body was light as an infant's. But I shall feel it until they put dust on my eyes.

4

I went back home and lit the light. I opened a window and sat down to rest. The wind blew and threw the letter at my feet. I looked at the letter, and at my feet, and was too lazy to lift it, for I was so weary that my limbs had begun to fall asleep. I undressed and went to bed, thinking about the things that had happened to me and that saint I had seen, and I knew that a great event had happened that day. No greater event will ever happen to me again. I do not remember whether I was sad or joyful, but I remember that another feeling, to which no term of joy or sadness can apply, moved my heart. If I had departed this world at that hour I would not have been sorry.

I lay in bed and thought: Why do we fear death? Something whispered to me: Raise the blanket. Immediately my fingers were filled with that thing to which no term of joy or sadness applies. And it too, namely, that thing, spread gradually to my shoulders, and the nape of my neck, and the crown of my head. I still belonged to this world, but I knew that if I raised the blanket and put it over my head I could enter into another world in the twinkling of an eye. May all my wellwishers be privileged to experience such a good hour.

The wind blew again and moved the letter. The letter began to roll this way and that. I said to myself: If I die, the letter will remain without anyone to send it. I pushed off the blanket.

The moon peeped into the room, illuminating the floor, and a pale light covered my letter. I raised my right hand and made a kind of circle in the air. When I opened my eyes a second time I heard a bird twittering at my window. It noticed me and fell silent. Then it raised its voice and flew away.

A pleasant languor spread throughout my limbs, a languor that filled them with a pleasure beyond compare. My bones seemed to dissolve in my body and my spirit was light. Although I was lying among pillows and covers and blankets, I imagined that I was not lying among them, but was one of them, inanimate as they. I closed my eyes and lay still.

As I lay like this, a band of Arabs passed by; they sounded as if they were quarreling with each other, and the silence of the street doubled and redoubled their voices. I covered myself up to my head and over with my blanket, but the voices pierced the blanket. My peace had been interrupted, so I got out of bed.

Remembering my letter, I lifted it from the floor and spread it before me; then I put it aside and picked up a book to read, but I did not read it. I set aside my studies and sat down to copy out the glosses I had discovered, like those students of the Torah who write down comments and glosses in their notebooks. I dipped my pen in the ink, arranged the sheet of paper in front of me, and concentrated my thoughts in order to set them down. An hour passed, but nothing happened. Apart from the shadow of the pen, there was no shape of a letter to be seen on the paper. I bent my head over the sheet and looked at the shadow of my pen, which was coupled with the shadow of my fingers, like two different species who cannot be fertile.

I rose and picked up the pages I had written a few days before. As I read them, I began to feel a kind of writer's itch in my hand, that sweet tingling one gets before starting work. I stretched out my hand over the paper and clothed my ideas in words. But the ideas disintegrated, like the snowman a child has made and wants to cover with a garment, which melts away as he tries to clothe it.

I read over again what I had written a few days before. When I started to read it, I thought I had got into the subject. I picked up the pen again. And again the pen cast a pale shadow on the blank paper.

As I found it hard to sit idle, I looked for something to do. I began to shake my books free of dust. Once I had started to shake a book, I began to regret the waste of time, for while I was shaking the dust off the book I might have studied it. When I sat down to study, it all started up again from the beginning. Things that used to refresh my soul turned to ashes in my mouth. An hour passed and another hour. I was trying to impress the words of the Torah on my heart, and my heart was giving me idle thoughts.

I went back to my writings and sat down to copy out what I had written recently; perhaps, while doing that, I could add something. And indeed I did not labor in vain. The pen moved on of its own accord, and added more and more.

When I examined what I had written, I saw that it did not add up to anything at all. I held the pen upright and made circles in the air with it. I remembered I had meant to kindle a light in memory of my grandfather. So I got up and went into town.

Before I went out I read the letter and saw that it was no worse than any other epistle of condolence. If Job said to his companions, who were privileged to have their words recorded in the Holy Scriptures, "How then comfort ye me in vain?" what can we write? I put the letter in an envelope and sent it off.

I went into town and walked from street to street and lane to lane until I reached the yard of the House of Study where I had been the evening before with Mr. Gedaliah Klein, and I heard a voice emerging from inside the yard saying, "Blessed be the glory of the Lord from His place." I went into the yard and asked: "Where is the House of Study?"

A girl replied, "There's no House of Study here."

An old woman came out and asked, "What are you looking for?"

I told her.

"There is no House of Study here," she said with a sigh.

"But I was here last night," I said to her.

"Last night?"

The old woman struck her forehead and said, "Well, Lord Almighty, now I remember! When I was a little girl, they used to show this place; they said there used to be a big House of Study here, and they used to study in it and pray, but because of all our sins it had disappeared."

I bade her farewell and went to another House of Study. This one was built many years ago, and it was built with the aid of a gentile king. His forefathers had destroyed Jerusalem and he helped to rebuild it, and we heard from the righteous men of that generation that when the righteous Messiah comes he will come and pray there. Some say this meant the gentile king, who would be converted and come to pray, but others said it meant the King Messiah. And it seems that those who applied the words to the King Messiah were right, for converts are not accepted in the world to come. When this synagogue was built, books and candelabra and Ark-cloths were donated from many countries, and the sages of Jerusalem used to adorn it with teaching and prayer. Now the house is empty, the plaster has peeled off the walls, the furnishings are broken and the books torn, the Ark-cloths are tattered and the candelabra rusted, and the students of the Torah have passed away. Hardly a bare quorum assembles there. And if the gates of Heaven are still open, nothing reaches them but a pennyworth of prayer.

I went in and found a blind old man sitting at a rickety table, shaking his head and muttering verses from the Psalms.

"Where is the sexton?" I asked.

"I am the sexton," he replied.

I asked him to kindle a light in memory of my grandfather.

The sweet, clear smile of the blind gleamed in his two blind eyes, and he nodded, saying "I will."

He went up to the lectern, took out a glass and raised it to the light, put in some oil, cut a length of wick and put it in the glass, set it on the lectern again, and said, "I will light it for the prayer."

I took out four small coins and gave them to him. He took three and left one.

"I gave you four," said I.

"I know," he said, nodding.

He took the coin and put it into a charity box.

"Are you wary of even numbers?" I said to him.

He smiled and said, "A charity box should not be empty."

I kissed the *mezuzah* and went out.

In the morning, when I sat down to study, my mind was not at rest. I stopped, and said: If I had looked longer for that House of Study I would have found it. I knew that this had come into my mind only to confuse me, but I thought of nothing else.

I tried to remember the faces of the worshippers who had appeared to me the night before in the House of Study.

Apart from that illustrious scholar, whom I had recognized from a drawing, I knew no one there. And even he was not like any picture I knew.

To gather up enthusiasm for my work, I reminded myself how our recent sages, of blessed memory, devoted themselves to the Torah. For instance, there was the story of the author of the *Face of Joshua*, whose disciples once arrived late. "Why are you late?" he asked them when they came. "We were afraid to go out because of the cold," they replied. He raised his face from the book—and his beard was frozen hard to the table. "True," he said, "it is cold today." Or like the story of Rabbi Jacob Emden, who hired a servant to announce to him every hour, "Woe, another hour has gone," so that that illustrious scholar should give himself an account of what he had put right during that hour. But the acts of the righteous did not bring me to the point of action.

Since I was sitting idle, I became a breeding place for strange reflections, for idle men beget idle thoughts. My study lost its savor, and I felt my work was of little worth. I began to ask myself: What is the point of this work when the land is being regenerated, when a new generation is regenerating the land by its deeds?

I rebuked myself and said to myself: Go and rake over your own dunghill. And I started again to read the words of our sages, of blessed memory, but I found no contentment in their teachings.

I remembered the days when I dedicated myself to the Torah, but the memory did not bring me to the point of action.

I tried to arouse myself by idle acts. I started to arrange my books, one day according to the date when they were written and the next day according to subject, or in alphabetical order. I also prepared handsome notebooks and other accessories. Every day I invented something new. But before I managed to do it, I set it aside.

During that year and a half when I had dedicated myself

to the Torah, I had received letters, books, and brochures which I had not taken the trouble to read. Now that I was idle, I looked at them.

I set aside all the books and brochures, and all the futile epistles, and turned to the letters of individuals I had left behind in exile in Poland and Germany, where they bewailed their exile and begged me to help them come to the Land of Israel.

I rested my hand on my table and spoke to myself: How shall I bring you up, how shall I bring you here, when you have no money to show the authorities?

I do not know whether it was in waking or in a dream, in vision or fancy, or perhaps it is neither dream nor fancy. Once a certain man wanted to come to the Land of Israel, and he did not have a thousand pounds to show the authorities. He took his wife and his sons and daughters, and wandered with them for several years until he reached the boundary of the Land of Israel, but the officers of the law would not let them in, so they threw themselves down before the gates of the land and wept. Sleep overtook them and they slumbered. Trees grew up around and concealed them, and they slept a long time. When they awoke, the father said to his son, "Take a coin and bring some bread."

He went out and saw people plowing and sowing in gladness, with never a policeman or an officer. He came back and told his father, who took his wife and his sons and daughters, and they entered into the land. The whole city was astonished at them, for they thought all the exiles had already arrived, and there was no Jew left who had not come. They gave them a dwelling and food and a field to plow and sow. The father took out money to pay. "What are these scraps of metal?" the people said to him. "You call these scraps?" he replied. "If I had had a thousand like them, I would have been with you long ago." Immediately it became a great joke throughout the city: for the sake of such things Jews had been prevented from entering the land, and the sons

of the land had not been allowed to return. How foolish the
world had been to torment the Jews for scraps of metal and
paper notes.

The letters lay before me, and I had to answer them. I
stretched out my hand and took the pen. I set a clean sheet
before me and started to write, but apart from greetings and
apologies I could not write a thing. I could not study the
Torah, because of my confused mind: I could not stay at
home for boredom. What could I do? I got up and went out
to wander for a while in the streets of Jerusalem.

5

I walked about the streets of Jerusalem. Jerusalem, which
had been still, gave voice. Buses and automobiles raced about
as if pursued by demons; the noise of them rose into the
heart of the heavens, and people dodged out of the way to
avoid being run over. Every street and corner was full of
soldiers, policemen and detectives, tarbushes red as blood
and eyes angry and black with hatred. And the precious sons
of Zion—some of them were dressed in velvet and satin, but
others lay in the dunghills.

Even as the streets of Jerusalem have changed, so have
its houses. Not all the prophecies have yet been fulfilled in
the city, but some of its ruins have been rebuilt. The Lord
buildeth Jerusalem, at any rate, even through gentiles, even
through speculators. And there are houses that rise up to the
sky. In the past, when the sons of Israel were lowly in their
own eyes, He would, as it were, lower all the seven firmaments
to be close to them; today, when they are proud and He is
getting further away from them, they build their towers up to
the sky.

There are other buildings in Jerusalem where you can find
anything, whether you want it or not: shops where no one

knows the use of the utensils they sell, or banks and coffee-houses and places of amusement and entertainment. If you find the night hangs heavy on your hands, and you do not know what to do with it, borrow money in a bank and go to a cinema or a coffeehouse or some other place of enter-tainment. And if you find it hard to wait until evening, stand at the side of the street and you will hear choruses on the gramophone. When Elijah, of blessed memory, comes to bring tidings of redemption, we can only hope his voice will be heard above the noise of the automobiles and the screech-ing of the gramophones.

I stand in front of a large building full of shops selling clothing and foodstuffs, jewelry and ornaments for males and females. Signs hanging over the shops proclaim their wares in every possible tongue, and the building emits a vapor like the vapor of foreign lands.

"And I will make thy windows of agates, and thy gates of carbuncles, and all thy borders of pleasant stones." And the sages say: "One day the Holy One, blessed be He, will make Jerusalem of precious stones and diamonds." And even now we can see in Jerusalem something like a pattern of the days to come, for its mountains are covered with all kinds of pleasant colors, were it not for the tall buildings that conceal the face of Jerusalem.

I wandered in the streets and squares of Jerusalem without seeking anything, and when I recalled that House of Study and those old men I had seen there, I knew that I would never find it and never see it.

But I saw new faces. These were the immigrants from Germany who had lately arrived. Where was their dignity, their property, their wisdom, their power? Those who had displaced the Divine Presence with their pride now walked along bowed with care. From time to time the Holy One, blessed be He, shows favor to one of the tribes of Israel and gives it wealth and honor, that they may help their brethren, but they ascribe all their good fortune to their own merits, to their clever behavior, to the masters of the land who have given them good laws because they are better and more honest than the rest of their brethren. When the Holy One, blessed be He, sees this, He, as it were, turns His face away from that tribe. Immediately the wicked men among the gentiles bring down ruin upon them and they go down into the dust.

As I was walking, I met one of the German immigrants whom I knew. I stopped and asked how he was.

He began to tell me the same things he had told me recently, all that the wicked men had done to him there in Germany, what he had suffered, how much money they had taken from him, and how at last he and his wife and his children had escaped without a penny.

I comforted him as I had comforted him before. "You are fortunate to have come here," I said, "for from now onwards, no wicked hand has power over you."

Now that I had mentioned the Land of Israel in his presence, he began to abuse the nation and the population, their behavior and demeanor; his room was minute, and the rent, to boot, would not be too small for a baronial hall; the maid downstairs put on ladylike airs; the workers were all Left, and the merchants bent on theft. The phones had gone crazy, the children were lazy; immigrants from many lands talked with their hands; the trains were always late, the beer was second rate. People didn't know how to pray, and they spat on the floor; the politicians made you pay, always asking for more; the men at the top talked and talked without a stop; mosquitoes were a pest, and gave you no rest; at funeral rites there were barbarous sights. In short, life was vile at home and outside, above and below, whatever you tried.

I said: "'And thou shalt see the good of Jerusalem,' the Scripture said. A Jew ought to see the good of Jerusalem and not its evil." And I went on: "Perhaps you have heard from the old men of Jerusalem how many troubles our fathers found in the Land of Israel, for the land was in ruins at that time, and they were plagued by diseases; when they got out of one trouble, along came another, worse than the first. But they paid no heed to their troubles; they were happy to live in the land and gave praise and thanks to the Creator of all the worlds for choosing us out of all the nations and giving us the Land of Israel."

He took the cigar out of his mouth and said, "Those people had God in their hearts."

I said to him in a whisper, "God exists now too."

"But not within us," he said.

I said to him: "A certain hasidic master was asked where the Holy One, blessed be He, dwells. He told them: Wherever He is allowed to enter, there He dwells."

6

In these days I visited some of the new neighborhoods at whose dedication ceremonies I had rejoiced. Most of the little houses were rickety; their builders no longer lived in them, for they had built them with loans and could not pay, so the banks had sold their houses to others. The same thing happened to the purchasers: they borrowed from the banks— borrowed from one bank and paid to another, so they had to go to the moneylenders—and anyone who falls into their hands never recovers. But so long as they paid the interest they were allowed to stay.

One day I found myself in a certain neighborhood in Jerusalem which Mr. Gedaliah Klein had an affection for, because he had helped some of its people with a loan at one or two per cent less than the banks usually take.

I walked about in the neighborhood. A row of houses on one side and a row of houses on the other, with a kind of road winding between, producing weeds and growing thorns, and a broken-down car sunk in the ground. Some of the houses are unpainted; others have their walls calcimined to look like slabs of marble. Some are on the point of collapse; the builders did not want to invest their money in deepening the foundations, for if they had sunk deeper foundations they would not have had enough to build the houses. The soil of Jerusalem, which was accustomed to sanctuaries, does not like the light houses, so it undermines them until they collapse. Another thing this soil does is to grow bushes and trees inside the houses. Usually, bushes and trees that are planted need care; here they flourish and grow of themselves, and break up the floor and the walls. And why does the soil not make the gardens grow around the houses? Because if the people of the neighborhood plow and hoe and water to grow a little greenery, their bad neighbors come along and loose their goats on them. From the Talmud we learn that the wicked Titus laid waste our land, but the evidence of our eyes teaches us that the goats are laying it waste, and it is still far from clear which did more damage.

I walk about in the neighborhood. Peace and quiet everywhere; not a living soul but goats and cats and dogs. Those who have work in town have gone to town, and those who have nothing to do have gone to look for work. And there are some people who have despaired of work, so they stay at home and recite psalms, or study Mishnah or Midrash. As for the women, some of them have kinds of shops in towns and some have gone to buy vegetables in the market, for the two shopkeepers in the neighborhood have nothing to sell and are going around the town to plead with their creditors. And where are the children? Those who have shoes for their feet have gone to town to study, and those who have no shoes are playing with their brothers at home, for the rainy days have come, and if their clothes are tattered and they have no shoes they cannot play outside.

I walk through the neighborhood, in the length of it and in the breadth of it, looking at the rickety windows with their slackly hanging shutters. On one house at the top of the neighborhood hangs a tin sign bearing the name of a certain benefactor after whom the street is named. The rains and winds of two or three winters have obliterated the name of the man who has taken to himself the name of a street in Jerusalem, and left him no name, but only a buckled sign.

As I walked through the neighborhood the silence was broken by the arrival of a bus full of people. They stretched their limbs as they got off, some to collect taxes and some to collect charity, and some to examine the houses to see which were fit to be security for loans. As they found no one, they started to pester me. As I could tell them nothing, they insulted me. If Mr. Gedaliah Klein were alive and I were walking with him, no one would dare to speak to me like that.

The driver went into one of the houses to rest awhile from the fatigue of the journey, for part of the way from the main road to the neighborhood is covered with holes and pitfalls, and part with spikes and stones; the bus is also rickety, and unless the driver lent it some of his strength it would not go more than a yard or two. Since the visitors wanted to leave and could not find him, they went in to have a look at the synagogue.

The synagogue is a fine building outside and inside. Pious women in America donated the money to build it, but they left one place unfinished, for in the course of construction a great deal of money was wasted to no purpose, and when the donors were asked to make up the difference they could not do it, for America was short of money at the time. So one corner was left uncompleted, but if you do not look in that direction you do not see what is missing.

The synagogue rises higher than any of the houses in the neighborhood—a fine building outside and inside. The floor is made of large stones, and the ceiling is white as the white-wash of the Temple. The walls are straight, and there are twelve windows in them, like the number of the gates of prayer in the Heavens. Our father Jacob, on whom be peace, produced twelve tribes, and the Holy One, blessed be He, correspondingly opened twelve windows in the firmament to receive the prayers of each tribe. But the seed of the tribes were fruitful and split up into Sephardim and Ashkenazim, Perushim and Hasidim—and the Hasidim, too, are split up according to their rabbis, each group praying in a different style. But the Heavens are still intact and no new gates are opened in them, and every worshipper wants the prayers to be recited in his own style, so that there is great confusion, and quarrels break out.

At last the driver came out, sat down in the bus, hooted and blared and hooted again. The travelers pushed their way in. The driver hooted and blared, started up the bus, and set off for town. Again the neighborhood was silent, and were it not for the thick, heavy smell of burnt gasoline which defiled the air there would be no sign that human beings had been here.

I saw a man sitting beside his house and reading the *Book of Legends*. I went up to him and talked to him, praising the late Mr. Gedaliah Klein, without whom there would be no one living here. The man put down the *Book of Legends*, sighed and smiled, and said, "It's a hopeless mess. Half my house is a wreck and the other half a ruin—and the whole of it is mortgaged. If it were sold to pay the debt, not even a small part of the debt would be settled, and if it remains in my hands—where will I get the money to repair it? And so far I've only been talking about myself. The others are in the same predicament. And there's another difficulty: we're far from town, where the people work, and to get to town we need the bus. The bus isn't always there, and the money's not there either. So we go on foot, but you cannot be sure you will get there safely. In times of peace our bad neighbors threaten your money, and in times of stress they threaten your life."

"Well," I asked him, "what will you do?" "What we ought to do we certainly shall not do," he replied with a smile.

"But I only hope the future is no worse than the past, for nothing is so bad that there's nothing worse. Master Gedaliah Klein, may he rest in peace, was a great man and meant to help the builders of the neighborhood. He came forward when they were in difficulties and found them money at a low rate of eight per cent when people pay nine or ten and up to twelve. But anyone who gets into debt has to leave his house in the end."

"And is there no hope for your neighborhood?" I asked. "There is one hope," he replied. "And what is it?" I asked. "When the Messiah comes," he said, "and the wolf dwells with the lamb, we shall no longer be afraid of our bad neighbors, and the goats will do no more harm either." "And until the Messiah comes?" I said. He smiled and replied, "The Old Man of Shpoli used to say, 'Master of the universe, I can assure Thee that the world will go on degenerating in this way until the coming of the Redeemer.' True, there was once a chance to put things right. You see the two rows of houses, on the road to our neighborhood, that separate us from the town and the next neighborhood? All these houses, as you see them, are new, recently built. But before they were built, that was virgin soil, and we could get from one neighborhood to the other in a short time. The owners of the land offered to sell it to us, and we agreed. So we went to our wealthy neighbors and said to them, 'This land is up for sale; buy it, and both of us will no longer be surrounded by the Arabs, who terrorize us so long as we are few. And we will pay our share for the bus and the watchmen and all the other public facilities that every Jewish community must have to survive.' But our neighbors sent us away empty-handed. After all, they had moved away from the town and its paupers, and then paupers come along and propose to get closer. We started going around from one institution to another, but they put us off, some for budgetary reasons and some for economic. 'It isn't enough that you haven't succeeded,' they said, 'but you want to drag other people into this mess.' So we were in despair. Meanwhile, along came Syrians from Syria, bought the land, and built themselves large houses. So we are still living in fear and trembling, and we can't keep up any public facility, not even a grocery. Our dignified neighbor has also suffered for its pride, for the Arabs have surrounded it, and it is far from any Jewish settlement, and the bus hardly comes for lack of passengers, for anyone who has no house of his own moves to town, and new houses are not being built there, for no one builds his home in a neighborhood whose people are leaving. And even those who own their own houses would be glad to leave, and this garden city, builded in beauty, is gradually being abandoned."

As we were talking, a bus came from town and the whole neighborhood went out to meet it. Women and children got off, carrying torn and tattered baskets, with a little cabbage, a little beet, a little turnip, a little garlic and onion in them, and a loaf or two on top—all those things a poor man covets. They set down the baskets and sacks, got into the bus again, and threw out bundles of rusty spikes and old iron hoops they had bought in town to reinforce their tottering houses; some brought out crates and some cradles.

The neighborhood began to hum and bustle. Even those who had been hidden in their houses came out and asked what news there was in town and when they would say the afternoon prayer. Little by little, the rest of the people re-turned from town with their sons, the young ones from the *cheder* and the older ones from the *yeshivah*. And from end to end of the neighborhood, people came running to the synagogue.

In the meantime, Arabs came by, on their way back from their work in town to the neighborhood villages. They were followed by shepherds with their flocks, who stirred up clouds of dust. The people of the neighborhood pushed their way through the sheep, groaning and panting.

It was time for me to return to town, so I got into the bus. An hour passed but it did not move. I asked the driver when he would start. "What's wrong with staying here?" said the driver. I said to him, "If you are not going, tell me and I will go on foot." "Do you think I'm a prophet, that I should know if I'm going?" he said. "If you're not afraid of tiring out your legs, get up and walk. If I find passengers and start off, I'll pick you up on the way and take you in; if I don't, I'll stay the night here. Nice neighborhood, isn't it? Refreshing air! Pity you can't live on air."

I got off the bus and set out on foot. Fine, big houses accompanied me most of the way. When were they built? We did not read about them in the papers; we were not invited to the dedications, but there they are, sound and solid. Every house is surrounded by a garden, with an iron fence around it, so that no goat can get in. The Lord buildeth Jerusalem, sometimes by means of Jews and sometimes by means of gentiles.

7

Once I was going to and fro, as usual, in the streets of Jerusalem, when I saw large posters announcing a memorial meeting that night on the thirtieth day after the passing of Mr. Gedaliah Klein. Ah, thirty days had passed since the day I wrote the letter of condolence.

I took out my watch to see if the time had not yet come for the commemoration, and I saw that the time had not yet come. To pass the time I went from wall to wall and from poster to poster. I doubt if there was a man in Jerusalem that day who was so well versed as I in the names and titles of the eulogists.

I began to be afraid I might have made a mistake in the order of the days, and the day of the commemoration had passed. I went into a bookshop to buy a calendar tablet.

The shopkeeper said, mockingly, "We are just going to

print a calendar for next year and you are looking for yester-year." "I am content with the old tablets," I said.

To pass the time I bought a newspaper. Since I had the paper, I read all the articles that were printed on the thirtieth day of Mr. Gedaliah Klein's passing. In the past, all the deeds of men were included in a single verse, such as "And Enoch walked with God: and he was not; for God took him," but now that knowledge has expanded and the deeds of men have multiplied, we cannot complete all their praises in one sentence.

It is almost eight o'clock. The shopkeepers are locking up their shops, with double locks, for fear of the thieves who have multiplied in Jerusalem. Buses race by, and so do passers-by. As they run, they bump into pedlars and broom-sellers, beggars and flute-players, reformers, crazy men and crazy women, distributors of leaflets and advertisers of merchandise, a dog who has lost his master and a mistress who has lost her dog.

As you escape from these, the shoeshine boys take hold of your feet. While they are sharing out your feet, paperboys offer you their newspapers. As you stand and read, agitators come up and fill your hands with pamphlets. If you get rid of them, women come along and pin all kinds of tags on you. You stop to pay, but your pocket is empty, for in the meantime pickpockets have extracted your purse. As you stand in despair, wanting to go home, along comes a procession of boys. While you wait for them to pass, a bus goes by and runs over an ass. You run to lift it; along come the police and strike you with their batons for obstructing the populace and holding up the traffic. When you run away and find a place to hide, you come across a girl who has been attacked by zealots. While they are punishing her because they saw her going with the English, a young man throws vitriol in another girl's face and blinds her. The gramophone shrieks, "How goodly are thy tents, O Jacob," while the radio sings back, "Happy are ye, O Israel." Meanwhile, the whole street lights up, revealing the picture of a naked woman, and a loud-speaker proclaims to the heavens, "Come and see the enchantress!"

The streetlamps, square and round and semicircular, illuminate the streets of the city, in addition to the moon and the stars. I walk in their light and read all kinds of placards about new productions of plays like *Thy People* and *Hard to Be a Jew*. And the gramophone screeches, "How goodly are thy tents, O Jacob," while the radio replies, "Happy are ye, O Israel," and the loudspeakers drown their voices, and the smell of *falafel* permeates the air. Little by little the street returns to normal. Buses rush and people push; some of their heads are hairy, and some of their chins are double; some of them float on air, and some are always in trouble; men with serious mien and women with delicate hands chatter in all the tongues of all the far-off lands; every stalwart lad and every maiden ripe puffs at a cigarette or pulls away at a pipe. The coffeehouses are full of people young and old; the men make eyes at the girls, and the girls are just as bold; the men drink beer and whiskey, the women paint their faces—O Muse, what have you to do with such peculiar places? The bars are full of soldiers, the British Mandate's men—"Drink up and then bring up, my lads, and fill your mugs again!" And now I go to mourn a man who is no more—O Muse, be silent now, and do not weep so sore.

8

The platform is draped in black, and a candelabrum draped in black illuminates a picture of the deceased hanging over the platform. His face is the face of a successful man, unmarred even by death.

The assembly hall is full and still the people come. The first arivals have been seated by the ushers on the middle benches, while the latecomers are seated above, near the platform. Last come those for whom the platform is waiting.

Mr. Schreiholz mounted—he is the principal speaker everywhere. He made a sad face and started in a whisper, like a man who cannot speak for grief. Suddenly he raised his voice and stretched his hand upwards with his fingers spread, seeking a word to express the full depth of his thought. When he found the word he began to spout with growing fluency, declaiming at the top of his voice: "The deceased was . . . , the deceased was . . . ," describing, between one "was" and the next, his recollections of where he had seen the deceased, and all the rest of it.

When he had finished, he got off the platform, pressed the hands of the mourners, climbed onto the platform again, and sat down, like an orator who knows his place.

Next came a teacher who had become a banker. As a man who knew the taste of learning and the value of money, he emphasized the virtues of the deceased, who had combined learning with trading, and by virtue of his talents had succeeded in setting several of Jerusalem's alms-hunting institutions on a sound financial basis and making them into national institutions, which added to the national capital and increased the strength of the nation.

After he had finished, he got down off the platform, pressed the hands of the mourners, and found a place to stand, like a man who seeks no more than a station for his feet.

Next came a townsman of the deceased. He recalled the honor of his house abroad, which was a place of assembly for Lovers of Zion and devotees of the Hebrew tongue. And first and foremost of all the deceased's achievements in his town was the splendid edifice of the modernized *cheder*, which was the archetype of the Hebrew school, whose waters we drink and in whose shade we shelter.

After he had finished, he got down off the platform, pressed the hands of the mourners and pushed his way in somewhere, for during his eulogy someone else had taken his place.

Next came the last of the eulogists, Mr. Aaron Ephrati, a
dignified old man respected by all. He started to sing the
praises of the deceased, who had served the entire community
without distinction of rich or poor, for since he had grown
up in wealth and lived all his days in wealth, he regarded
wealth as a matter of course, and not as a special virtue that
entitles its possessors to make distinctions between rich and
poor. And when he had set up the modernized *cheder*, he
had not behaved like those wealthy men who have their sons
and daughters educated in the schools of the gentiles and
leave the modernized *cheder* for the common people, but
sent his sons and daughters to the same modernized *cheder*,
so that they should get a plain Jewish education. And so as
to combine the light of Judaism with the beautiful and the
useful, he had sent them to high school and the university,
so that they might fulfill the maxim: "Be a man and a Jew
both in your tent and outside." Finally, Mr. Ephrati turned
to the sons and daughters of the deceased and said to them:
"Your father has still left you things to do, for his aspirations
were in keeping with his greatness. Though he is dead, you
are alive, and the sons must add to the deeds of their
fathers."

After Mr. Ephrati had finished speaking, the cantor of the
synagogue climbed onto the platform, took out a hexagonal
velvet biretta, bent down and put the biretta on his head, took
out a cantor's tuning fork and put it in his mouth, bent and
struck the tuning fork on the table, stuck it in his mouth
again, put it close to his ear, and began to sing "O God, full
of mercy."

Since I am no judge of music, I was free to think my own
thoughts. This prayer used to make my heart throb, I mused
as I stood there, but today it just bores me. And another
thought occurred to me: there are theater melodies which
sound, when sung by the performers, like prayers and supplications, but sometimes prayers and supplications, when they
are sung by the cantors, sound like theater tunes. On the

cantor's head the biretta quivered; on his throat his Adam's apple shivered; around the hall the echoes rolled, over consolers and consoled; while biretta and pate, with every nod, invoked the infinite mercy of God.

I stand looking at the distinguished people who have come to pay their respects to the memory of Mr. Gedaliah Klein. Although I would not compare my work with theirs, I feel sorry that I do not succeed in doing my own work. And the man with the biretta, with his cantor's tongs, warbles his notes like a bird's sweet songs, stretching his throat toward God on high, emitting each word with a groan or a sigh; and everyone listens to the lamentation—wiping his tears, or his perspiration.

All the people are on their feet, including the daughter of the deceased. Her black veil quivers over her comely features, and she is surrounded by important people, whose faces are pink with satiety and complacency, like practical men rooted in the life of the nation, who can adapt their behavior to the nation's needs, or the nation's needs to their behavior. Fine clothes like theirs were never seen in Jerusalem until Hitler started killing the Jews, so that all the great craftsmen fled, and some of them settled in the Land of Israel.

I look at the clothes and say to myself: I will get some clothes like these too; perhaps I will raise my spirits. But I am afraid the great tailors may see how humble I am and not take much trouble with such a fellow; they may not even make me as good a garment as this one, which was made by the Jerusalem tailor. And if they make me a fine garment, my friends and relatives will be ashamed of their clothes when they meet me, as I am ashamed to be seen by these men with their fine clothes. But all these were futile thoughts, for to get fine clothes you need money, and to get money you need the desire for money, and to have the desire, you must have a desire for the desire. And where will I get the strength for those desires?

The memorial light was still burning there, when the cantor finished the memorial prayer. He doffed his biretta and wiped his pate, and put on his hat, brooding on his fate: "If I sang in the theater, at home or abroad, all the beautiful women would applaud; but here not a soul has a word to say—that's your reward when you sing to pray."

After the recital of the mourners' kaddish, the audience mingled with each other, shook out their clothes, which had got wrinkled with sitting, and took out cigarettes for a smoke. "If anyone tells you there's such a thing as free will," said Mr. Schreiholz, "don't believe him. For two and a half hours I was waiting to smoke, but I didn't do it out of respect for this solemn occasion."

People from the suburbs who were in the hall started to push their way out to get their buses. I should have hurried, too, and run for my bus, but I wanted to pay my respects to Mr. Gedaliah Klein's daughter.

She sat like a mourner, her black hat adding to her charm; a peaceful sadness covered her face, like a well-bred woman who has been bereaved, but has not been bereft of her distinction. Public leaders, men and women, came up to her one after another and pressed her hand, and she pressed the hands of them all.

I bowed my head and greeted her. But she did not notice me. I bowed and greeted her again. Perhaps she nodded slightly, and perhaps she did not nod to me at all. I felt no grudge against her. Why should she have to move her head in return for two or three lines I had written her? Countless letters of condolence had been sent her, and they were still being sent.

I left the assembly hall. The entire square was full of cars for Mr. Klein's family and the eulogists. A little while later, nothing was left of them but the odor of burnt gasoline and cosmetics and dust.

I set off for the bus station, but when I reached it the bus had gone. I waited for the next, but it did not come, so I gave up the idea of riding home and set out on foot.

An old carriage came along. The coachman reined in his

horses and said to me, "Get in." I felt no desire to get in. The horses set off without me. Silently, silently, they moved off without lifting their feet, and, if I am not mistaken, the motion of the carriage was not visible either.

The air was clear; the moon and the stars shone. The earth was soft; it would have been easy to open it and cover oneself up with it like a blanket. How tired I was, how I wanted to rest. The coachman came back and rode around me with his coach. I looked up at him, hoping that he might take me into the coach, but he took no notice and did not take me in. The horses lifted their feet; not a sound was heard as they moved, but the echo quivered in my ears until I reached home and went in.

9

When I entered, I found Mr. Gedaliah Klein sitting at my table. His head was bowed toward his breast, and his cane lay between his knees. He stirred, raised his head, and whispered: "You here?" "I have just come," I replied in a whisper. He rubbed his eyes. "I felt sleepy and dropped off," he said.

His face was weary and aged. Since I last left him, he had suddenly become very old. Apart from the fox-fur coat he wore, there was nothing about him that was not old.

I pretended not to notice that he had aged considerably, for Mr. Gedaliah Klein desired the honor of age coupled with the vigor of youth, and not the old age which is a burden and a shame. He looked at me and said, "I have not seen you for decades. Tell me now, my dear friend, why do you not come to visit me? Or perhaps I have seen you in the meantime? Where have you been all the time? And where, for instance, did you spend the whole evening?" I could not bring myself to tell him where I had been, so I was silent.

He pricked up his right ear, supported it on his right hand,

and said, "I did not hear what you said. Now for another matter: Where did I leave you that night I saw you last? If I am not mistaken, there was an old courtyard, and candles were burning low, and some man, a sexton, pestered me. Don't you remember, my dear friend?" I told him.

"One thing is clear," said Mr. Klein; "there was a House of Study there. You see, my dear friend, I forget nothing. What did we go to that House of Study for? If I remember rightly, you wanted to kindle a light for the repose of your grandfather's soul. I hear the sound of horses. Did you come home in a carriage?"

"No, I came on foot."

"So what is the carriage doing here?"

I said to him, "Perhaps you know where that House of Study is? I am looking for it but cannot find it."

Mr. Klein smiled at me as people do at a child who is trying to get something easy. He raised his hands to his eyes to settle his spectacles. Then he pried open his eyes with his fingernails and looked straight at me. "Did you put out the light?" he said. "You didn't? So why don't I see? What did you say? You are looking for the . . . What are you looking for? Speak into my ear. When one's eyes are affected, all one's limbs are weakened."

I went up close to him and said, "I am looking for the House of Study."

"You are looking for the House of Study?" he repeated in a tone of surprise. "Which House of Study are you looking for? Perhaps the one where you were with me? Give me my cane and I will draw you where it is."

I took his cane from between his knees and put it in his hand.

He took the cane and began to grope with it like a blind man in an unfamiliar place. The cane in his hand quivered, his hands quivered, and he quivered with the cane. He gripped the cane with all his strength, but his strength was gone. His face was no longer the same, and he, too, began to change, until he was entirely changed, and no longer resembled himself. And perhaps it was not he, but that old man, that blind old man who had kindled the memorial light for my grandfather, may he rest in peace.

I waited for him to look kindly on me, as he had done at first in the Great Synagogue when he whispered verses from the psalms. But his face was frozen and his eyes devoid of laughter. I felt it hard to stand in front of a man who used to be courteous to me but now paid me no attention, so I turned my face away from him. When I turned my face away, he stood up over me with his cane. I felt afraid of him and closed my eyes. He took hold of the cane and began to draw with it, making six marks. A house emerged and rose up, like that House of Study. I tried to enter but could not find the door. The old man raised his cane and knocked twice on the wall. An opening appeared, and I went in.

Translated by Misha Louvish

Fernheim

1

WHEN HE RETURNED he found the house locked. After he rang once, twice, and then a third time, the doorkeeper appeared, folded her hands on her stomach, leaned her head on her shoulder, and stood gaping a moment. "Well," she said, "who do I see? Mr. Fernheim! Bless my soul, it *is* Mr. Fernheim. So, then, Mr. Fernheim's come back. Then why did they say he wouldn't come back? And all this ringing—it's really quite useless, because the house is empty and there's no one to open it for him, because Mrs. Fernheim left and locked the house and took the keys with her. She didn't imagine there'd be any need for keys, like now, for instance, that Mr. Fernheim's back and wants to get into his house."

Fernheim felt he had better say something before the woman inundated him with more derision. He forced himself to speak, but his reply was short, stammering—and meaningless.

The doorkeeper went on, "After the baby died, her sister Mrs. Steiner came, and Mr. Steiner with her too. They took Mrs. Fernheim with them to their summer home. My son Franz, who carried her bags for her, heard that the Steiners plan to stay there in the village until the big Israelite holy days at the end of the summer, right before the fall, and I'd guess Mrs. Fernheim won't come back to the city before then. Why should she hurry, now that the baby's gone? Does he need a kindergarten? Poor little thing, he kept getting thinner and thinner till he died."

Fernheim pressed his lips together tightly. Finally he nodded at the doorkeeper, stuck his fingertips into his vest pocket, took out a coin, and gave it to her. Then he turned and left.

Fernheim spent two days in the city. He left no cafe unvisited, nor did he neglect to speak to each and every one of his acquaintances. He went to the cemetery to his son's grave. On the third day he pawned the present he had bought for his wife, went to the railroad station, and bought himself a round-trip ticket to Lückenbach, the village where Hans Steiner, his brother-in-law, had a summer home. There, years back, Fernheim had met Inge when he was friendly with Karl Neiss, who had brought him along to see her. But Karl Neiss had not realized what was to come of it all.

2

When Fernheim entered the villa, Gertrude, his sister-in-law, was standing on the porch in front of a basket of laundry, folding linens she had taken down from the line. She greeted him politely and poured him a glass of lemonade, but without the least show of joy, as if he had not returned from prison camp, as if years had not passed without her having seen him. When he asked her where Inge was, she looked shocked, as if that were too personal a question. Finally, when he looked at the door opening to another room, Gertrude said, "You can't go in; Zigbert's bed is there. Remember Zigbert, the child of my old age?" As soon as she mentioned Zigbert she smiled inwardly for calling him "the child of my old age" when at that very moment a new child was stirring inside her. As she was speaking, Zigbert entered.

Gertrude stroked her boy's head, arranged the curls tumbling over his forehead, and said, "Moved your bed again? Now didn't I tell you, 'Don't move the bed'? But you, Zigbert, you don't listen, and you went and moved it again. You shouldn't have done that, my son."

The little boy stood wondering what bed his mother was talking about. And if he had moved the bed, why shouldn't he have moved it? But there wasn't any bed in the first place. And if there really had been a bed and he had moved it— why, his mother should have been proud that he was big and strong enough to move a bed if he wanted to! But everything that Mother was saying was strange, because there wasn't any bed. Zigbert wrinkled up his face at this yoke he had to bear. Nevertheless, he was ready to overlook it if there were the least bit of truth in what his mother had said.

By this time Fernheim realized nothing was in the way, but because he respected Gertrude and did not want to make a liar of her, he did not open the door.

Hans must be told that Fernheim is here, thought Gertrude, but if I leave Fernheim alone he could open the door, cross the room, and go right into Inge's room; and it won't do for him to see her before Hans talks with him. Anyway, it's not good that he came just today, with Inge sitting there waiting for Karl Neiss. Maybe Neiss has arrived already, maybe he's sitting with Inge. There's no need for these two to come across each other right in front of her.

She saw Zigbert standing by. "Go to Daddy and tell him that . . ."

"Whom do we have here?" Fernheim stretched his arms out to the little boy and began speaking affectionately. "Why, this is young Steiner of the house of Starkmat and Steiner. What's this, Zigbert, you don't say hello to your dear uncle, Uncle Werner, as though you weren't happy that he came back from prison where the enemy fed him live snakes and gave him snake poison to drink? Come, Zigbert, my sweet, let me kiss you." He caught hold of the child, lifted him up, and kissed him on the lips.

Zigbert wrinkled up his mouth and glowered. Fernheim took out half of a cigar, lit it with his lighter, and said to Zigbert, "Don't you want to put the flame out? Open your mouth and blow on it; it goes out almost by itself."

Gertrude addressed her son. "Go, sweetheart, and tell Daddy that—that Uncle Werner has come and would like to see him."

As he was leaving she called him back. Gertrude wanted to warn the child not to tell anyone, least of all Aunt Inge, that Fernheim had come, until he told his father first. But realizing that it was impossible to speak in front of Fernheim, she sent him off.

Zigi stopped, waiting for his mother to call him back as she had the first time. Seeing that she remained silent, he left.

"Daddy, Daddy," he called, "Mommy wants you. A man is here."

"Who's here?" Steiner called down from the attic.

"A man," the child repeated, saying nothing more.

"Go on and tell Mother that I'm coming."

"I don't want to," said the child.

"You don't want to what?" asked the father.

"I don't want to go to Mother."

"Why don't you want to go to Mother?"

"Because."

"Because why?"

"That man."

"What about that man?"

"Because."

"You're acting stubborn, Zigbert; I don't like stubborn people."

The child went off crying.

Fernheim sat himself down, as did Gertrude. While she

folded her linens, he clenched a cigar stub between his lips. She sat quietly, uttering not a word, while he was astounded at himself for sitting next to his wife's sister and saying nothing. She waited for her husband to come; he puffed away furiously.

The cigar stub had almost vanished, but still he gripped it between his lips. I see, thought Gertrude, that the new laundress does a good job. The sheet is sparkling white. It needs scrubbing, though. Werner's coming back—it's not good. But now that he's come, maybe there can be an end to this business. The towels gleam more than the sheets, but their edges are crumbled. Obviously, the laundress ironed two towels as though they were one. What's this, pigeon droppings? Doesn't she know you have to clean the rope before hanging the wash? Hans still hasn't come, and I can't make up my mind whether or not to invite Werner to lunch, since we've already invited Karl Neiss. But just so he shouldn't feel insulted, I'll pour him another glass of lemonade. He's looking for an ashtray. He's already thrown the cigar into the garden.

3

The footsteps of Hans Steiner resounded, and the aroma of the fine cigar in his mouth wafted into the room. He had a vexed look, the kind he wore regularly when having to appear before a stranger. As soon as he came in and saw Fernheim, his pent-up anger doubled. Utter amazement covered his face. Scratching his moustache and scarcely opening his lips, he muttered, "You're here?"

Fernheim, trying to look cheerful, answered, "There's a good deal of truth in that, Hans," immediately extending both hands in greeting.

Hans presented him with two fingertips and said something indistinguishable, without moving lips or tongue. "You're back," he added.

Fernheim replied jokingly, "That, we must admit, is correct."

"When did you come back?"

"When did I come back? I came back two days ago; to be precise, three days ago."

Hans flicked the cigar ashes into the glass of lemonade. "You've been here three days. Then I would assume you've come across some people you know."

"What if I did?" answered Fernheim heatedly.

"If you happened to meet some people you know," said Hans, "maybe you happened to hear a little something."

" 'A little something,' meaning—"

"Meaning there have been some changes made."

"Yes," said Fernheim, "lots of things have changed. I wrote that I would come on a certain day, at a certain hour, on a certain train; and when I got there I found the railroad station empty. Actually it wasn't empty. On the contrary, it was filled with mobs of noisy people who had come to welcome their brothers and sons and husbands returning from the war; but Werner Fernheim, who shed his blood in the war, who was a prisoner of war, who spent a year in a prison camp—no one was available to come welcome him."

Steiner raised his head above Fernheim's. "In your opinion, Werner, who should have come?"

"Heaven forbid that I meant you," he replied. "I realize that Mr. Steiner is an important personage, a man weighed down with serious business, so serious it even exempted him from army duty; but there is someone here who, had she come to greet her husband, would not have been acting altogether outrageously. What do you think, brother-in-law, suppose Inge had come? Does that sound so very unreasonable?"

Steiner tried to smile, but, as he was not used to smiling, his face assumed a look of surprise. He made a fist of his left hand, looked at his fingernails, and said, "If my ears aren't liars, Inge should have rushed to the railroad station to meet you. Is that it, Werner?"

"Why are you so surprised?" asked Fernheim. "Isn't it usual for a wife to greet her husband returning from a distant country? And what a distant country I'm returning from! Anyone else in my place would have died a hundred deaths by now and wouldn't have lived to see the face of his loved ones." Suddenly he raised his voice and asked fiercely, "Where's Inge?"

Steiner looked straight at his brother-in-law and then turned his eyes away. Then he looked at him again and calmly flicked off the cigar ash. "Inge is on her own; we don't pry into her affairs. And let me advise you, Werner: don't be prying into her affairs."

Gertrude sat thinking, This is a man, this is a man. This is a man who can handle anyone. Tonight I'll tell him my secret—that I've got a new child ready for him. But now I'll leave them alone.

The whites of Fernheim's eyes reddened as though they had been pricked and blood were trickling out. "What do you mean," he shouted, " 'Don't be prying into her affairs'? It seems to me I still have some authority over her."

Gertrude rose to leave.

"Sit down, Gertrude," said Hans. "If you don't want to hear what this fellow has to say, maybe you'd like to hear what I have to say. Now, you, Werner, look here. If you haven't told it to yourself, I'll tell you. The world you left behind when you went to war has changed, and what concerns us most has changed, too. I don't know just how clear these things are to you, or just how pleasant you find them. If you like, I'm ready to explain them to you."

Fernheim raised his eyes and tried to look straight at his brother-in-law, whose face at that moment was not pleasant to look at. He lowered his head and his eyes and sat despondent. Steiner shouted suddenly, "Is there no ashtray here?

Excuse me, Gertrude, if I say that here, on this spot, there should always be an ashtray."

Gertrude rose and got an ashtray.

"Thanks very much, Gertrude. The ash has already dropped onto the rug. What were we talking about? You want an explanation, Werner. In that case, let me begin at the beginning. Once there was a daughter of a well-to-do family who was engaged to a certain man; only the ceremony had not yet taken place. It chanced to happen that a certain fellow started to frequent this man's company. The man who was engaged to the girl disappeared, and this other fellow who had been trailing along after him came and started courting the girl, until finally he won her and she married him. Why did he win her and why did she marry him? This I leave to riddle solvers. I can't say why. From the very start the match was no match, but what happened happened. At any rate, there's no need that it be so forever. Do you understand, my dear fellow, what I'm driving at? You don't understand? Amazing. I'm speaking quite frankly."

"Is that the only reason?" said Werner.

"What I've said seems trivial?" Hans replied.

"At any rate," said Werner, "I'd like to know if that's the only reason."

"There's that and there's another reason . . ."

"And what's the other reason?"

Steiner fell silent.

Werner went on, "I beg of you, tell me what that other reason is. You say, 'There's that and there's another reason.' What is that other reason?"

"What you speak of as another reason," said Steiner, "is something else again."

"And if I want to know?"

"If you want to know," said Steiner, "I'll tell you."

"Well?"

"Well, the same man to whom the young woman was engaged was found alive, and we trust that you won't go about setting up obstacles. You notice, Werner, that I'm not bringing up your absconding with the funds and staining the firm's reputation."

Fernheim whispered, "Karl Neiss alive?"

"Alive," repeated Steiner.

"Have the dead revived already, then? I myself, everybody with me—we all saw him disappear beneath a landslide and I never heard of his having been pulled out of the debris. Hans, my dear fellow, you are joking with me. And even if they did get to him, he couldn't possibly have come out alive. Tell me, Hans, what led you to say such a thing? Didn't—"

"Story-telling is not my business," clipped Steiner, "but I'll tell you this: Karl is alive and well, alive and well. And, let me add, Inge is counting on you, on your not setting yourself as a barrier between them. And as to your coming back empty-handed, we've taken that into consideration; we won't send you away empty-handed. I haven't as yet set aside a definite sum for you, but at any rate you can be sure it will be enough to set you on your feet, unless you mean to go idle."

"Won't you let me see Inge?" pleaded Fernheim.

"If Inge wants to see you," said Steiner, "we won't stand in her way."

"Where is she?"

"If she hasn't gone out for a walk, she's sitting in her room."

"By herself?" asked Fernheim derisively.

Steiner did not catch Fernheim's derision and answered calmly, "She may or may not be by herself. Inge is on her own and may do as she pleases. At any rate, she can be asked if she is free to receive visitors. What do you think, Gertrude? Shall we send Zig to her? What was wrong with Zig that he was acting so stubbornly? Doing nothing is good for no one, especially children."

4

Inge greeted Fernheim politely. If we did not know what we do know, we would think that she was glad to see him. A new light, a deep contentment shone from her eyes. Happiness is a wonderful thing: even when it is not intended for you, you bask in its light. At that moment, all that he had to say fled him. He sat looking at Inge in silence.

"Where were you all these years?" she asked.

"That I know perfectly well," said Werner, "but were you to ask me where I am now, I doubt that I could answer."

Inge smiled as though she had heard a joke.

Werner moved uncomfortably in his chair. He leaned his right hand on the arm of the chair, lifted his left hand to his nose, smelled his fingernails, yellowed from smoking, amazed all the while that after all the years that he had been way from Inge he was once more sitting beside her, even looking at her while she looked at him—but not one of the thoughts that filled his heart reached his lips, even though his heart urged him to say something.

"Tell me," said Inge, "I'm listening."

Werner stuck his hand into his pocket and started groping about. But the present he had bought for Inge had been pawned for travel expenses to Lückenbach. He smiled painfully and said, "You want to know what I did all that while?"

She nodded her head. "Why not?"

As soon as he started speaking he saw that she was not listening.

"And how did the Bulgarians treat you?" asked Inge.

"The Bulgarians? The Bulgarians were our allies."

"But weren't you a prisoner of war? I thought I heard that you had been captured."

"I was a prisoner of war of the Serbs," Fernheim answered.

"You fail to distinguish between friend and foe. I heard he came back."

Her face reddened and she did not reply.

"You suspect me of having purposely deceived you when I came and told you that I saw Karl Neiss buried in a land-slide. I was ready to tell a hundred lies in order to win you. But that was true."

"True and not true."

"True and not true? What's not true about it?"

"It's true that a landslide fell on top of him, but it didn't buiy him."

"Then where was he all those years?"

"That's a long story."

"You're afraid to tell me," said Werner, "for fear I'll stay here with you that much longer."

"I wasn't thinking of that."

"But rather—"

"Rather—I don't know how to tell stories."

"At any rate," said Werner, "I'd like to know what hap-pened and what didn't happen. With my own eyes I saw a landslide bury him, and you say there was a landslide, but not on him. Forgive me if I repeat myself, but where was he, then, all those years? He wrote no letters, he wasn't inscribed among the living. Suddenly he comes and says, 'Lo and behold, here I am, and now, now all we need to do is pluck Werner Fernheim out of the world and take his wife.' Right, Inge?"

"Please don't, Werner."

"Or it would be better were this same Werner, this same Werner Fernheim, Inge's husband, to pluck himself out of the world, so that Mr. Karl Neiss might take to wife Mrs. Inge Fernheim, excuse me, Miss Ingeborg of the house of Starkmat. This is the woman Werner took in holy matri-mony, who even bore him a child, and though God did take him, his father is still alive, and means to go on living; yes, to go on living after all the years he was half dead. But this same Werner Fernheim, this unlucky fellow, doesn't want to pluck himself out of the world. To the contrary, he seeks new life. Yesterday I was at our son's grave. Do you think that with him we buried everything that was between us? Don't cry, it's not tears I'm after."

Suddenly he changed his tone. "I didn't come to force myself on you against your will. Even the lowest of the low isn't utterly lacking in honor. But you do understand, don't you? I had to see you, I have to speak to you; but if you don't want me to, I'll go. And maybe the future will be brighter for me than Mr. Hans Steiner and Miss Ingeborg of the house of Starkmat think. My black fate isn't sealed forever. Not yet. Tell me, Inge, is he here? Don't be afraid of me, I don't want to do anything to him. What could I do, if even mountains make a fool of me?"

Inge sat silently sorrowful. Werner looked at her two or three times. Since he had last seen her she had put on a little weight. Or maybe she looked that way because she was wearing black. The black skirt she had on went with her slender figure and her shiny blonde hair. The white of her neck shone, but the radiance that had beamed from her eyes had dimmed. Fernheim knew that this happiness had not come on his account, on his returning from the prison camp; no, her happiness had been held in readiness for the coming of Karl Neiss. And even though at first he had been saddened by the cause, her happiness had made him happy. Now that all happiness had left her, he was overwhelmed with pity for her.

Again he looked at her. She sat hunched over, her face in her hands, wet with tears. Suddenly she shook herself in alarm, as if a hand had touched her shoulder. She extended her hands as if to defend herself and looked at him angrily.

"Well, now I'll leave," he said.

"Goodbye, Werner."

He returned. "You won't give me your hand?"

She gave him her hand in farewell. Clasping it, he said, "Before I leave, I want to tell you something."

She removed her hand and shook her shoulders in refusal.

"Still, maybe it would be worth your while to listen. And if not for the sake of the Werner standing here as an uninvited guest, then for the sake of that Werner who was lucky enough to stand under the wedding canopy with Ingeborg. But if you refuse, I won't impose upon you. And now—"

"And now, goodbye," said Inge.

"So be it. Goodbye, Ingeborg, goodbye."

Seeing her turn to go, he stood up.

She stared at him, wondering why he was not leaving.

"At any rate," said Werner, "it's rather strange that you don't want to hear a little of what I went through."

"Haven't you told me?"

"When I started to tell you, your ears were already in another place."

"My ears were in their proper place, but you didn't say a thing. Really, I don't recall that you said a thing."

"Would you like me to tell you?" asked Werner.

"You must have told Hans or Gertrude or both of them," she replied.

"And if I did?"

"If you did, they'll tell me."

"If I understand what you're really getting at," said Werner, "you don't want to hear it."

"Why do you say that? I expressly said that Gertrude or Hans would tell me, so I do want to hear it."

"And if I myself were to tell you?"

"What time is it?" said Inge.

Werner smiled. "So goes the proverb doesn't it? *Dem Glücklichen schlägt keine Stunde:* the happy person is beyond time."

"I don't know what answer to give to that sort of question," said Inge.

"And are you ready to answer other questions?" he countered.

"That depends on your questions. But now my head aches and I can't keep talking on and on, and anyway—"

"Anyway what?"

"You have a strange way of latching on to every word," said Inge.

"Does it seem strange to you that after all the years I haven't seen you I'm drawn by what you say?"

Inge clutched her temples. "My head, my head! Don't be difficult, Werner, if I ask you to leave me alone."

"I'm already leaving," he said. "Are you looking at my shoes? They're old, but easy on the feet. You're quite à la mode, though; you've even cut your hair. I can't say it's unattractive, but when you had all your hair it was prettier. When did the baby die? I was at his grave and I saw his stone, but I forget the date. Are you crying? My heart cries too, inside of me, but I get hold of myself. If you look at my eyes you won't find even a trace of a tear. Tell the fellow who's knocking at the door you can't get up and open it for him because of your headache. Zigi, are you here? What do you have to say, Zigi? Come here, sweetheart, let's make up. What's this in your hand, a letter? You're a mailman, are you, my dear nephew?"

Zigi gave a note to his aunt and left.

Inge took the note while looking at Werner with a furrowed brow, trying her best to understand why on earth the man would not go away. He should have left long since.

After a while she stopped thinking about him and began saying to herself, I have to leave, I simply must leave, it's impossible for me not to leave, every wasted minute is precious.

Her mind came back to Fernheim. Can't he see that I have to go?

She looked at him and said, "Excuse me, Werner, but I'm wanted and I have to go."

"How do you know you're wanted? The note is still folded in your hand and you haven't looked at it."

Inge dropped her shoulders. It seemed that she abrogated her will before his, and that it did not matter whether she went or stayed. Her eyes were extinguished, as it were, and her lids fell down over them.

"Are you tired?" Werner whispered.

Inge opened her eyes. "I'm not tired," she replied.

A new spirit clothed Werner. "Good, good," he said, "it's good that you're not tired and we can sit and talk with each other. You can't imagine how I've longed for this moment when I should see you. Had it not been for this hope, I would have died long since. Now I see that all that longing is nothing compared to this moment when you and I are seated here together as one. I have no words to express it, but I think you read some of it in my face. You see, my darling, how my knees bend of themselves and kneel before you. So did they bend whenever I thought of you. How lucky I am to be with you once again under the same roof. I'm not an eloquent man, but I tell you this: From the moment that I stepped over the threshold of your room, my soul was stirred as on that day when you placed your hand in mine and agreed to become my wife. Do you remember that moment, when you rested your head on my shoulder while we sat together as one, your hand in mine? Your eyes were closed, as were mine, as I close them now and pass before me all the events of that matchless day. Throw away the note, Inge, and give me your hand. My eyes are closed, but my heart sees how good you are, how good you are to me."

Inge shrugged her shoulders and left.

Fernheim opened his eyes. "Inge!" he cried.

But Inge had vanished. Fernheim was alone. What now? he thought. Now I have no choice but to leave this place. That's clear; but everything else is "something else again," as my worthy brother-in-law would put it.

His mind was already vacant of thought, and his former

tension began to dissolve. But his toes were burning and the soles of his feet as well. It seemed that the shoes he had said were comfortable were not so comfortable after all.

He put his hand into his pocket and took out his ticket: one half had allowed him to visit his wife and the other half would allow him to return. Holding the ticket in his hand he thought, Now I'll go to the railroad station and leave. And if I've missed the afternoon train I'll take the evening train. Not only the happy ones stand beyond time, but the unfortunate, too. All times are ripe for misfortune.

For a little while he stood in the room that Inge had left. Then he turned around and went to the door. He looked about the room, walked out, and shut the door.

Translated by David S. Segal

At the Outset
of the Day

AFTER THE ENEMY destroyed my home I took my little daughter in my arms and fled with her to the city. Gripped with terror, I fled in frenzied haste a night and a day until I arrived at the courtyard of the Great Synagogue one hour before nightfall on the eve of the Day of Atonement. The hills and mountains that had accompanied us departed, and I and the child entered into the courtyard. From out of the depths rose the Great Synagogue, on its left the old House of Study and directly opposite that, one doorway facing the other, the new House of Study.

This was the House of Prayer and these the Houses of Torah that I had kept in my mind's eye all my life. If I chanced to forget them during the day, they would stir themselves and come to me at night in my dreams, even as during my waking hours. Now that the enemy had destroyed my home I and my little daughter sought refuge in these places; it seemed that my child recognized them, so often had she heard about them.

An aura of peace and rest suffused the courtyard. The Children of Israel had already finished the afternoon prayer and, having gone home, were sitting down to the last meal before the fast to prepare themselves for the morrow, that they might have strength and health enough to return in repentance.

A cool breeze swept through the courtyard, caressing the last of the heat in the thick walls, and a whitish mist spiraled up the steps of the house, the kind children call angels' breath.

I rid my mind of all that the enemy had done to us and reflected upon the Day of Atonement drawing ever closer, that holy festival comprised of love and affection, mercy and prayer, a day whereon men's supplications are dearer, more desired, more acceptable than at all other times. Would that they might appoint a reader of prayers worthy to stand before the Ark, for recent generations have seen the decline of emissaries of the congregation who know how to pray; and cantors who reverence their throats with their trilling, but bore the heart, have increased. And I, I needed strengthening —and, needless to say, my little daughter, a babe torn away from her home.

I glanced at her, at my little girl standing all atremble by the memorial candle in the courtyard, warming her little hands over the flame. Growing aware of my eyes, she looked at me like a frightened child who finds her father standing behind her and sees that his thoughts are muddled and his heart humbled.

Grasping her hand in mine, I said, "Good men will come at once and give me a prayer shawl with an adornment of silver just like the one the enemy tore. You remember the lovely prayer shawl that I used to spread over your head when the priests would rise up to bless the people. They will give me a large festival prayerbook filled with prayers, too, and I will wrap myself in the prayer shawl and take the book and pray to God, who saved us from the hand of the enemy who sought to destroy us.

"And what will they bring you, my dearest daughter? You, my darling, they will bring a little prayerbook full of letters, full of all of the letters of the alphabet and the vowel-marks, too. And now, dearest daughter, tell me, an *alef*

and a *bet* that come together with a *kametz* beneath the *alef*
—how do you say them?"

"Av," my daughter answered.

"And what does it mean?" I asked.

"Father," my daughter answered, "like you're my father."

"Very nice, that's right, an *alef* with a *kametz* beneath and
a *bet* with no dot in it make 'Av.'

"And now, my daughter," I continued, "what father is
greater than all other fathers? Our Father in Heaven, who is
my father and your father and the father of the whole world.
You see, my daughter, two little letters stand there in the
prayerbook as if they were all alone, then they come together
and lo and behold they are 'Av.' And not only these letters
but all letters, all of them join together to make words and
words make prayers and the prayers rise up before our Father
in Heaven who listens very, very carefully, to all that we pray,
if only our hearts cling to the upper light like a flame clings
to a candle."

Even as I stood there speaking of the power of the letters
a breeze swept through the courtyard and pushed the memorial candle against my daughter. Fire seized hold of her
dress. I ripped off the flaming garment, leaving the child
naked, for what she was wearing was all that remained of her
lovely clothes. We had fled in panic, destruction at our heels,
and had taken nothing with us. Now that fire had consumed
her dress I had nothing with which to cover my daughter.

I turned this way and that, seeking anything my daughter
could clothe herself with. I sought, but found nothing. Wherever I directed my eyes, I met emptiness. I'll go to the corner
of the storeroom, I said to myself, where torn sacred books are
hidden away, perhaps there I will find something. Many a
time when I was a lad I had rummaged about there and
found all sorts of things, sometimes the conclusion of a
matter and sometimes its beginning or its middle. But now
I turned there and found nothing with which to cover my

little girl. Do not be surprised that I found nothing. When
books were read, they were rent; but now that books are not
read, they are not rent.

I stood there worried and distraught. What could I do for
my daughter, what could I cover her nakedness with? Night
was drawing on and with it the chill of the night, and I had
no garment, nothing to wrap my daughter in. I recalled the
home of Reb Alter, who had gone up to the Land of Israel.
I'll go to his sons and daughters, I decided, and ask clothing
of them. I left my daughter as she was and headed for the
household of Reb Alter.

How pleasant to walk without being pursued. The earth is
light and comfortable and does not burn beneath one's feet,
nor do the Heavens fling thorns into one's eyes. But I ran
rather than walked, for even if no man was pursuing me,
time was: the sun was about to set and the hour to gather
for the evening prayer was nigh. I hurried lest the members
of Reb Alter's household might already be getting up to leave
for the House of Prayer.

It is comforting to remember the home of a dear friend
in time of distress. Reb Alter, peace be with him, had cir-
cumcised me, and a covenant of love bound us together. As
long as Reb Alter lived in his home I was a frequent visitor
there, the more so in the early days when I was a classmate
of his grandson Gad. Reb Alter's house was small, so small
that one wondered how such a large man could live there.
But Reb Alter was wise and made himself so little that
his house seemed large.

The house, built on one of the low hills surrounding the
Great Synagogue, had a stucco platform protruding from it.
Reb Alter, peace be with him, had been in the habit of sitting
on that platform with his long pipe in his mouth, sending
wreaths of smoke gliding into space. Many a time I stood
waiting for the pipe to go out so I could bring him a light.
My grandfather, peace be with him, had given Reb Alter

that pipe at my circumcision feast. "Your grandfather knows pipes very well," Reb Alter told me once, "and knows how to pick just the right pipe for every mouth."

Reb Alter stroked his beard as he spoke, like one well aware that he deserved that pipe, even though he was a modest man. His modesty showed itself one Friday afternoon before sunset. As he put out the pipe, and the Sabbath was approaching, he said, "Your grandfather never has to put out his pipe; he knows how to smoke more or less as time necessitates."

Well, then, I entered the home of Reb Alter and found his daughter, together with a small group of old men and old women, sitting near a window while an old man with a face like a wrinkled pear stood reading them a letter. All of them listened attentively, wiping their eyes. Because so many years had passed I mistook Reb Alter's daughter for her mother. What's going on? I asked myself. On the eve of the Day of Atonement darkness is falling, and these people have not lit a "candle of life." And what sort of letter is this? If from Reb Alter, he is already dead. Perhaps it was from his grandson, my friend Gad, perhaps news had come from Reb Alter's grandson Gad, who had frequented the House of Study early and late. One day he left early and did not return.

It is said that two nights prior to his disappearance his wetnurse had seen him in a dream sprouting the plume of a peculiar bird from his head, a plume that shrieked, "A, B, C, D!" Reb Alter's daughter folded the letter and put it between the mirror and the wall. Her face, peeking out of the mirror, was the face of an aged woman bearing the burden of her years. And alongside her face appeared my own, green as a wound that has not formed a scab.

I turned away from the mirror and looked at the rest of the old people in Reb Alter's home and tried to say something to them. My lips flipped against each other like a man who wishes to say something but, upon seeing something bizarre, is seized with fright.

One of the old men noticed the state of panic I was in. Tapping one finger against his spectacles, he said, "You are looking at our torn clothing. Enough that creatures like ourselves still have skin on our flesh." The rest of the old men and old women heard and nodded their heads in agreement. As they did so their skin quivered. I took hold of myself, walked backwards, and left.

I left in despair and, empty-handed, with no clothing, with nothing at all, returned to my daughter. I found her standing in a corner of the courtyard pressed against the wall next to the purification board on which the dead are washed. Her hair was loose and wrapped about her. How great is Thy goodness, O God, in putting wisdom into the heart of such a little girl to enable her to wrap herself in her hair after her dress has burned off, for as long as she had not been given a garment it was good that she covered herself with her hair. But how great was the sadness that enveloped me at that moment, the outset of this holy festival whose joy has no parallel all the year. But now there was no joy and no sign of joy, only pain and anguish.

The stone steps sounded beneath feet clad in felt slippers and long stockings, as Jews bearing prayer shawls and ritual gowns streamed to the House of Prayer. With my body I covered my little girl, trembling from the cold, and I stroked her hair. Again I looked in the storeroom where the torn pages from sacred books were kept, the room where in my youth I would find, among the fragments, wondrous and amazing things. I remember one of the sayings, it went approximately like this: "At times she takes the form of an old woman and at times the form of a little girl. And when she takes the form of a little girl, don't imagine that your soul is as pure as a little girl; this is but an indication that she passionately yearns to recapture the purity of her infancy when she was free of sin. The fool substitutes the *form* for the *need*; the wise man substitutes *will* for *need*."

A tall man with a red beard came along, picking from his teeth the last remnants of the final meal, pushing his wide belly out to make room for himself. He stood about like a man who knew that God would not run away and there was no need to hurry. He regarded us for a moment, ran his eyes over us, then said something with a double meaning.

My anger flowed into my hand, and I caught him by the beard and began yanking at his hair. Utterly astonished, he did not move. He had good cause to be astonished too: a small fellow like me lifting my hand against a brawny fellow like him. Even I was astonished: had he laid hold of me, he would not have let me go whole.

Another tall, husky fellow came along, one who boasted of being my dearest friend. I looked up at him, hoping that he would come between us. He took his spectacles, wiped them, and placed them on his nose. The whites of his eyes turned green and his spectacles shone like moist scales. He stood looking at us as though we were characters in an amusing play.

I raised my voice and shouted, "A fire has sprung up and has burned my daughter's dress, and here she stands shivering from the cold!" He nodded his head in my direction and once more wiped his spectacles. Again they shone like moist scales and flashed like green scum on water. Once more I shouted, "It's not enough that no one gives her any clothing, but they must abuse us, too!" The fellow nodded his head and repeated my words as though pleased by them. As he spoke he turned his eyes away from me so that they might not see me, and that he might imagine he had made up the story on his own. I was no longer angry with my enemy, being so gripped with fury at this man: though he had prided himself on being my friend, he was repeating all that had befallen me as though it were a tale of his own invention.

My daughter began crying. "Let's run away from here."

"What are you saying?" I answered. "Don't you see that night has fallen and that we have entered the holy day?

And if we were to flee, where would we flee and where could we hide?"

Where could we hide? Our home lay in ruins and the enemies covered all the roads. And if by some miracle we escaped, could we depend upon miracles? And here were the two Houses of Study and the Great Synagogue in which I studied Torah and in which I prayed and here was the corner where they had hidden away sacred books worn with age. As a little boy I rummaged about here frequently, finding all sorts of things. I do not know why, on this particular day, we found nothing, but I remember that I once found something important about *need* and *form* and *will*. Were it not for the urgency of the day I would explain this matter to you thoroughly, and you would see that it is by no means allegorical but a simple and straightforward affair.

I glanced at my little girl who stood trembling from the cold, for she had been stripped of her clothing, she didn't even have a shirt, the night was chill and the song of winter birds resounded from the mountains. I glanced at my daughter, the darling of my heart, like a father who glances at his little daughter, and a loving smile formed on my lips. This was a very timely smile, for it rid her of her fear completely. I stood then with my daughter in the open courtyard of the Great Synagogue and the two Houses of Study which all my life stirred themselves and came to me in my dreams and now stood before me, fully real. The gates of the Houses of Prayer were open, and from all three issued the voices of the readers of prayer. In which direction should we look and whither should we bend our ears?

He who gives eyes to see with and ears to hear with directed my eyes and ears to the old House of Study. The House of Study was full of Jews, the doors of the Ark were open and the Ark was full of old Torah scrolls, and among them gleamed a new scroll clothed in a red mantle with silver points. This was the scroll that I had written in memory of the souls of days that had departed. A silver plate was hung over the scroll, with letters engraved upon it, shining letters. And even though I stood far off I saw what they were. A thick rope was stretched in front of the scroll that it might not slip and fall.

My soul fainted within me, and I stood and prayed as those wrapped in prayer shawls and ritual gowns. And even my little girl, who had dozed off, repeated in her sleep each and every prayer in sweet melodies no ear has ever heard.

I do not enlarge. I do not exaggerate.

Translated by DAVID S. SEGAL

The Night

WHEN NIGHT FELL I went home; that is, I went to the hotel room I had taken for my wife and myself. I was hurrying, as I knew that my wife was tired out by all the travel and wanted to sleep, and I had no intention of disturbing her.

There was a multitude of people in the streets, mainly new immigrants, who were arriving here from all over the world. For many years they had wasted away in the death camps, or wandered aimlessly over hill and valley, and through forests, all this time without seeing so much as the flicker of a candle, and now that they'd stepped from the dark into this sudden brightness, they seemed puzzled and somewhat suspicious, not being able to grasp whether all the lights had been left burning by an oversight, or whether it was part of some scheme of the authorities.

An old man came toward me, wearing a greenish coat that came down to his knees, exactly like the coat Mr. Halbfried, the bookseller in our town, used to wear for as long as I remember. The coat had lost most of its color, but had kept its original shape. Short coats are better at keeping their shape than long ones, because long coats sweep the ground and get frayed, whereas short coats flutter in the air, and the ground cannot harm them in any way. Even though their appearance might have changed, their hems remain as the tailor finished them and seem to have retained their perfection.

While I was wondering whether this was really Mr. Halbfried, he ran his weary eyes over me and said: "From the day that I arrived here I've been looking for you, and now that we've met I'm happy twice over, once because I've found someone from my home town, and twice because that someone happens to be you." The old man was so excited that he forgot to greet me properly, instead of which he straightway reeled off a string of names, people he'd asked about me, and after each name he'd express his amazement that So-and-so didn't know me, and had he himself failed to recognize me the moment he saw me, he could have passed me as if we were not fellow townsmen. Having come around to mentioning our town, he began talking about the past, the time when we were neighbors, and his bookstore was filled with books that united all the learned people of the town, who were passing in and out of the shop all day, and having heated discussions about what was going on in the world, and about the future, and coming to the conclusion that the world was evolving into a better place, and there was I, a small boy, fingering the books, climbing the ladder, standing at the top reading, not realizing that I was endangering myself; for had someone blundered into the ladder by mistake, I could very easily have fallen off. But as if the large stock of books which he kept were not sufficient for me, I had asked him to get me *The Poem of Jerusalem Liberated*. However, he couldn't remember any more whether he'd placed the order before I emigrated to the Land of Israel, or whether I did so before he'd placed the order.

Another thing he was reminded of, said Mr. Halbfried, was the time they showed my first poems to that old mystic who had written two interpretations of the prayerbook, and the old man had looked at them and murmured, *"Kehadin kamtza dilevushe mine uve"* ["like the snail whose garb is a part of it"], and the learned listeners tried hard to understand the meaning of these words, and did not succeed. He, Mr. Halbfried continued, was still puzzled that they never took the trouble to look them up in a dictionary, and that he himself did not do so, although he had a number of dictionaries in stock, and could have done so quite easily, yet somehow never did.

He broke off his story and asked me was I angry with his brother?—Why? His brother had just passed us and greeted me, and I made as if I didn't see him.

Mr. Halbfried's last words shocked and saddened me. I had not noticed anyone greeting me; as for the man who had passed us, I was under the impression that it was Mr. Halbfried himself. As I didn't wish him to think that I would turn my eyes away from people who greet me, I said to him: "I swear I didn't notice your brother; had I noticed him, I would have been the first to greet him." So Mr. Halbfried began talking once more of the good old days, of his bookshop and the people who came to it. Every time Mr. Halbfried mentioned a name, he did so with great warmth, the way we used to talk about good friends in those long-lost days before the war.

After a while, Mr. Halbfried stopped and said: "I shall leave you now, as I do not want you to keep a man waiting who wishes to see you." With that he shook my hand and went away.

The man Mr. Halbfried had mentioned was not known to me, nor did he seem to be waiting for me; however, Mr. Halbfried's mistake came in handy, as it enabled me to shake the old man off politely, and so avoid disturbing my wife's sleep.

But Mr. Halbfried had not been mistaken; after I'd gotten rid of him, this man barred my way, then poked his stick into the ground and leaned on it with both hands, while looking at me. Then he lifted his hand in greeting, lifted it to his cap, a round cap of sheepskin leather, and while he was doing so, he said: "Don't you know me?" I said to myself: Why tell him I don't know him? So I gave him a warm look and said: "Certainly I know you, you're none other than —" He interrupted me and said: "I was sure you'd know me, if not for my own sake, then for the sake of my son. What do you think of his poems?" From this I realized that he was the father of someone or other who had sent me his book of poems. I said to myself: Why tell him that I haven't looked at them yet? So I gave him a warm look and said whatever it is one says on these occasions. Yet he didn't seem satisfied with it. So I said to myself: Why not add a few nice words? So I added a few compliments; but he was still unsatisfied, and began singing his son's praises himself, and I kept nodding my head in agreement, so that an onlooker would have thought that the praise came from my mouth.

Having done, he said: "No doubt you wish to make my son's acquaintance, so go to the concert hall, that's where you'll find him. My son is a well-loved man, all the doors are open to him, not only the doors of music but the doors of all the important houses in town. Why, if my son desired, let's say, to ride on a mouse, why, the animal would rush up to him with its tail between its legs and beg him to take a ride. Truly, I myself would love to go to that concert, all the best members of our intelligentsia will be there, the trouble is they won't let you in if you haven't got a ticket." Saying this, he rubbed two fingers together and made a noise with his lips, as if to say, you need real coins for that.

I kept quiet and did not say a word. It was some years now that I hadn't gone to a concert. I could never understand how a crowd of people could assemble at a fixed date and hour, in a special hall, just to hear some singing. Nor could I understand how it was that the singers were ready to lift up their voices in song at the exact hour the ticket holders were filling the hall, ready to listen.

I'm just a small-town boy; I can grasp that someone is singing because his heart is full; but this singing in front of an audience rich enough to buy tickets, because some impresario organized it all, was beyond me. So when I saw how much this man wanted to go to the concert, I asked myself whether I should help him, and decided to buy him a ticket. He saw what I was thinking, and said, "I won't go without you."

I asked myself whether to go with him, and then I said, "All right, I'll buy two tickets, and we'll go together." He started feeling the air, as if it were full of tickets. Again he rubbed two fingers together, and made a popping noise, like a cork coming out of a bottle.

So we walked together, and he kept praising the concert hall, where there was so much music one could almost drown in it. Then he told me about this violinist whose violin was so precious that even the case he carried it in was worth more than the instruments of other violinists. Then he returned to his son, to whom poetical rhymes came for the sole purpose of the matching of words. Then he returned to the subject of the tickets, out of respect for which the doors used to open themselves. Suddenly he began worrying, as it occurred to him that he could be wasting his time, for, although I seemed willing enough to buy him a ticket, what if every seat was sold out, or supposing there was only one single ticket left— wouldn't I buy it for myself, and leave him standing outside. Thus we came to my hotel.

I said to him: "Wait here, I'm going in to change, and then we're off to the concert." He poked his stick into the ground, leaned on it with both hands, and stood there.

I left him outside and told the doorman I wanted two tickets for the concert. The doorman said: "I have two good tickets, which were ordered by the Duke of Ilivio, but he left them with me, as he cannot come since he has been called to the Emperor." Here the doorman whispered to me that the Emperor had arrived secretly in town, with most of his retinue, dukes, lords, and officers, and that some of them were actually staying at our hotel.

I took the tickets and went up to my room, leaving the door open so that I could change by the light in the corridor, and not have to turn on the light in the room, which would have awakened my wife. I walked in on tiptoe, noiselessly, and to my surprise and distress I found a strange man in the room. Who was that who dared to enter my room in the dark of the night? Should the earth refuse to open at his feet and swallow him, then I would be forced to throw him out myself, and not too politely, either.

As I approached him, I saw that it was Moshele, a relative of mine. This Moshele and I had grown up together, and we went through difficult times together, until one day he was called up into the army, where he stayed until he was wounded and dismissed. We thought that he had been burned in the gas chambers of Auschwitz, but here he stood, alive, in my room.

I said, "What brought you here?" He said, "My troubles brought me here. I have been shuffling from one mound of refuse to another without a roof over my head, and when I heard you were here I came running, for I was sure that you would put me up."

I said to him: "Do I have a home that you should ask to sleep here? As you can see, I'm myself but a guest for the night."

He said: "All I'm asking is a place on the floor."

I began laughing. A hotel where dukes and lords live, and he wants to sleep on the floor.

I don't know if his brain succeeded in grasping what I meant and if his heart accepted my words. In any case, he got up and left.

I went to the window to watch him go, and I saw him in the street, cowering as he was hit by the whips of the coachmen who drove the coaches of the nobility. I called to him, but he didn't answer me; I called to him again and he didn't answer, probably being too busy trying to evade the whips to hear my voice. I decided to call louder, but then I remembered that my wife was sleeping, so I didn't. And it is probably just as well, for, had I shouted, all the other coachmen would have seen him too, and joined in beating him.

I looked after Moshele until he disappeared from view. Then I went to the wardrobe to change.

Two small children came in and started walking around

me in circles. As I opened the door of the wardrobe to take
some clothes, one of them jumped in, and his brother jumped
after him, and they shut the wardrobe door behind them. I
was somewhat perplexed; as they were probably the sons of a
duke or a lord, I couldn't very well be rude to them. On the
other hand, I couldn't let them go on playing, as they were
liable to wake my wife.

Their governess came and helped me out of this trouble.
She said to them: "If I may be so bold as to say, it behooves
not the princes to enter the room of a strange person."

I apologized to the governess for having left the door of
my room open and caused the two king's sons to enter my
room. I added that I was going to the concert and had only
come to dress.

The governess examined my clothes with her eyes and
said: "You can't show yourself in that collar you're wearing."
I said to her: "Yes, you're quite right." She said: "Surely, you
can find another collar." "Probably," I said. She said: "Go
on, put it on." I said to her: "I am afraid that when the
king's son did me the honor of jumping into my wardrobe,
he trampled on my collars, and they got soiled." She said:
"In that case, I'll tie your tie. Your gracious highnesses, would
you be so kind as to leave the room until I finish tying the
tie of this gentleman, who is the brother of your teacher."
The little boys stood there and looked very surprised that
this creature, which had been created to serve them, should
now wish to serve a simple mortal.

The graciousness of the young lady and the envy of the
king's sons put me into a much better mood. I stuttered somewhat and said: "It is not my custom to go to concerts, but
what is a custom worth if you're not ready to disregard it for
the sake of another person." The young lady didn't pay much
attention to my words; she was too busy tying and then
untying every knot she tied, saying, "It wasn't such a knot
I meant to tie, now I shall tie one that is much handsomer."
Finally, she stroked my arm and said: "Look in the mirror

and see how beautifully tied your tie is." I said to her: "I cannot look in the mirror." "Why?" "Because the mirror is screwed onto the inside of the wardrobe door, and if I opened it wide it would squeak and wake my wife." "Your wife?" screamed the young lady in a rage. "And here you were talking to me as if we were alone in the room. If your wife is here, then go and be happy with her." With that the young lady went away.

"Who were you talking to," asked my wife. I said to her: "No one." She said: "I must have been dreaming." I said to her: "Dream or not, I'm going out for a walk, and won't be back till after midnight."

I went looking for the man who was waiting for me in front of the hotel, but he was nowhere to be seen. I asked the doorman about him; he answered: "Some time ago I did see a person loitering in front of the hotel. Had I known he was a friend of yours, sir, I would have looked at him more carefully." I said to the doorman: "Where could he be now?" "Where? I really don't know." "Which way did he go?" "Well," said the doorman, "I seem to remember that he turned right, or maybe it was left, people like these have round shoulders and one never knows quite which way they turn." I gave him a tip. He bowed low and said: "If your excellency would care to listen to my advice, he would visit the servants' quarters in the hotel, as the serfs of the nobles have brought a Jewish clown with them, and it is quite possible that the man your excellency is looking for has gone there to see the fun."

I went to the servants' quarters of the hotel, and saw the serfs sitting like masters, their bellies shaking with laughter, and a small man, shrunken and beautiful, standing on the big stage doing tricks, and talking all the while. When the tricks were funny, his voice was sad, and when they were sad, his voice was funny. I wondered whether he did it on purpose. It seemed to me to be great art, being funny in a sad voice, and being sad in a funny voice. I looked around and found the man I was searching for. I waved the two tickets at him, but he pretended not to see me, and left. It seemed as if his leaving were only temporary, because of me, that is, and he was likely to return as soon as I had gone.

Another man came up to me; he had a long face and a cheerful beard. He stroked his beard and said: "Who are you looking for?" I told him. He said: "I could manage to go with you to the concert." I threw a look at him and shouted in amazement: "What! You?" He shook his beard and said: "Why not?" I repeated what I had said before, only with a great deal of sarcasm: "What! You?" He disappeared, and so did his beard. "What do we do now?" I thought to myself. I waved the tickets in the air, but nothing happened. The man I was waving at didn't show up. So I said to myself: Not only can't I give him the pleasure of a concert, I'm even preventing him from the pleasure of seeing the clown, as he won't show his face in the audience as long as I'm here. I got up and left.

As this man didn't wish to come, I gave up the idea of going to the concert; but, having told my wife that I wouldn't be in before midnight, not until the singer had finished his recital, I had time to take a walk. I began thinking about what had happened, about these incidents which seemed to grow each out of the other, and yet there was no connection between them. I started from the beginning, from the ladder in the bookstore, *The Poem of Jerusalem Liberated*, and that small creature whose garb is a part of him.

After skipping over some matters, I got to thinking of Moshele, my own flesh and blood, who had escaped the fires of cremation and now was shuffling from one mound of refuse to another. As the concert had not yet come to an end and it was not yet time for me to return to my room, I was able to think a great many thoughts. As I strolled along I thought: If only I could find Moshele now that I am just strolling and have nothing else to do, I would talk to him and let him tell me all his troubles; I would appease him and bring him to the inn, give him food and drink and order a soft, warm bed, and we would part from each other with a hearty goodnight. As I was strolling and thinking such thoughts, it suddenly dawned on me that there could be nothing finer. But favors do not come at all times, or to anyone. Moshele had been saved from cremation, and as an added favor it had been given him to find his own flesh and blood. Whereas I, who was his flesh and blood—no favors at all were granted to me, and I couldn't find Moshele again.

Finally, the singer ended his song and the audience went home. I too returned to the room at the hotel and closed the door behind me carefully, as an open door calls to uninvited guests. But there are guests who come no matter how tightly one's door is shut, as they are the thoughts surrounding our actions. So many guests came that the air in the room got fouler and fouler, and I was afraid I was going to choke. I then untied the knot which the young lady had made in my tie, and that helped a little. Now there was more air to breathe, and the guests brought some more guests, and very soon I was choking again.

Translated by Yoram Matmor

First Kiss

FRIDAY AFTERNOON; Sabbath eve. Father was out of town on business and had left me alone, like a kind of watchman, to take care of the store. Dusk. Time to lock up, I said to myself, time to go home and change my clothes. Time to go to the House of Prayer.

I took down the keys from where we keep them hidden, but as I went outside to lock the door, three monks appeared. They were bareheaded and wore heavy, dark robes and sandals on their feet. "We want to talk with you," they said.

I thought to myself, If they've come to do business, Friday afternoon close to sunset is no time to do business; and if they've come to have a talk, I'm not the man for them. But they saw that I was hesitant to reply, and they smiled.

"Don't be afraid," one of them said, "we're not about to delay you from your prayers."

"Look to the heavens and see," added the second. "The sun has yet to go down, we still have time."

The third one nodded his head, and in the same words, or in different words, repeated what the first two had already said. I locked the door and walked along with them. It so happened that we came out opposite my house. One of the monks raised his left hand.

"Isn't this your house?"

"This is his house," answered the second.

"Of course it's his house," added the third. "This is his house." And he pointed three fingers at Father's house.

"If you'd like, we can go in," I said.

They nodded their heads: "By your leave."

We made a circuit of the entire street and walked down a short incline that took us below street level. I forgot to say that there are two entrances to Father's house, one onto the street, where his shop is, and another onto an alleyway, opposite his House of Study. Both entrances are kept open on weekdays, but at dusk on Friday afternoon we close the door that gives onto the street and unlock the one to the House of Study.

I pushed open the door and we went in. I brought them into the parlor. They sat on chairs that in preparation for the Sabbath meal had been arranged around a table set for the Sabbath. Their robes dragged behind their sandals over the special rug that Mother lays out in honor of the Sabbath.

The eldest of the three, who sat at the head of the table, was fat and fleshy. The others sat on either side of him: one was long and thin, with pale hair and a small wound that glowed red on the back of his head where the monks leave a round spot without hair. The other had no distinguishing marks except for a large Adam's apple. Myself—I didn't sit down, but remained standing, as is only reasonable for a man who is in a hurry but has had to receive guests.

They began to talk; I kept quiet. When they saw the two candlesticks on the table they said, "There are three of you, aren't there? There's you, your father, and your mother. Why doesn't your mother light a third candle for her son?"

"Mother is simply continuing a custom she began on the first Sabbath after her marriage," I told them, "which is to light two candles only."

They started discussing the various regulations that pertain to the ritual of candle-lighting, and what each one of them means.

"No," I broke in, "it's not for any of the reasons you've

mentioned, it's just that one candle is for the Written Law and one is for the Oral Law. And the two are actually one, which is why we refer to the Sabbath candles in the singular. But, anyway, I see you're all quite expert in Jewish custom."

They smiled, but the smile disappeared into the wrinkles in their faces.

"Well, and why shouldn't we be experts in Jewish custom," said the one that I've been calling the third. "After all, we belong to the order of—"

I thought he said they were Dominicans; but outside the monastery Dominicans don't usually wear their habits, and these three had their habits on. So he must have named a different order, but his Adam's apple got in the way and I didn't catch what he said.

The conversation was preventing me from keeping track of time, and I forgot that a man has to make himself ready to greet the Sabbath. I asked the maid to serve refreshments. She brought in the special delicacies that we prepare in honor of the Sabbath. I put a flask of brandy in front of them. They ate and drank and talked. Since I was agitated about the time, I didn't hear anything they said.

Two or three times it occurred to me that the hour had come to welcome the Sabbath. But when I looked out the window, the sun was in the same place it had been when the monks first accosted me. Now you can't say there was some kind of black magic here, because I had mentioned the name of God any number of times during the conversation; and you can't say that I'd made a simple mistake in time, because the sexton had not yet called for prayers. The whole thing was quite astonishing: when the monks first came, the sun was close to setting, and all this time they'd been eating and drinking and talking, yet the sun was precisely where I'd last seen it before they ever appeared. And it's even harder, for that matter, to explain away the problem of our clock, because even if you claim that I was so preoccupied with my guests I didn't think to set it for the Sabbath, all the same I assure you it's a fine instrument, and would keep proper time even without a daily winding.

Mother came in to light the candles. The monks stood up, and in the selfsame movement walked out.

I got up to accompany them. In the street, one of them shoved me aside.

I was stunned. After all the honor I'd shown him, to be treated like that—while the other two, who saw him push me, didn't even bother to rebuke him.

I didn't want Mother to notice that something had happened to me, so I decided not to return home. And I didn't go to the House of Prayer, because, by the time I could have washed myself from the touch of the monk's hand, they would have already finished the prayers. I stood there like a man with nothing to do, neither here nor there.

Two young novices came along.

"Where did the Fathers go," they said.

I was dumbfounded by what I heard. Men like that they call Father. Before I could rouse myself to answer, one of the novices disappeared. Vanished, right before my eyes. He left the other one behind.

I just stood there, shocked and speechless. For a while it was as if no one else existed. Then I glanced at him and saw that he was very young, about the height of a small youth, with black eyes. If it hadn't been for the commandment that tells us not to show them grace, which also means not to impute grace to them, I would even have said that his eyes were graceful, and sweet. His face was quite smooth, without the slightest trace of a beard. He had the kind of beauty you used to be able to see in every Jewish town, the beauty of young Jewish boys who have never tasted the taste of sin. And beyond that there was something else about him that imparted all the more grace to his graceful features.

I began talking with him so that I could examine him more

closely. As I talked, I laid my hand on his shoulder and I said to him, "Listen my brother, aren't you a Jew?"

I felt his shoulders tremble beneath my hand; I felt his eyes tremble; he lowered his head on his chest and I felt his heart tremble.

"Tell me," I repeated my question, "aren't you a Jew?"

He raised his head from his heart: "I am a Jew."

I said to him, "If you're a Jew, what are you doing with them?"

He bowed his head.

"Who are you," I said, "and where are you from?"

He stood in silence before me.

I brought my face close to his, as if to transfer my sense of hearing to my mouth.

He lifted his head, and I could see how his heart was shuddering, and my heart too began to shudder. I felt his black, sweet eyes upon me. He looked at me with such loving grace, with such tender faith, such glorious kindness, and above all with such grief—like a man trying to control himself before he finally reveals a long-kept secret.

I said to myself, What is all this?

As much time went by as went by, and still he said nothing.

"Is it so hard for you to tell me where you're from?"

He whispered the name of a city.

I said, "If I heard you correctly you're from the town of Likovitz."

He nodded his head.

"If you're from Likovitz," I said, "then you must certainly know the Zaddik of Likovitz. I was in his House of Prayer once on New Year's Day, and the Zaddik himself led the prayers. Let me tell you, when he came to the verse 'And all shall come to serve Thee,' I imagined that I heard the approaching footsteps of all the nations of the world who fail to recognize the people of Israel or their Father in Heaven.

And when he sang 'And the wayward shall learn under-standing,' I imagined they were all bowing down as one to worship the Lord of Hosts, the God of Israel. . . . My brother, are you in pain?"

He shook with sobs.

"What are you crying about?"

Tears flooded his eyes. He wiped them away. Still weeping, he said, "I am his daughter. His youngest daughter. The daughter of his old age."

My heart thundered and my mouth fastened to hers, and her mouth to mine. And the purest sweetness flowed from her mouth to mine and—it is possible—from my mouth to hers. We call this in Hebrew "the kiss of the mouth," and it must be the same in other languages too. I should say here that this was the first time I ever kissed a young girl, and it seems almost certain to me that it was her first kiss as well: a kiss of innocence that carries with it no pain, but goodness and blessing, life, grace, and kindness, whereby a man and a woman live together till calm old age.

Translated by NEAL KOZODOY

Editorial Postscript

S. Y. Agnon, winner of the Nobel Prize for literature in 1966, is the author of three long novels, over two hundred stories, and compilations of classical materials, such as *Days of Awe* (*Yamim Noraim*, 1938; English edition, 1948). Many of the stories appeared first in periodicals. The collected narrative work in the Hebrew original was issued first by Schocken Verlag (Berlin), then by Schocken Publishing House (Jerusalem–Tel Aviv): the first edition, in eleven volumes, appeared 1931 to 1952 ("Schocken I"); the second, revised and newly arranged, edition, in eight volumes, appeared 1952 to 1962 ("Schocken II").

Of the novels two have appeared to date in English versions: *The Bridal Canopy* (*Hakhnasat Kallah*, 1931; English editions, 1937 and 1967) and *A Guest for the Night* (*Oreah Natah Lalun*, 1939; English edition, 1968). *In the Heart of the Seas*, a novella, appeared in English in 1947 (*Bilvav Yamim*, 1933). The volume *Two Tales*, 1966, contains "Betrothed" ("Shevuat Emunim," 1943) and "Edo and Enam" ("Edo ve-Enam," 1950). The anthology *Israeli Stories*, 1962, contains Agnon's "Tehilah" (1950) and "Forevermore" ("Ad Olam," 1954). For a fuller perspective of Agnon as a master of the Hebrew short novel and story, the present volume of tales (some of the translations appear here for the first time) should be read in conjunction with the aforenamed narratives.

Roughly one half of the stories included in the present selection come from *The Book of Deeds* (or *Book of Happenings, Sefer Ha-Maasim*), written in the 'thirties and 'forties. These surrealistic, introspective, dreamlike tales are told with a clarity and precision that remind some readers of Kafka's style. So, too, does the content: Man is lonely, homeless, in exile; meaning disintegrates, lines of communication break down; there is no exit. Deep faith is a matter of the past; the present forms of religion are full of ambivalence, paradox, even of decay. Time itself disintegrates. In 1966 Agnon spoke of himself as "a stranger both to his time and to his place."

After the interpreters—accustomed to Agnon the artful, sensitive recorder of pious traditions—recovered from the shock of these modernistic, anguished, disturbing stories, it became clear that most of both Agnon's early work and that which followed *The Book of Deeds* contained the same elements: decline of the old order, loss of innocence, ambivalence, and exile. In this sense, *The Book of Deeds* "provides the best introduction to the entire corpus of Agnon's writings" (A. J. Band).

It may be assumed that the tragedy that befell the Jewish people in the 'thirties and 'forties prompted Agnon to accentuate in *The Book of Deeds* the motives that incited his creative life from its inception, though in less stark, less turbulent forms. Against the background of the frightful events, the artist must have felt compelled to abandon the form of the well-composed tale, the quiet, orderly progression of events, and the appearance of simplicity. Now, the experience of chaos penetrated the very form of the story and pervaded style and expression.

The following notes to the individual stories can do no more than attempt to point to key motifs and symbols, to the basic structure of the story, to possible meaning of some of the proper names. No authentic interpretation is in order in multilevel work such as Agnon's. Many details, evoked by a stream of consciousness, defy coherent explanation. The reader ought to feel free to make his own choice of emphasis within a story and intuit its meaning. I found it helpful to consult Arnold J. Band's comprehensive *Nostalgia and Nightmare: A Study in the Fiction of S. Y. Agnon* (Berkeley and Los Angeles, 1968); Baruch Kurzweil's *Masot al Sippure Shay Agnon* (Jerusalem–Tel Aviv, 1962); and Dov Sadan's *Al Shay Agnon* (Tel Aviv, 1959). I have benefited much from talks on the author with Professor Naftali C. Brandwein. Of inestimable value to me have been the intermittent but intensive talks with Mr. Agnon in the course of four decades and more.

The master himself is reputed to have remarked that after publishing a story he waits to read the critics to understand what he meant by it. This, I suspect, is a bit of irony, so typical of Agnon. It strangely contrasts with what he said to me in July, 1968: "I write things simply as they are."

THE TALE OF THE SCRIBE
Agadat ha-sofer; Schocken I, vol. III, 1931; Schocken II, vol. II, 1953. Tr. Isaac Franck. *Midstream* XIII, 2 (February, 1967). Copyright © 1967 by Schocken Books Inc.

The motif of this tale (first published in 1919) occupied Agnon for many years before the story reached its present form. The tale is all purity, sanctity of life, devotion to a holy task—out of these very qualities comes also the irony: their devoutness leaves no place for normal marriage. This life of perfection in which the scribe and his beloved wife share is suffused with tragedy: childlessness (viewed as denial of fulfillment), the wife's death, the scribe's withdrawal from human company and ultimately from reality. Only his death brings about the union between himself, the Torah, and the appearance of his wife. The Song of Songs of piety turns into Lamentations over life's destructiveness; both, however, are transcended in a higher, no longer earthly, vision.

FABLE OF THE GOAT
Maase ha-ez, 1925; Schocken I, vol. III, 1931; Schocken II, vol. II, 1953. Tr. Barney Rubin. *Commentary* XLII, 6 (December, 1966). Copyright © 1966 by Schocken Books Inc.

On the surface this is a simple folk talk. Underneath it, however, pulsates the tragic tension between young and old, trusting faith and disbelief, the realm of spirituality (Land of Israel, Sabbath) and that of exile. By having the goat slaughtered the sick old man severs (unwittingly) his link with salvation. In the last passages of the story, Agnon makes use of biblical phrases, such as the lament of David over Absalom (II Samuel 19:1) and the lament of Jacob over Joseph (Genesis 37:34).

AGUNOT
Agunot; *Besod Yesharim*, 1921; Schocken I, vol. III, 1931; Schocken II, vol. II, 1953. Tr. Baruch Hochman. *Congress Biweekly* XXXIII, 14 (November 7, 1966). Copyright © 1966 by Baruch Hochman.

This is Agnon's first major tale (1908); from its title the author, whose original name was Czaczkes, took the name under which he has published his works ever since. An *agunah* (singular of *agunot*) is a deserted wife who, according to Jewish law, cannot remarry till the husband has been proven dead or has sent her a bill of divorce. In this tale everybody is in a state of desertion, including the *shekhinah*, the Divine Presence in the world.

THE KERCHIEF

Ha-mitpahat, 1932; Schocken I, vol. VI, 1935; Schocken II, vol. II, 1953. Tr. I. M. Lask. *The Jewish Caravan*, ed. Leo W. Schwarz (New York: Holt, Rinehart & Winston, 1935). Copyright © 1935, 1963, 1965 by Leo W. Schwarz. By permission of Holt, Rinehart & Winston.

The father's absence from home is felt by the family to be as sad as the week of the Ninth of Ab, observed in memory of the destruction of the Jerusalem Temple. Destruction, however, evokes the thought of redemption. While awaiting the father's return, the son (i.e., the narrator) dreams of the coming of the Redeemer who, according to pious legend, until his coming sits among the beggars at the gates of Rome, binding his wounds. The beggar toward the end of the story symbolizes this Messiah; on the day of his maturity (Bar Mitzvah) the boy hands over to him the precious kerchief—originally a gift of the returning father to the waiting mother and representing the sacredness of the home.

TO FATHER'S HOUSE

Le-vet abba. In *The Book of Deeds*, 1941; Schocken I, vol. X, 1950; Schocken II, vol. VI, 1953. Tr. Jules Harlow. Copyright © 1970 by Schocken Books Inc.

Unable to do his work, the narrator decides to go to his home town, to his father's house, i.e., to renew contact with his childhood. There are distracting elements in the way: the narrator's hesitance to interrupt his father's celebration of the feast; a twice-beheld enigmatic candle suspended in the air; meeting the eighteenth-century enlightener Isaac Euchel; the inn that tries to replace the home. Finally, a child—innocence—points the way.

TO THE DOCTOR

El ha-rofe. In *The Book of Deeds*, 1932 and 1939; Schocken I, vol. VIII, 1941, and vol. X, 1950; Schocken II, vol. VI, 1953. Tr. Arnold J. Band. *Midstream* VI, 4 (Autumn 1960). Copyright © 1960 by the Theodor Herzl Foundation Inc.

It may be assumed that the father and the cantor symbolize the religious tradition of the past. But the father is sick, and it is doubtful whether the doctor, even if he were reached, could cure the patient. The element of delay and detraction is introduced by Mr. Andermann (Mr. Otherman).

THE DOCUMENT

Ha-teudah. In *The Book of Deeds*, 1932 and 1939; Schocken I, vol. VIII, 1941, and vol. X, 1950; Schocken II, vol. VI, 1953. Tr. Joseph Moses. Copyright © 1970 by Schocken Books Inc.

Here the helpless individual, conscious of himself and his memories, aware of his surroundings, and there a mindless bureaucratic machine, moving automatically, blindly disregarding the petitioner. And between the two: hordes of people, pushing, squeezing, shoving; seemingly composed of individuals, they are in effect part of the machine.

FRIENDSHIP

Yedidut. In *The Book of Deeds*, 1932 and 1939; Schocken I, vol. VIII, 1941, and vol. X, 1950; Schocken II, vol. VI, 1953. Tr. Misha Louvish. Copyright © 1970 by Schocken Books Inc.

The narrator leaves his home in order not to be bothered by clinging neighbors; but having left it, he cannot find his way back and has even forgotten the address. Who will help? Not Mrs. Klingel (Jingle), whose jokes are insulting; not Dr. Rischel, whose linguistic discourse the narrator seems to interrupt; the narrator's wife, who had come "home" when the story started, has walked off. The unfriendly, uncommunicative situation (of which the narrator is a part!) is suddenly changed when a former friend appears after an absence of many years. His kind though half-hearted readiness to help leads the narrator to find his home (he was standing right beside it)—and himself.

A WHOLE LOAF

Pat shelemah. In *The Book of Deeds,* 1933; Schocken I, vol. VIII, 1941, and vol. X, 1950; Schocken II, vol. VI, 1953. Tr. I. M. Lask. *A Whole Loaf,* ed. S. J. Kahn (New York: The Vanguard Press, 1957). Copyright © 1957 by Karni Publishers, Ltd. By permission of The Vanguard Press.

To Baruch Kurzweil this tale represents the tension between the narrator's pursuit of egoistic, material desires (the wish to order "a whole loaf") and his obligation toward the sacred book and its ineffable author, the Lord, indicated by four dots in parentheses (the Tetragrammaton) and transmitted to us by Dr. Yekutiel (one of the names of Moses) Ne'eman ("Faithful"—an attribute of Moses); the doctor's letters symbolize the commandments; the worldly Mr. Gressler is the persistent hinderer in the narrator's attempt to mail the letters (*Masot al Sippure Shay Agnon,* chap. VIII). Arnold J. Band sees here an antithesis between a life structured by well-defined commandments (the doctor's letters) and a vague pursuit of wholeness, of sanctity, symbolized by the "whole loaf"—part of the Sabbath meal; the yearning for such wholeness remains unfulfilled (*Nostalgia and Nightmare,* pp. 190, 193).

FROM LODGING TO LODGING

Mi-dirah le-dirah. In *The Book of Deeds,* 1939; Schocken I, vol. VIII, 1941, and vol. X, 1950; Schocken II, vol. VI, 1953. Tr. Jules Harlow. *Midstream* XIII, 2 (February, 1967). Copyright © 1967 by Schocken Books Inc.

A room in a quiet, comfortable house surrounded by pleasant trees versus a narrow, low-ceilinged room in a hot, noisy city. Why does the sensitive narrator choose to return to the latter? Because of the presence here of a child—sick, groaning, awkward, but ever so human. "The child's cries and groans are dearer to me than all the musical instruments in the world, for then I know that he is alive." The child's need for attention turns the otherwise unpalatable lodging into a home.

METAMORPHOSIS
Panim aherot, lit. A Different Face, 1941. Schocken I, vol. VIII, 1941; Schocken II, vol. III, 1952. Tr. I. Schen. A *Whole Loaf*, op. cit. Copyright © 1957 by Karni Publishers, Ltd. By permission of The Vanguard Press.

Divorce ended the meaningless marriage between Toni and Hartmann—and initiated a new phase of communication, concern, awareness of the other person, and tenderness. Will the couple be reunited? The story does not reveal this, only that Hartmann's "spirit began to hover in the world of dreams, where no partition separated them."

THE DOCTOR'S DIVORCE
Ha-rofe u-gerushato, 1941. Schocken I, vol. VIII, 1941; Schocken II, vol. III, 1952. Tr. Robert Alter. *Hebrew Short Stories*, ed. S. Y. Pnueli and A. Ukhmani, vol. I (Tel Aviv, 1965). Copyright © 1965 by the Institute for the Translation of Hebrew Literature.

The doctor, trained to deal soberly, rationally with life situations, cannot free himself of the nagging notion that his wife, a nurse, had an affair with another man before their marriage. Alienation grows deeper and deeper; the union is forced to come to an end. But the doctor's heart preserves the woman's warm smile and at night he stetches out his hands, calling for the nurse "like the patients she used to take care of." No one can say which of the conflicting inner forces is stronger than the others.

THE FACE AND THE IMAGE
Ha-panim la-panim. In *The Book of Deeds*, 1942; Schocken I, vol. X, 1950; Schocken II, vol. VI, 1953. Tr. Misha Louvish. Copyright © 1969, 1970 by Schocken Books Inc.

The Hebrew title of the story is taken from Proverbs 27:19, which the standard translations render as, "As in the water face answereth to face, so the heart of man to man." The narrator is quietly planning a study on mirrors (in which face is "answered" by face). This plan is strangely counteracted (or challenged?) by a call to visit his sick mother. A series of absurd interferences prevents this homecoming. The story ends with the narrator's surprised look into a mirror that reflected his face "without partiality."

THE LADY AND THE PEDLAR
Ha-adonit veha-rokhel, 1943. Schocken I, vol. X, 1950; Schocken II, vol. VI, 1953. Tr. Gershom Schocken. *Ariel* XVII (1966–67). Copyright © 1966 by Schocken Books Inc.

A violent, murderous gentile lady and a lone, wandering, peddling Jew: a nightmare of attraction and repulsion, fascination and cruel response, primordial suspicions, hatreds, distorted symbols; a dreamlike, grotesque happening, without purpose or resolve.

ON THE ROAD
Ba-derekh. In *The Book of Deeds*, 1944; Schocken I, vol. X, 1950; Schocken II, vol. VI, 1953. Tr. Misha Louvish. Copyright © 1970 by Schocken Books Inc.

Note the narrator's (Agnon's) interest in remnants of Jewish communities; here it is a group of Jews speaking "antique German," survivors of persecutions. The narrator lovingly records their ways of life and religious customs. A number of references to rituals, meaningless to the general reader, have been omitted with Mr. Agnon's consent. The "factual" observation turns into a personal experience when the narrating visitor becomes a substitute for the "tenth man" required to complete the quorum for Jewish worship; the dying Samuel Levi is replaced by the visitor, whose Hebrew name roughly corresponds to Agnon's own. After having experienced ruins and memories of exile, the narrator is ready to return to the living Land of Israel.

THE ORCHESTRA
Ha-tizmoret. In *The Book of Deeds*, 1946; Schocken I, vol. X, 1950; Schocken II, vol. VI, 1953. Tr. Judah Stampfer. *Mosaic* I, 1 (Spring 1960). Copyright © 1960 by Judah Stampfer. By permission of Harold Ober Associates Inc.

The narrator, a writer, tries to prepare himself for the awesome

New Year's Day. The attempt fails. In A. J. Band's view, the two figures Charni (Black) and Ora (Light) represent traditional faith and artistic involvement, respectively, while the orchestra is "nothing but a projection of [the writer's] guilt-stricken imagination, his remorse at having allowed his artistic preoccupations to distract him from repentance" (*Nostalgia and Nightmare*, pp. 338f.).

THE LETTER

Ha-mikhtav. In *The Book of Deeds*; *Schocken* I, vol. X, 1950; Schocken II, vol. VI, 1953; *Keshet* II (1959). Tr. Misha Louvish. Copyright © 1970 by Schocken Books Inc.

How illusive is reality; how real unreality. How ambiguous the present and strongly assertive the past. The new city of Jerusalem is full of activity; the old city, symbolized by its House of Study, is more profoundly alive. But will we find the entrance? Mr. Gedaliah Klein (God is great, [man is] small), the energetic builder of the secular new city, has died; yet on several occasions he meets the narrator who detects in him the likeness of his pious grandfather. Another representative of the Jerusalem of the past, the old, saintly scholar "chosen to bear the burden of the Torah," moved through life as if directed by an other-worldly force; Mr. Klein, dead, was still boasting of his achievements on behalf of the new city. Note the passages in rhymed prose in chapters five, seven, and eight.

FERNHEIM

Fernheim, 1949. Schocken I, vol. XI, 1952; Schocken II, vol. VII, 1953. Tr. David S. Segal. Copyright © 1970 by Schocken Books Inc.

The name signifies "distant home" or "home is distant." Such is the experience of the hero, a soldier and prisoner of war, who, returning "home," finds his wife and family estranged. His quest for human contact fails. Home is not merely distant; it is non-existent.

AT THE OUTSET OF THE DAY

Im kenisat ha-yom, 1951, Schocken I, vol. XI, 1952; Schocken II, vol. VII, 1953. Tr. David S. Segal. *Hadassah Magazine* XLVIII, 9 (May, 1968). Copyright © 1967 by Schocken Books Inc.

Destruction of the home, terror, flight by night. Help seems to lie in the Great Synagogue and its worshippers, now getting ready for the Day of Atonement. But even from the sanctuary issues fire, and it consumes the dress of the narrator's daughter (his soul?), and the storeroom for pages from sacred books (the *genizah*) offers no relief beyond the enigmatic reference to the three elements of faith: need, form, and will (*tzorekh, tzurah, ratzon*; note the assonance). Despair gives way to hope when the narrator beholds among the Torah scrolls in the Ark the one he himself had written "in memory of the souls of days that had departed," and when he joins in prayer with the congregation; his daughter, who has dozed off, repeats the prayers in her sleep—"melodies no ear has ever heard."

THE NIGHT

Laila min ha-leilot, lit. One Night, 1951. Schocken I, vol. XI, 1952; Schocken II, vol. VII, 1953. Tr. Yoram Matmor. Copyright © 1970 by Schocken Books Inc.

The time: the period shortly after World War II. The place: Jerusalem, to which many refugees from the death camps of Europe flocked. The central episode: the arrival of Moshele, the narrator's relative, believed to have perished in Auschwitz. In awe of some nobility that have taken up quarters at the hotel where the narrator rented a room (he has no home), he refuses hospitality to Moshele. Soon, however, remorse sets in, and the narrator sets out to find his relative, to involve himself in his fate rather than relishing childhood memories (the bookseller Halbfried), the luxury of going to a concert, and the enticing graciousness of a young governess.

FIRST KISS

Ha-neshikah ha-rishonah. *Keshet* XX (1963). Tr. Neal Kozodoy. *Commentary* XLII, 6 (December, 1966). Copyright © 1966 by Schocken Books Inc.

The Sabbath transforms secular, natural time into sacred time; on that day time reaches fulfillment, presaging life eternal. (Note the references to "time" in the first part of the story.) Here, the Jew is in his very own sphere; an intrusion from the outside cannot but create a disturbance in the innermost sense. But the outside world does intrude, consciously; the three monks (note the number) are no innocent visitors; they suggest there should be three Sabbath candles, only to be informed that the two candles are "actually one." The three monks are followed by two novices, one of whom confesses to be a woman (conversion—perversion). In fact, she is "the daughter of old age" of a hasidic master whose mighty New Year's prayer for the unity of mankind in the service of the one God led his listeners to imagine this union to be a reality. The narrator, representing this tradition of Israel, and the "novice," representing the return of the wayward, become one in a holy kiss. The transforming power of the Sabbath is restored.

N.N.G.

During the final preparation of this volume for the press, word came of the death of S. Y. Agnon on February 17, 1970.